Essential Concepts in Sociology

Second Edition

ANTHONY GIDDENS & PHILIP W. SUTTON

polity

First edition published in 2014 by Polity Press
This second edition first published in 2017 by Polity Press
Reprinted 2017

Polity Press
65 Bridge Street
Cambridge CB2 1UR, UK

Polity Press
350 Main Street
Malden, MA 02148, USA

ISBN-13: 978-1-5095-1666-7
ISBN-13: 978-1-5095-1667-4 (pb)

A catalogue record for this book is available from the British Library.

Library of Congress Cataloging-in-Publication Data

Names: Giddens, Anthony, author. | Sutton, Philip W., author.
Title: Essential concepts in sociology / Anthony Giddens, Philip W. Sutton.
Description: Second edition. | Malden, MA : Polity, 2017. | Revised edition
   of the authors' Essential concepts in sociology, 2014. | Includes
   bibliographical references and index.
Identifiers: LCCN 2016042570 (print) | LCCN 2017006778 (ebook) | ISBN
   9781509516667 (hardback) | ISBN 9781509516674 (paperback) | ISBN
   9781509516698 (Mobi) | ISBN 9781509516704 (Epub)
Subjects: LCSH: Sociology. | BISAC: SOCIAL SCIENCE / Sociology / General.
Classification: LCC HM585 .G51973 2017 (print) | LCC HM585 (ebook) | DDC
   301--dc23
LC record available at https://lccn.loc.gov/2016042570

Typeset in 9.5 on 12 pt Utopia by
Servis Filmsetting Ltd, Stockport, Cheshire
Printed and bound in Great Britain by CPI Group (UK) Ltd, Croydon

For further information on Polity, visit our website: politybooks.com

Contents

Introduction

Social life is never static but is in a constant process of change. Over the last thirty years or so the modern world has been transformed by fluid gender relations, shifting migration patterns, multiculturalism, the digital revolution in communications, the Internet and social media, financial crises, global terrorism and numerous political upheavals. Sociology, originally a product of the nineteenth century, cannot afford to stand still but must move with the times or risk becoming irrelevant. The discipline today is theoretically diverse, covers a very wide range of subjects and draws on a broad array of research methods to make sense of the human world. This is the inevitable outcome of attempts to understand and explain the increasingly globalized environment we are entering, and it means that our familiar concepts need to be reassessed and new ones created. This book includes a mix of both long-established and newly minted concepts.

Concept Development in Sociology

Some sociological concepts are very longstanding and have stood the test of time exceptionally well. Class, status, bureaucracy, capitalism, gender, poverty, family and power, for example, remain fundamental to the business of 'doing' sociology. Others have been developed much more recently. Globalization, postmodernity, reflexivity, environment, life course, restorative justice and the social model of disability – all are now part of the conceptual lexicon, representing some of the enormous social changes of recent decades. All of this means that it becomes more difficult to grasp the overall shape of the discipline. The book makes a contribution to this task by introducing some of sociology's essential concepts, many of which act as signposts for particular theoretical developments in sociology over the last 150 years or so. Understanding these essential concepts, their origins and contemporary usage should help readers to see how the subject matter of sociology has developed over time.

Concept development in sociology is usually tied to theories and empirical studies which demand new concepts to make sense of their findings. Some concepts, such as status, class and risk, are already in wide circulation in society but are lifted out of that context into sociology, where they are debated and refined, becoming more precise and useful in the process. Others, including alienation, moral panic and globalization, are specifically created by sociologists to help them study social phenomena but then slip into everyday life, where they

1

influence people's perceptions of the world in which they live. This is quite unlike the situation in the natural sciences. Regardless of how many concepts from the natural sciences are created, those concepts do not have the potential to change the behaviour of animals and plants. As Giddens has argued, this is an example of a 'one-way' process. In sociology, concepts, research findings and theories do make their way back into society at large, and people may alter their ideas and behaviour as a result. This means that sociological research is part of a continuous 'two-way' process between sociologists and the subjects they study.

This two-way process means that sociological concepts are inherently unstable and open to modification and change, not just within professional sociological discourse but in the social world itself. It also means that some concepts – perhaps even a majority – are 'essentially contested'. That is, they are used in a variety of theoretical positions and there is no general agreement on their meaning. However, this probably overstates the level of variation and disagreement. In practice, the competing theories in sociology are relatively small in number and conceal the fact that there is more consistency and integration between them than might first appear.

Concepts developed within one theoretical perspective are very often used in others. The concept of alienation, for instance, was originally devised by Karl Marx, enabling him to understand better the nature of work in capitalist societies. Yet it was revived more than a century later, lifted out of its original Marxist theoretical frame and given a new lease of life by industrial sociologists to assess how employees feel about their working environment. In the process, the concept was modified, and, though some Marxists may object, the revised version has given us some very worthwhile insights into how different workplaces and management systems impact on the lives of workers.

The Essential Concepts

We did not set out to produce a comprehensive compendium of sociological concepts. Instead we have carefully selected about seventy concepts that have helped to shape, or are currently shaping, particular fields of inquiry. We have chosen some concepts that have stood the test of time – power, class, ideology, society and culture, for example. Concepts such as these have been in use over the entire course of sociology's history, yet they continue to stimulate debate and guide research projects today. Others, such as gender, consumerism, identity and life course, do not have such a long history, but their impact has been significant. Such concepts have not only stimulated large bodies of research but have also reshaped the older debates, forcing sociologists to reassess the value of earlier concepts. Finally we have included some very recent concepts, among them intersectionality, globalization, risk and restorative justice. It is our assessment that these have already generated some innovative research studies and are very likely to become embedded within their specialist fields as essential.

The entries are longer than is usual for a typical 'key concepts' book. Our aim is to give more than just brief definitions. Instead we provide an extended discussion of each concept which sets it into historical and theoretical context, explores its main meanings in use, introduces some relevant criticisms, and points readers to contemporary pieces of research and theorizing which they can read for themselves. This structure enables readers to link the history of sociology with its contemporary form through the development of its concepts. In addition many other concepts are discussed and briefly defined within the entries. 'Industrialization', for instance, also includes the related concepts of urbanization, post-industrialism and ecological modernization. Hence, readers are advised to use the Index as a guide to locating the many other concepts that are not in the Contents list.

We also accept that some of the concepts we have selected will be queried. Some sociologists will no doubt think we have missed out some crucial concept or included others that have become irrelevant. Such disagreements are quite normal in sociology, even over such fundamental things as what constitutes an 'essential' concept. This is mainly because of the varied theoretical commitments and perspectives of sociologists. As a community of scholars, sociologists are intensely disputatious, but, even so, they do speak to and understand each other. One reason for this is precisely because of the shared conceptual heritage derived from numerous theories and explanatory frameworks that have waxed and waned over the years.

How to Use the Book

Entries are in ten major themes, internally listed alphabetically. As a quick reference guide, this makes finding entries in particular subject areas much simpler and quicker. The book is a stand-alone text that can be used by anyone looking to understand sociology's essential concepts. However, students who use our *Sociology: Introductory Readings* (2010) will appreciate that the matching structure across both books facilitates cross-referencing of concepts with associated readings by theme. Concepts are cross-referenced within the present text using the simple device of highlighting in **bold** the first use of other concepts within individual entries. We have also taken a few liberties with the concept of 'concept', as it were. For example, **'race'** and **ethnicity** are covered in one rather than two entries because the two are generally discussed together, though the key differences between 'race' and ethnicity are made clear in the discussion. We decided to do something similar with **structure/agency** and **qualitative/quantitative** methods. Some entries may also be thought of as primarily theories or general perspectives rather than concepts. **Globalization**, for example, is both a concept and a theory of social change, while the **social model of disability** is a particular approach to the study of disability. These are included in order that the book is able to fulfil its purpose, which is to provide an accurate conceptual map of contemporary sociology.

Thinking Sociologically

Discourse

Working Definition

A way of talking and thinking about a subject that is united by common assumptions and serves to shape people's understanding of and actions towards that subject.

Origins of the Concept

The concept of discourse originates in linguistics – the study of language and its use. In this context, discourse refers to speech or written communication such as that involved in face-to-face conversation, public debates, online chatrooms, and so on. In linguistics, discourses are analysed in order to understand how communication operates and is organized. However, in the 1950s, the British philosopher J. L. Austin (1962) argued that written and spoken communications were not just neutral, passive statements but 'speech acts' which actively shaped the world as it is known. Michel Foucault connected the study of language to the mainstream sociological interest in **power** and its effects within **society**. From this starting point the concepts of discourse and 'discursive practices' became much more interesting to sociologists.

Meaning and Interpretation

Studies of language and communications focused mainly on the technical aspects such as the role of grammar and grammatical rules to construct meaning. However, from the late 1950s, discourse came to be understood as a type of action and, as such, an intervention in the world. The way we act is influenced, for example, by whether we discuss political groups as 'terrorists' or 'freedom fighters', or whether news reports home in on the causes of industrial strikes or the disruption it produces. The notion of the 'speech act' altered the way that language and everyday conversation was viewed. What had previously appeared marginal soon became central to our understanding of social structures and power relations, as well as to studies of **culture** and the **mass media**. Sociologists were able to study the way language is used to frame political arguments, exclude certain ideas from debate and control the way people discuss issues.

Undoubtedly the most influential theory of discourse is that of Michel Foucault, who studied the history of mental illness (in his terms, 'madness'), crime, penal systems and medical institutions. Foucault ([1969] 2002) argued that a variety of discourses create frameworks which structure social life, through which power is exercised. In this way, discursive frameworks operate rather like paradigms, setting limits to what can be sensibly said about a particular subject as well as how it can be said. Discussions of crime, for example, are structured according to the dominant discourse of law and order, which makes conformity to the law and acceptance of policing a common-sense part of normal life. To suggest that mass policing should be opposed or that the law should be routinely disobeyed by the poor would be almost unintelligible. Because the crime discourse precedes people's entry into society, their behaviour and attitudes are partly shaped by it, as they imbibe the norms and values of society during **socialization**. In this way, discourses help to create people's very sense of self and personal **identity**. This is a useful reminder that people do not have total freedom to think, say and do whatever they want, as there are limits to human agency.

Foucault's concept of discourse goes even further, making discourse and discursive practices central to the study of power. He argued that knowledge and power are intimately connected rather than being opposed. Academic disciplines such as criminology and psychiatry, which seek objective knowledge of criminal behaviour and mental illness respectively, also produce relations of power that shape the way that crime and mental illness are understood and acted upon. Psychiatric discourse creates its own boundary between sanity and madness, legitimizing specialized medical institutions for the isolation, treatment and cure of mental illness. Similarly, shifting discourses of crime do not just describe and explain criminal behaviour but help to bring into being new ways of defining and dealing with criminals (Foucault 1975).

Critical Points

The concept of discourse is undoubtedly thought-provoking and has generally been well received in sociology. But Foucault's central idea that discourses are disembodied and unconnected to a specific social base – such as a social **class** – is at odds with other research on power. Many studies of power see it as something to be gained and used for personal or group advantage, as in the patriarchal power that men hold and exercise over women or that ruling classes have over subordinate ones. The idea that power anonymously 'oils the wheels' of social relations seems to ignore the very real consequences of major inequalities of power. A further criticism is that the primary focus on language, speech and texts tends to give these too much importance. For some critics, this has produced a 'decorative sociology' that submerges social relations within the sphere of culture, avoiding difficult and genuinely sociological issues of shifting power balances (Rojek and Turner 2000). Not just discourses but real social relations and material culture are more significant in shaping social life.

Continuing Relevance

The central idea that discursive frameworks are a key part of social life remains a productive one which informs the study of many diverse subjects. For example, Lessa (2006) evaluated a UK government-funded agency working with teenage single parents using discourse analysis to understand the narrative accounts given by teenagers, their parents and carers. In contrast to the dominant discourse in society which presents single mothers as irresponsible, feckless welfare 'scroungers', this agency helped to generate an alternative discourse of teenage mothers as 'young parents' with a legitimate right to social support. This alternative discourse has had some success in garnering resources and shifting perceptions. What this study shows is that currently dominant discourses are rarely unopposed and can potentially be subverted, albeit in this case at a local level and in a very specific area of the welfare system. Discursive contestations of this kind are perhaps the norm rather than the exception.

At a much broader level are studies of global political discourses. Following the attacks on American targets on 11 September 2001 (known as '9/11'), a new discourse of a global 'war on terror' was launched by the US government. In this discursive frame, the attacks committed by terrorists were not just against the United States but 'against democracy' as such (Hodges and Nilep 2007: 3). This discourse then shaped public debate among a range of social actors, who reacted to them, sought to explain them or tried to justify them. In doing so, the 'war on terror' discourse set the terms of an 'us and them' public discussion, which helped to create new identities, enemies and friends.

Although the language and rhetoric of war seems to have changed very little over time and across numerous wars, Machin (2009) argues that the visual representations of war – also a type of 'narrative' – have changed significantly. Using multimodal analysis (combining communicative sources such as text, images, body language, and so on) to study press images of the Iraq War presented in 2005–6, he shows that ongoing wars, such as that in Afghanistan, tend to be portrayed as highly professional 'peacekeeping' missions with soldiers carefully protecting vulnerable civilians, while 'enemy' casualties are excluded from view. Rather than documenting specific events, war photographs are increasingly used to structure page layouts representing general themes such as 'suffering', 'enemies', 'combat' or 'civilians'. In particular, Machin argues that cheaper images from commercial image banks are used more and more in generic, symbolic ways. Hence war photography can be seen as an important element in the new discursive framing of contemporary warfare.

References and Further Reading

Austin, J. L. (1962) *How to Do Things with Words* (London: Oxford University Press).
Foucault, M. ([1969] 2002) *The Archaeology of Knowledge* (London: Routledge).
Foucault, M. (1975) *Discipline and Punish* (Harmondsworth: Penguin).

Hodges, A., and Nilep, C. (eds) (2007) *Discourse, War and Terrorism* (Amsterdam: John Benjamins).

Lessa, I. (2006) 'Discursive Struggles within Social Welfare: Restaging Teen Motherhood', *British Journal of Social Work*, 36(2): 283–98.

Machin, D. (2009) 'Visual Discourses of War: Multimodal Analysis of Photographs of the Iraq Occupation', in A. Hodges and C. Nilep (eds), *Discourse, War and Terrorism* (Amsterdam: John Benjamins), pp. 123–42.

Rojek, C., and Turner, B. (2000) 'Decorative Sociology: Towards a Critique of the Cultural Turn', *Sociological Review*, 48(4): 629–48.

Globalization

Working Definition

The various processes through which geographically dispersed human populations are brought into closer and more immediate contact with one another, creating a single **community** of fate or global **society**.

Origins of the Concept

The idea of a worldwide human society can be traced back to discussions of the prospects for 'humanity' as a whole during the eighteenth-century Enlightenment period. Globalization can also be distilled from the nineteenth-century ideas of Marx on the expansive tendencies of **capitalism** and Durkheim on the geographical spread of the **division of labour**. However, the first dictionary entry for 'globalization' in the modern sense was in 1961, and only in the early 1980s was the term in regular use in economics (Kilminster 1998: 93).

A significant forerunner of the globalization thesis in sociology is Immanuel Wallerstein's 'World Systems Theory' (1974, 1980, 1989). Wallerstein argued that the capitalist economic system operates at the transnational level, constituting a world system with a core of relatively rich countries, a periphery of the poorest societies, and a semi-periphery squeezed in between. However, contemporary debates stem from a perceived acceleration of globalization from the 1970s caused by the growth and **power** of multinational corporations, concerns about the decline of the **nation state**, the rise of supranational trading blocs, regional economic and political entities (such as the European Union), cheaper travel leading to more widespread foreign tourism and **migration**, and the advent of the Internet enabling rapid global communication. By the 1990s, the concept of globalization had entered the sociological mainstream, impacting on all of the discipline's specialist fields.

Meaning and Interpretation

Although most sociologists could accept our working definition above, there are many disagreements on the underlying causes of globalization and whether it is a positive or negative development. Globalization alerts us to a process of change or perhaps a social trend towards worldwide interdependence. But this does not mean it will inevitably lead to a single, global society. Globalization has economic, political and cultural dimensions (Waters 2001). For some, globalization is primarily economic, involving financial exchange, trade, global production and consumption, a global division of labour and a global financial system. *Economic globalization* fosters increased migration, altering patterns of movement and settlement, creating a more fluid form of human existence. For others, *cultural globalization* is more significant. Robertson (1995) devised the concept of *glocalization* – the mixing of global and local elements – to capture the way that local communities actively modify global processes to fit into indigenous **cultures**. This leads to multidirectional flows of cultural products across the world's societies. Those more impressed with *political globalization* focus on increasing regional and international governance mechanisms, such as the United Nations and the European Union. These institutions gather nation states and international non-governmental organizations into common decision-making forums to regulate the emerging global system.

Globalization involves several processes. Trade and market exchanges routinely take place on a worldwide scale. Growing international political cooperation, as in the notion of an active 'international community' or the use of multinational peacekeeping forces, demonstrates political and military coordination beyond national boundaries. Recent developments in information technology and more systematic (and cheaper) transportation also mean that social and cultural activity operates at a global level. In addition, the globalizing of human activity is becoming *intensified*. That is, there is *more* global trade, *more* international politics, *more frequent* global transport and *more routine* cultural interchanges. The sheer volume of activity at the global level is increasing. And many sociologists perceive a *speeding up* of globalization since the 1970s with the advent of digitization, information technology and improvements in the transportation of goods, services and people. This rapid globalization has far-reaching consequences. Decisions taken in one location can have an enormous impact on other, distant societies, and the nation state, so long the central actor, appears to have lost some of its power and control.

Critical Points

Globalization theorists see the process as fundamentally changing the way people live, but others argue that such claims are exaggerated (Held et al. 1999). Critics (also called 'sceptics') argue that, despite greater contacts and trade between nation states today than in the past, these have not created a unified global economic system (Hirst et al. 2009). Instead, there has been a trend towards intensified *regional* trading within the European Union, the Asia-Pacific region and North America. Given that these three regional economies operate relatively independently from each other, the sceptical argument is that any notion of a worldwide, global economic system remains fanciful.

The idea that globalization has undermined the role of the nation state can also be challenged. National governments continue to be key players because they regulate and coordinate economic activity in trade agreements and policies of economic liberalization. Pooling of national sovereignty does not mean its inevitable loss. National governments have retained a good deal of power even though global interdependencies are stronger, but states adopt a more active, outward-looking stance under the conditions of rapid globalization. Globalization is not a one-way process of ever closer integration but a two-way flow of images, information and influence with diverse outcomes.

Continuing Relevance

Because globalization forms the essential conceptual backdrop to sociology, it is present in an enormous range of recent research studies on diverse subjects, including transnational terrorism, **social movement** activity, **conflict** and war, migration studies, environmental sociology, multiculturalism and many more. As research has progressed, some of the unintended consequences of large-scale globalization have been discovered. For instance, Renard (1999) studied the emergence and growth of the market for 'fair trade' products, which aims to reward small-scale producers in developing countries fairly by selling to ethical consumers in the industrialized nations. Mainstream globalization processes are dominated by large transnational companies, and it is extremely difficult for small businesses to break into their mass markets. However, Renard found that economic globalization actually creates smaller gaps, or niches, which small producers can move into and develop. This is an interesting piece of research which shows how globalization can open the way for small producers (in this case, of fair-trade coffee) to succeed based on the shared values of fairness and solidarity among sections of the population in both the developed and developing countries.

If globalization has a political dimension, we might expect social movements to organize above the level of local and national politics. A quantitative analysis by Barnartt (2010) looked at possible evidence for this in disabled people's movements. She analysed more than 1,200 protest events in the USA and over 700 outside events in 1970 and 2005. The project found that the number of disability protests in the USA increased rapidly after 1984 and outside America after 1989. Barnartt argues that disabled people's protests have indeed increased and spread across the world. Yet this is not necessarily indicative of globalization. The majority of these events were concerned with local or national issues rather than global ones. Similarly, there were 'few if any' transnational organizations involved. Despite similarities across the various movements, Barnartt concludes that disabled people's movements are not part of globalization processes.

Assessments of globalization differ markedly, but Martell's (2016) evaluation returns to the familiar theme of inequality. He argues that, although many sociologists see globalization as partly or mainly a cultural phenomenon, sociologists need to acknowledge the key role played by **capitalist** economics and material interests. Martell takes issue with cosmopolitan theories of an emerging transnational political sphere, which he sees as too optimistic. To the extent that it is real, globalization is uneven, reproducing existing inequalities and unequal power chances. Global free movement, for instance, means 'those least in need, rich elites, being the most free, while those most in need of mobility, the poor and those beyond the rich core, are most restricted' (Martell 2016: 251). Although cultural change is important, for Martell, capitalist economics remains the crucial driving force.

References and Further Reading

Barnartt, S. (2010) 'The Globalization of Disability Protests, 1970–2005: Pushing the Limits of Cross-Cultural Research?', *Comparative Sociology*, 9(2): 222–40.

Held, D., McGrew, A., Goldblatt, D., and Perraton, J. (1999) *Global Transformations: Politics, Economics and Culture* (Cambridge: Polity).

Hirst, P., Thompson, G., and Bromley, S. (2009) *Globalization in Question* (3rd edn, Cambridge: Polity).

Kilminster, R. (1998) *The Sociological Revolution: From the Enlightenment to the Global Age* (London: Routledge).

Martell, L. (2016) *The Sociology of Globalization* (2nd edn, Cambridge: Polity).

Renard, M.-C. (1999) 'The Interstices of Globalization: The Example of Fair Coffee', *Sociologia Ruralis*, 39(4): 484–500.

Robertson, R. (1995) 'Glocalization: Time–Space and Homogeneity–Heterogeneity', in M. Featherstone, S. Lash and R. Robertson (eds), *Global Modernities* (London: Sage), pp. 25–44.

Wallerstein, I. (1974, 1980, 1989) *The Modern World-System*, 3 vols (New York: Academic Press).

Waters, M. (2001) *Globalization* (2nd edn, London: Routledge).

Modernity

Working Definition

The period from the mid-eighteenth-century European Enlightenment to at least the mid-1980s, characterized by secularization, **rationalization**, democratization, individualization and the rise of **science**.

Origins of the Concept

The word 'modern' can be used to refer to anything that is contemporary, though the contrast between the ancient and the modern had become more commonplace in Europe by the late sixteenth century (Williams 1987). The idea of modernization – making something more contemporary – was seen as a retrograde step until the nineteenth century, when modernization took on a more positive hue. Over the first three-quarters of the twentieth century, the modernization of transport, houses, social attitudes, fashions and much more was widely seen as necessary and progressive. However, in social theory, 'modernity' has a much broader meaning, referring to an entire historical period from the mid-eighteenth century to the 1980s. Enlightenment philosophers attacked tradition, religious **authority** and received beliefs, proposing instead that human progress could come only through the application of rational thinking, scientific methods and the pursuit of freedom and equality. Sociology itself is a product of modernity which aims to gather reliable knowledge of the social world through scientific methods in order to intervene and improve **society** for the betterment of all.

Meaning and Interpretation

The period of modernity followed from European feudalism and is an umbrella for all of the distinctive aspects of post-feudal societies. These include industrialization, **capitalism**, urbanization and **urbanism** as a way of life, secularization, the establishment and extension of **democracy**, the application of science to production methods, and a broad movement towards equality in all spheres of life. Modernity also instituted an increase in rational thinking and action characterized by an unemotional 'matter of fact' attitude, which contrasted sharply with the previous emotional and religious orientations to the world. Max Weber described this process as the gradual 'disenchantment of the world', spreading across the globe by an expanding, legal-rational form of capitalism.

As a social formation, modernity has been spectacularly successful in exploding the limits to the production of material goods, generating vast wealth for the relatively rich countries and bringing about more equality in many areas of life. During the twentieth century, many sociologists theorized that modernity represented a societal model that all nations would aspire to or be forced into eventually. This generic thesis came to be known as modernization theory, arguably the most famous version of which was devised by Walt Rostow (1961). Rostow argued that modernization was a process moving through several stages as societies 'caught up' with the early modernizers and their economies began to grow. From a traditional, agrarian or agricultural base, societies could modernize by shedding their longstanding traditional values and institutions and investing for future prosperity in infrastructural projects and new industries. From here, a continuous investment in advancing technology leads to higher levels of production and a drive towards mass consumption, which in turn creates a sustainable pattern of economic growth. Although countries such as Hong Kong, Taiwan, South Korea and Singapore have followed a pattern somewhat akin to this, Rostow's model is seen today as too optimistic, as many countries, particularly in Africa, have not modernized in this way.

For some theorists, notably Zygmunt Bauman (1987), the key to understanding modernity lies in grasping its distinctive **culture** and mentality, which can be compared to gardening. The modern mentality is one that privileges order over randomness. Hence, if society is likened to a wild garden, then wilderness and wild nature had to be tamed and domesticated, and the growing **power** of **nation states** to do the gardening provided the means to achieve this. The gardening metaphor is not restricted to nation states, though, as the desire for order and orderliness became a normal aspect of people's everyday modern lives.

Critical Points

The main problem with the concept of modernity is that it is overgeneralized. Critics see it as really a *post hoc* description of some modern societies – but by no means all – and the concept fails to offer any explanation of the causes of modernization. Modernization theory also fails to account for the persistence of gross inequalities in the global system and the apparent 'failure' of many developing economies to take off as predicted. Because the concept of modernity incorporates several key social processes, it is too vague and is largely descriptive rather than analytical. It is not clear which of the constituent elements is the main driving force in the modernization process. Is capitalist economics the main causal factor or is it industrialization? What role is played by democratization? Where does urbanization fit in – is it a cause or a consequence?

Neo-Marxist critics also take issue with the idea that there is an inexorable logic to modernization that will propel the less developed societies into a period of strong economic growth and prosperity. Rather, at the global level, the relatively poor countries are kept in a permanent state of dependency by the rich world, their resources are plundered, and their populations are used as cheap labour by Western-based multinational capitalist corporations. Hence, not only is the concept too vague, the modernization thesis is deeply flawed.

Continuing Relevance

Following the emergence of postmodern theorizing of an end to modernity, there have been reassessments of the concept. Some sociologists argue that we are not entering a period of **postmodernity** but one of 'late' or 'reflexive' modernity (Giddens 1990). Rather than this sounding the death knell for modernity, it means revealing and facing up to its negative aspects, such as **environmental** damage, which make social life much less certain as both the previous faith in science as the way to truth and deference to authorities start to wane. Jürgen Habermas (1983) argued that postmodern theorists gave up too early on what he saw as the ambitious project of modernity. Many of its essential features are only partially complete and need to be deepened rather than abandoned. There is much still to do in relation to ensuring meaningful democratic participation, equalizing life chances across the social **classes**, creating genuine **gender** equality, and so on. In sum, modernity is an unfinished project that deserves to be pursued, not allowed to wither away.

A more recent body of developing work is based on the notion of 'multiple modernities' – a critique of the illegitimate conflation of modernization with Westernization (Eisenstadt 2002). This idea counters the earlier assumption of a single, linear route to modernity and a standardized, uniform version based on Western societies. Empirical studies of modernity around the world suggest that this is wrong. In fact, there have been numerous diverse routes to modernity (Wagner 2012). Japanese modernity is markedly different from the American version, and it seems likely that the developing Chinese model will be different again. Some modernities, even that in the USA, have not become as secular as forecast but remain staunchly religious in character, while at the same time embracing industrialism and continuous technological development. Others, such as the Saudi Arabian version, are not only explicitly religious but also selective in relation to what they take from Western forms before adding their own unique aspects. The multiple modernities agenda seems likely to produce more realistic evaluations that may reinvigorate the concept into the future.

References and Further Reading

Bauman, Z. (1987) *Legislators and Interpreters: On Modernity, Postmodernity and Intellectuals* (Cambridge: Polity).

Berman, M. (1983) *All That is Solid Melts into Air: The Experience of Modernity* (London: Verso).

Eisenstadt, S. N. (2002) 'Multiple Modernities', in S. N. Eisenstadt (ed.), *Multiple Modernities* (New Brunswick, NJ: Transaction), pp. 1–30.

Giddens, A. (1990) *The Consequences of Modernity* (Cambridge: Polity).

Habermas, J. (1983) 'Modernity – an Incomplete Project', in H. Foster (ed.), *The Anti-Aesthetic* (Port Townsend, WA: Bay Press), pp. 3–15.

Rostow, W. W. (1961) *The Stages of Economic Growth* (Cambridge: Cambridge University Press).

Wagner, P. (2012) *Modernity: Understanding the Present* (Cambridge: Polity).

Williams, R. (1987) *Keywords: A Vocabulary of Culture and Society* (London: Fontana).

Postmodernity

Working Definition

An historical period, following **modernity**, which is less clearly defined, pluralistic and socially diverse than the modernity that preceded it. Postmodernity is said to have developed from the early 1970s onwards.

Origins of the Concept

The 'postmodern turn' in social theory began in the mid-1980s, though the concept of the postmodern lies a decade earlier in **culture** and the arts. In architecture, for instance, a new style emerged that took elements from a range of existing genres to produce strange-looking buildings – such as the Lloyd's building in London – that somehow 'worked'. This method of playfully mixing and matching genres and styles was described as postmodern. In film, the strange worlds created by the director David Lynch (see, for instance, *Blue Velvet*, 1986) mixed historical periods, combining extreme violence and sexual **'deviance'** with old-fashioned tales of romance and morality. In many other areas of artistic work and culture the postmodern trend continued, and in the late 1980s the social sciences finally caught up.

The single key work in sociology was Jean-François Lyotard's (1984) *The Postmodern Condition*, in which the author outlined his thesis that some of the main planks of modern **society** were losing their central place. In particular, Lyotard saw **science**, which had been the dominant form of knowledge during the modern period, losing legitimacy as people began to seek out local forms of knowledge, such as older folk knowledge and religious and common-sense beliefs. The decentring of scientific thinking, argued Lyotard, was a symptom of the emerging postmodern society. Other theorists whose work has had a major impact on theories of postmodernity include Zygmunt Bauman (1992, 1997) and Jean Baudrillard (1983, 1995).

Meaning and Interpretation

Postmodern thinking is diverse, and theorists prioritize different elements associated with the suggested shift to a postmodern society. One target of most postmodernists is the attempt by social theorists, from Comte and Marx to Giddens, to discern the direction and shape of history. For these theorists, the process of historical change is structured and 'goes somewhere' – it makes progress. In Marxist theory, for example, this progressive movement is from **capitalism** to the more egalitarian societies of socialism and communism. However, postmodern thinkers reject such grand theorizing.

The trust people invested previously in science, politicians and human progress in history has been eroded as fears of nuclear war or **environmental** catastrophe, along with continuing **conflicts** and episodes of genocide, puncture the civilized veneer of modern societies. Lyotard described this process as the collapse of 'metanarratives', those big stories of continuous progress that justified deference towards scientists, experts and professionals. Instead, the character of postmodernity is irrevocably diverse and fragmented, exemplified by the world-wide web, which teems with images, videos and other material from almost every culture around the world. The experience of web surfing can be one of randomness as we encounter a wide range of values and ideas very different from our own. This potentially disorientating experience is typical of a postmodern culture that is saturated with mass-media content.

Jean Baudrillard argues that the electronic media have destroyed our relationship to the past, creating a chaotic, empty world in which society is influenced, above all, by signs and images. For Baudrillard, the rising prominence of the **mass media** erodes the border between reality and its representation, leaving just one 'hyperreality' within which we all live. In a hyperreal world, our perception of events and our understanding of the social world become highly dependent on their being viewed through mass media such as television. Baudrillard's (1995) provocative newspaper articles 'The Gulf War Will Not Take Place', 'The Gulf War is Not Really Taking Place' and 'The Gulf War Did Not Take Place', published before, during and after the war in 1991, aimed to show how apparently primary 'real-world' events, such as armies fighting in Kuwait, and the apparently secondary media reports of it were actually part of the same hyperreality.

A good way of thinking about postmodern ideas as received in sociology is to distinguish between the main tenets of postmodern social change and socio-logical theory's ability to account for and understand this. The rapid growth and spread of mass media, new information technologies, more fluid movements of people across national boundaries, the demise of social **class** identities, and the emergence of multicultural societies – all of these changes, say postmodernists, lead us to conclude that we no longer live in a modern world ordered by national states. Modernity is dead and we are entering a postmodern period. The question then arises as to whether 'modern' sociology can adequately analyse a 'post-modern' world: Is there a *sociology of postmodernity*? Or are the consequences of postmodern change so radical that they render modern theories and concepts redundant? Do we need a *postmodern sociology* for a postmodern world?

Critical Points

There are many critics of postmodern theory. Some sociologists argue that post-modern theorists are essentially pessimists and defeatists who are so appalled by the dark side of modernity they would jettison its positive aspects as well. Yet there are clear benefits to modernity, such as the valuing of equality, individual freedom and rational approaches to social problems. Some of the social changes described in postmodern theory are also poorly supported by empirical studies. For example, the idea that social class and other collective forms no longer structure social life, leaving individuals at the mercy of mass media imagery, is an exaggeration. Though there are now more sources of **identity**, social class remains a key determinant of people's social position and life chances (Callinicos 1990).

Similarly, there is much evidence that the media do play a more important role than in previous periods, but it does not follow that people simply soak up media content. There is a large body of research which shows that TV viewers, for instance, actively read and interpret media content, making sense of it from their own situation. With the advent of the worldwide web there are also many alternative information and entertainment sources, many of which are based on **interactions** between providers and consumers, generating more rather than less critical comment and evaluation of mainstream media output. Finally, even if some of the changes proposed by postmodernists are genuine and influential, the evidence that they add up to a radical shift beyond modernity remains a matter of theoretical debate.

Continuing Relevance

The concept of postmodernity was bound to be controversial given that sociol-ogy itself is rooted in a modernist approach. What would be the point of sociol-ogy if we gave up on trying to understand and explain social reality and to apply that knowledge in order to improve it? Nonetheless, postmodernity has had a longer-lasting impact on the discipline. The opening up of plural viewpoints and diverse interpretations of the same social reality means that sociologists can no longer assume an unproblematic common culture or shared values within society but have to be sensitive to cultural diversity.

McGuigan (2006) provides an interesting account of the modern–postmodern debate. He argues that contemporary societies can best be seen as culturally postmodern but that, in all other respects, global modernity, especially capitalist economics, remains intact. In short, we are not living in or headed towards a postmodern age, but there are many examples of a culture of postmodernism. Postmodernism is not confined to a small artistic *avant garde* but can also be found in global cultural products as well as in academic and philosophical ideas. Like Jameson (1991) and others, McGuigan suggests that modernity and post-modernism are not opposed but complementary. As the mass, uniform produc-tion of Fordist manufacturing methods gave way to diverse production for niche markets in the 1970s, an individualized, pluralistic postmodern culture seemed to 'fit' the emerging mode of production very well.

References and Further Reading

Baudrillard, J. (1983) *Simulations* (New York: SemioTex(e)).
— (1995) *The Gulf War Did Not Take Place* (Bloomington: Indiana University Press).
Bauman, Z. (1992) *Intimations of Postmodernity* (London: Routledge).
— (1997) *Postmodernity and its Discontents* (Cambridge: Polity).
Callinicos, A. (1990) *Against Postmodernism: A Marxist Critique* (Cambridge: Polity).
Jameson, F. (1991) *Postmodernism or the Cultural Logic of Late Capitalism* (Durham, NC: Duke University Press).
Kumar, K. (2005) *From Post-Industrial to Post-Modern Society* (2nd edn, Oxford: Blackwell).
Lyotard, J.-F. (1984) *The Postmodern Condition* (Minneapolis: University of Minnesota Press).
McGuigan, J. (2006) *Modernity and Postmodern Culture* (2nd edn, Buckingham: Open University Press).

Rationalization

Working Definition

A long-term social process in which traditional ideas and beliefs are replaced by methodical rules and procedures and formal, means-to-ends thinking.

Origins of the Concept

To act in a rational way means to act reasonably and to think through the action and its consequences before performing it. The philosophical doctrine known as rationalism, which originated in the seventeenth century, contrasted knowledge based on reason and reasoning with that rooted in religious sources and received wisdom. Clearly, rationality has its origins in the connection between thinking and doing and the production of knowledge. In sociology, the theory of rationali-zation in **society** at large refers to a process rather than a fixed state of things and is central to the work of Max Weber. For Weber, rationalization and the elimination of magic was a long-term, world-historical social process that underpins any realistic understanding of the distinctiveness of the period of **modernity**. In more recent studies, debates have focused on whether the rationalization process has stalled as religious and spiritual beliefs appear to have risen to prominence again, or whether the process continues, albeit in new forms.

Meaning and Interpretation

Because Weber's rationalization thesis has been so influential in sociology, we will concentrate on this rather than on philosophical arguments around reason and rationalism. Rationalization is a process of change, beginning in the West, during which more and more aspects of social life come to be shaped by means-to-ends calculations and matters of efficiency. This is in stark contrast to earlier periods, in which traditional practices, customary actions and emotional commitments dominated people's thoughts and actions. Weber saw rationalization becoming cemented by the development of capitalist economics and its need for rational accounting and measurement, but also by the growth of scientific institutions promoting a rational outlook and by **bureaucracy**, which became the dominant, most efficient form of organization.

Weber discussed rationality in terms of four basic types: practical, theoretical, substantive and formal (Kalberg 1985). Practical rationality is in evidence where people generally accept the situation and their actions are guided by essentially pragmatic considerations of how they can make the most of it. Theoretical rationality exists where people try to 'master reality' by thinking through their experience and finding a meaning in life. Philosophers, religious leaders, political theorists and legal thinkers may be seen as adopting forms of theoretical rationality. Substantive rationality directs actions according to a cluster of values in a particular sphere of social life. For instance, friendship relations tend to involve the values of mutual respect, loyalty and assistance, and this value cluster directly frames people's actions in this area of life.

Weber's fourth type, formal rationality, is based on the calculation of the most effective means to achieve a specific goal in the context of a set of general or universal laws or rules. The rationalization of Western societies involves the growth and spread of formal rationality and calculation into more and more spheres of life as bureaucracy becomes the most widely adopted form of organization. Economic decisions are the paradigmatic form, though means–end calculations have become commonplace in many other areas of life too. Rationalized Western music, for example, uses a universal system of notation and measurement of rhythmic and tonal differences and is codified and written down, allowing the compositions of the towering geniuses to be performed by anyone who can read sheet music and play an instrument. Music has become rule-governed, calculable and predictable but less spontaneous and flexible.

As **capitalism** expanded along with state bureaucracies, formal rationality gradually became embedded in the major institutions of society, edging out other forms. Weber was quite clear that this process was likely to be permanent, as the impersonal, bureaucratic form of administration that was adopted throughout office environments, workplaces and state departments was simply the most efficient method of organization yet devised. By squeezing out all personal favours and emotional connections, bureaucracies ensure that the best-qualified people are appointed to each position and that career promotions are based on demonstrated evidence of competence and performance in the role. Remember, this is an **ideal type**! Similarly, the basic double-entry book-keeping associated with capitalist profit-making (recording credits and debits) produces a calculative mentality which encourages instrumentally rational action, and, as capitalist firms become ever larger and more geographically dispersed, an efficient administration becomes ever more important.

Although he saw the growth of this form of rationalization as inevitable, Weber also saw some clear dangers. The pursuit of efficiency and technical progress begins to produce a society that becomes increasingly impersonal, seeming like an external force that controls our destiny. In Weber's thesis, society turns into a 'steel-hard cage' from which there is no prospect of escape. A further consequence is that there is a tendency for the means to dominate over the ends. That is, bureaucracies are a means to achieving other ends, such as an efficient civil service, a well-ordered health service or an efficient welfare benefits system. But over time, as its **power** grows, the bureaucracy takes on a life of its own, so that, rather than being the servant to other ends, it becomes the master. Weber saw this as a process of rationalization towards irrational outcomes which can be observed in many areas of society.

Critical Points

As Weber himself saw, the process of rationalization does not inevitably lead to progressive development, but it can produce contradictory outcomes and new social problems. However, there are also criticisms of the rationalization thesis itself. Although capitalism continues to dominate the world's economies, the extent to which bureaucracies in the traditional mould remain dominant can be questioned. Over recent years, there has been a growth in looser organizational forms that are based more on a **network** structure than on the hierarchical model outlined by Weber (van Dijk 2012). The question is, do such networked organizations still promote formal rationality? Rationalization is also linked to the fate of **religion**, and some sociologists have argued that, far from receding, religion enjoyed a resurgence in the late twentieth century, with religious fundamentalism, televangelism and a range of new religions emerging. Does this represent a 're-enchantment of the world' which runs counter to Weber's rationalization thesis?

Continuing Relevance

Given the rise of critical **postmodern** ideas in the mid-1980s, Weber's rationalization thesis may appear outmoded, as trust in **science** has been eroded and a certain 're-enchantment' of the world seems to be growing (Gane 2002). However, the thesis has proved remarkably productive and applicable to contemporary social change (Cook 2004). Two key studies have been highly influential in extending and modernizing Weber's original ideas. Zygmunt Bauman's *Modernity and the Holocaust* (1989) rejects arguments suggesting that the Nazi policy and implementation of the mass murder of Jewish populations was an essentially 'uncivilized' aberration from the main, progressive direction of modernity. Instead, Bauman shows that the Holocaust could not have taken place without the rational, bureaucratic administration that organized transportation and record-keeping or the rational actions of the perpetrators and victims. In this sense the rationalization process does not inevitably create a bulwark against barbarism but, given the right context, is just as likely to facilitate it.

George Ritzer (2014) applied the rationalization thesis to contemporary fast-food restaurants. He noted that, in Weber's time, the modern bureaucratic office was the ideal-typical vehicle for further rationalization, but in the late twentieth century it became the ubiquitous fast-food restaurant, typified by the McDonald's restaurant chain, whose standardized products, highly efficient service, measurable staff targets and uniform customer experience represent the extension of rationalization into the heart of consumer societies. The McDonald's model has been taken up in many other areas of business and administration. However, Ritzer sees this rationalized model producing its own irrationalities: staff are deskilled and their jobs routinized, the experience for diners is degraded and waste becomes endemic. In the rational quest to reduce chaos and uncertainty, the McDonaldization process generates a new type of 'steel-hard cage'.

References and Further Reading

Bauman, Z. (1989) *Modernity and the Holocaust* (Cambridge: Polity).

Cook, C. (2004) 'Who Cares about Marx, Durkheim and Weber? Social Theory and the Changing Face of Medicine', *Health Sociology Review*, 13(April): 87–96.

Gane, N. (2002) *Max Weber and Postmodern Theory: Rationalization versus Re-enchantment* (Basingstoke: Palgrave Macmillan).

Kalberg, S. (1985) 'Max Weber's Types of Rationality: Cornerstones for the Analysis of Rationalization Processes in History', *American Journal of Sociology*, 85(5): 1145–79.

Ritzer, R. (2014) *The McDonaldization of Society* (8th edn, New York: Sage).

Van Dijk, J. (2012) *The Network Society* (3rd edn, London: Sage).

Society

Working Definition

A concept used to describe the structured social relations and institutions among a large **community** of people which cannot be reduced to a simple collection or aggregation of individuals.

Origins of the Concept

The concept of society can be traced to the fourteenth century, when the primary meaning was companionship or association, and this limited sense can still be seen in eighteenth-century usage to describe upper-class groups or 'high society'. The term was also used to describe groups of like-minded people, as in the 'Society of Friends' (Quakers) or various scientific 'societies'. However, alongside this was a more general and abstract definition of society, which became more firmly established by the late eighteenth century (Williams 1987). From this general concept, the specifically sociological meaning of society was developed in the nineteenth century.

A strong argument can be made that society has been the central concept in sociology, which Émile Durkheim used to establish the new discipline dealing with the collective reality of human life as opposed to studying individuals. Durkheim ([1893] 1984) saw society as an independent reality that existed *sui generis*, or 'in its own right', and that had a profound influence on individuals within a bounded territory. Durkheim's conception of society held its central place in sociology throughout much of the twentieth century and was seriously questioned only from the mid-1970s onwards. Theories of an emergent global level of social reality and theories of **globalization** called Durkheim's essentially nation-state-based concept of society into question. Studying social processes at the global level also drew attention to the movement of people, goods and **culture** across national boundaries, and in the 2000s there have been calls to move sociology beyond the concept of society altogether and into the potentially more productive analysis of 'mobilities'.

Meaning and Interpretation

In sociology, the concept of society has been fundamental to its practitioners' self-**identity**. Many dictionaries and encyclopaedias state as a matter of uncontested fact that sociology is 'the study of societies', defined as large communities existing within the bounded territories called **nation states**. Talcott Parsons added another important feature, namely the ability of a society to be 'self-perpetuating' – that is, its constituent institutions should be able to reproduce society without the need for external assistance. It is certainly the case that, for most of sociology's history, sociologists have studied, compared and contrasted particular societies and their central features, and some of the typologies that have been devised show this very clearly. The older division between First, Second and Third World societies aimed to capture the gross disparities in wealth and economic production across the globe, while contemporary discussions of the different living conditions and prospects of developed and underdeveloped countries now perform a similar function. Such typologies have been useful in alerting us to global inequalities as well as to issues of **power**. Nonetheless, such bald characterizations tell us little if anything about inequalities and power relations *within* national societies.

In addition, there have been many attempts to understand social change by extracting one specific driving force, which has led to many theories of the industrial society, the post-industrial society, the capitalist society, the postmodern society, the knowledge society, the **risk** society and probably many more. All of these theories of change remain essentially rooted in Durkheim's state-based conception, but, arguably, the temptation to extrapolate one aspect of social change as definitive of entire societies shows the limitations of this conception of society.

Critical Points

A theoretical problem with the concept of society is its relatively static, thing-like quality, which has sometimes created the impression that society and the individual are separate 'things'. Many sociologists have seen this dualism as unhelpful and misguided, none more so than Norbert Elias ([1939] 2000), whose own work has been described as a form of 'process sociology' that concentrates on shifting relationships at a variety of levels, from individual **interactions** to interstate **conflicts**. Elias was perhaps the first to dispense with such dualisms, which he saw as the legacy of Western philosophy and which hindered sociological thinking and analysis.

Since the late twentieth century, the concept of society has been brought into sharper critical focus by the realization that supranational social forces are impinging on the ability of individual nation states to determine their own destiny. Globalization has generated much discontent with the concept of society, which does not seem capable of capturing the dynamics of global social change. Large multinational corporations now have incomes that are larger than the GDP of many developing countries and move around the world seeking out sources of cheap labour and subsidized economic environments. National governments have to band together to avoid being drawn into a 'beggar's auction' of low-paid job creation. Terrorist groups such as al-Qaeda organize, recruit and mount attacks in all parts of the world, making international cooperation essential if they are to be effectively combated. These and many more examples show that the level above the nation state is becoming more effective in shaping social life, something which sociologists have to find ways of theorizing. Arguably the concept of society hinders rather than helps us understand global processes.

A more recent example of attempts to move beyond the concept of society is the 'mobilities' project associated with John Urry (2007). This does not deny the power of society altogether, but it does insist that there are other powerful entities as well, including multinational agencies, regional blocs, and so on. More than this, the suggestion is that sociology should be about the study of mobilities – processes of movement across national borders – which are becoming ever more effective in people's everyday lives.

Continuing Relevance

Given the rapid rise of globalization and a huge body of research exploring its contours and future direction, some argue that the concept of society (implying a series of discrete nation states) has no future. John Urry's (2000, 2007) work on 'mobilities' is a good case in point. Globalization involves the more rapid and extensive movement around the world of people, goods, images, finance and much more, which is reshaping the way we think about and study socie-ties. Mainstream sociology worked with the fundamental concept of society con-ceived as a bounded entity more or less coextensive with the nation state. The assumption here was that states were powerful enough to regulate and control their own development so that nation states embarked on different trajectories. However, as global networks and flows become more effective and powerful, they tend to cross national boundaries, which are now seen as more permeable than they once appeared. In this globalizing context, the concept of society becomes less relevant to the emerging sociology of the twenty-first century. The task for sociologists today is to devise ways of understanding the varied range of mobili-ties and what kind of social life they are producing.

In contrast to the mobilities paradigm, others see that the concept of society remains fundamental to the practice of sociology today (Outhwaite 2006). The assessment that the concept of society has little purchase rests in part on the claim that nation states are no longer key actors in human affairs, and this is far from conclusive. State-based societies continue to be the largest 'survival units' capable of mobilizing large populations to defend their territories and, by pooling elements of sovereignty in regional bodies such as the European Union, individual states retain much of their power. However, in June 2016 the UK's referendum on EU membership delivered a majority vote to leave. One key argu-ment of 'leave' campaigners was the idea of taking back control of 'our' country, suggesting that the nation state remains a major source of identification which continues to exert a strong emotional pull. Outhwaite argues that 'society' is also a collective representation, and as such the concept still resonates with people's perception of social reality as it is lived.

References and Further Reading

Durkheim, É. ([1893] 1984) *The Division of Labour in Society* (London: Macmillan).
Elias, N. ([1939] 2000) *The Civilizing Process: Sociogenetic and Psychogenetic Investigations* (Oxford: Blackwell).

Jenkins, R. (2002) *Foundations of Sociology: Towards a Better Understanding of the Human World* (Basingstoke: Palgrave Macmillan), esp. chapter 3.

Outhwaite, W. (2006) *The Future of Society* (Oxford: Blackwell).

Urry, J. (2000) *Sociology Beyond Societies: Mobilities for the Twenty-First Century* (London: Routledge).

— (2007) *Mobilities* (Cambridge: Polity).

Williams, R. (1987) *Keywords: A Vocabulary of Culture and Society* (London: Fontana).

Structure/Agency

Working Definition

A conceptual dichotomy rooted in sociology's attempts to understand the relative balance between **society**'s influence on the individual (structure) and the individual's freedom to act and shape society (agency).

Origins of the Concept

Although questions of human free will have been part of philosophical debates for centuries, in sociology this issue translated into the 'problem' of agency and structure. The problem itself is a direct result of the early sociologists' insistence that there were indeed such things as society and social forces limiting individual choice and freedom. Herbert Spencer and August Comte saw social structures as groups, collectivities and aggregates of individuals, but it was Durkheim's idea of social facts and of society as an entity in its own right that laid out the subject matter of the new discipline. The type of sociology which emerged focused on how individuals are moulded and shaped by social structures that are, to all intents and purposes, external to themselves and beyond their control. In twentieth-century functionalism, Talcott Parsons devised a theory of action which took social structures to be less 'thing-like' and closer to patterns of normative expectations and guidelines governing acceptable behaviour.

By the 1960s, the pendulum had swung against structure-led theories. Dennis Wrong (1961) and others argued that structuralist ideas left too little room for the creative actions of individuals, and many sociologists turned to more agency-focused perspectives, such as symbolic interactionism, phenomenology and ethnomethodology. This shift towards the actor's perspective was part of an emerging theoretical pluralism that students of sociology now experience as the normal state of affairs. However, since the 1980s there have been attempts to integrate structure and agency theoretically, such as the work of Archer (2003), Elias ([1939] 2000), Giddens (1984) and Bourdieu (1986).

Meaning and Interpretation

Structure/agency is one of several related conceptual dichotomies in sociology, including macro/micro and society/individual. The structure/agency distinction is perhaps the most enduring division, and it led Alan Dawe (1971) to argue that there were in fact 'two sociologies', with contrasting subjects, research methods and standards of evidence. Even those who would not go quite that far see grappling with agency/structure as fundamental to the practice of doing sociology.

It may appear that those studying social structures would look at large-scale phenomena at the macro level, ignoring individual action, while those studying agency would focus only on individual actions at the micro level. This is not a bad rule of thumb, but there are structured **interactions** and relationships at the micro level that involve the study of individual actions, and, conversely, it is possible to argue that not only individuals but also collective entities such as trade unions, **social movements** and corporations can be said to 'act' and therefore to exercise creative agency in shaping social life. Thus, the structure/agency dichotomy does not map neatly onto the macro/micro distinction.

Social structures such as the class system, the **family** or the economy are built from social interactions, which endure and change over time. For instance, the **class** system has changed significantly as a result of generally rising income levels, competing forms of **identity** (such as **gender** and **ethnicity**) and the creation of new types of occupation and employment. However, there is still a class system into which people are born and which has a major effect on their life chances. Similarly, family life today is far more diverse than it was even fifty years ago, as societies have become multicultural, more married women enter the workplace and divorce rates have risen sharply, but all families continue to perform important functions such as socialization, which provides the necessary training for life in society. At a general level, then, social structures create order and organize the various spheres within society.

For some the concept of social structure can be hard to accept. At best, social structures are seen as heuristic concepts, constructive fictions created by sociologists to assist their studies, and, at worst, reifications, the illegitimate concretizing as 'things' of what are really fluid sets of social relationships. A key element of interactionism is the interpretation of situations which are influenced by others and involve a certain **reflexivity**. Hence, the kinds of fixed, organizing structures proposed by structural theorists are much more malleable, impermanent and open to change than is supposed. The relatively peaceful 1989 gentle or 'velvet' revolution in Czechoslovakia shows how quickly apparently solid social structures and institutions can crumble under the creative action of individual and collective agency.

The separation of the 'two sociologies' has been seen as a problem for the discipline, because studying structure without agency and agency without structure would seem to limit the sociological imagination to partial accounts of social reality. The solution would seem to be finding a productive way of combining agency/structure which keeps the best insights of both while moving beyond the dichotomy.

Critical Points

Marx offered one way of reframing the problem, arguing that it is indeed people who make history (agency), but that they do not do so under circumstances they have freely chosen (structure). Giddens's (1984) structuration theory owes something to this idea. For Giddens, structure and agency imply each other. Structure is *enabling*, not just constraining, and makes creative action possible, but the repeated actions of many individuals work to reproduce and change the social structure. The focus of Giddens's theory is social practices that are 'ordered across space and time', and it is through these that social structures are reproduced. However, Giddens sees 'structure' as the rules and resources that enable social practices to be reproduced over time, not as abstract, dominating, external forces. This 'duality of structure' is a way of rethinking the previous dichotomy.

Pierre Bourdieu's theorizing is also explicitly aimed at bridging the structure-agency divide. Bourdieu uses the concept of practice to do this. People have embedded, internalized mental structures – their 'habitus' – enabling them to handle and understand the social world. Habitus is the product of a long period spent inhabiting the social world from a specific position (such as class location), and individual habitus therefore varies considerably. Like Giddens, Bourdieu sees many practices developing from this, but for Bourdieu practice always takes place within a 'field' – a sphere of life or realm of society such as the arts, the economy, politics, **education**, and so on. Fields are arenas for competitive struggle in which a variety of resources (types of capital) are used. So, in this model, structure and agency are again seen as intimately related, not opposed.

Continuing Relevance

It seems unlikely that the problem of structure and agency will ever be resolved to everyone's satisfaction. In recent theorizing it is noticeable that Giddens seems to work from an agency perspective while Bourdieu's theory remains closer to a structural position. Whether either has achieved a genuine integration remains a matter of debate. In the future, what we may see are more empirical and historical studies that are able to throw light on the relative balance of structure and agency in specific historical periods, particular societies and spheres of social life.

For instance, a comparative empirical study of the transition from school to work in Canada and Germany explored the decisions taken by young people on whether to apply to university or take on an apprenticeship (Lehmann 2007). Rejecting the notion that structures such as social class have collapsed, giving way to highly individualized forms of identity, this study found that social structure continues to play a large part in shaping the choices and opportunities available to people. However, structure does not entirely determine people's habitus or dispositions. Lehmann argues that the young people engaged actively with their structural, institutional, historical and cultural context and, in the process, formed perceptions of their position within the social structure. As a result, they arrived at their decisions as to which avenue they should pursue. Rather than 'learning to labour', as in Willis's (1977) famous study of class reproduction, the young people here were actually 'choosing to labour'.

References and Further Reading

Archer, M. (2003) *Structure, Agency and the Internal Conversation* (Cambridge: Cambridge University Press).

Bourdieu, P. (1986) *Distinction: A Social Critique of the Judgement of Taste* (London: Routledge & Kegan Paul).

Dawe, A. (1971) 'The Two Sociologies', *British Journal of Sociology*, 21(2): 207–18.

Elias, N. ([1939] 2000) *The Civilizing Process: Sociogenetic and Psychogenetic Investigations* (Oxford: Blackwell).

Giddens, A. (1984) *The Constitution of Society* (Cambridge: Polity).

Lehmann, W. (2007) *Choosing to Labour: School–Work Transitions and Social Class* (Montreal and Kingston: McGill–Queens University Press).

Parker, J. (2005) *Structuration* (Buckingham: Open University Press).

Swingewood, A. (2000) *A Short History of Sociological Thought* (3rd edn, Basingstoke: Palgrave Macmillan), esp. chapter 9.

Van Krieken, R. (1998) *Norbert Elias* (London: Routledge), esp. chapter 3.

Willis, P. (1977) *Learning to Labour: How Working-Class Kids Get Working-Class Jobs* (London: Saxon House).

Wrong, D. (1961) 'The Over-Socialized Conception of Man in Modern Sociology', *American Sociological Review*, 26: 183–93.

2 Doing Sociology

Ideal Type

Working Definition

The researcher's 'pure' construct of a social phenomenon, emphasizing only some of its main aspects, which is used to approach the similarities and differences in concrete, real-world cases.

Origins of the Concept

The concept of the ideal type was devised by Max Weber as part of his method for studying social action as a form of sociology. For Weber, understanding and explaining social life was not possible using the same methods as the natural **sciences**. Human beings, unlike other beings in the natural world, create a meaningful **environment**, and to understand their individual actions we have to set these within the context of that social environment. Of course, people create organizations and social institutions, which some sociologists see as their main object of research, but Weber ([1904] 1949) argued that a full account of social phenomena has to be understandable at the level of individual action. This approach to sociology is known as *Verstehen*, and Weber used it to explore the origins and key aspects of **capitalism** and its relationship to religious belief, the different types of economic life across societies, types of **authority** and leadership, and forms of organization in different historical periods. Constructing ideal types was an important element of Weber's method that allowed him to bring together the macro and micro levels of sociological analysis.

Meaning and Interpretation

Ideal types are 'constructs' – that is, they are created by researchers on the basis of criteria derived from their interest in a particular social phenomenon. For example, we could construct an ideal type of socialism, **democracy**, cybercrime, consumer **society** or **moral panic**. However, in making the construct, we do not aim to combine as many aspects of the phenomenon as possible in order to produce an accurate depiction of it. Because, Weber argued, sociology cannot replicate the experimental methods of the natural sciences, we need to find other ways of gaining valid knowledge of society, and the ideal type is one useful tool which helps us do that.

For example, if we want to understand the 'new terrorism' of al-Qaeda net-works and the self-styled Islamic State (*Daesh*), we can identify some typical aspects from our observations – perhaps their global connections, loose organizational forms, disparate aims and preparedness to use extreme violence against civilian targets. Then we can create our ideal type around these central features. Of course, real cases of the new terrorism will include more than just these elements and, in some cases, one or more elements may be absent while others are more prominent. For example, *Daesh* actions in Syria and Iraq involved creating an effective army, rather than a loose **network**, that succeeded in temporarily taking and holding territory. However, in creating an ideal type we are intentionally creating a one-sided model, a pure form, which probably does not or never could exist in reality. Those people, cells and organizations involved in the new terrorism may actually behave in ways that diverge from our ideal type. But the point of the exercise is to highlight a logically derived form of the new terrorism which will enable us to compare it with older forms and pick out significant similarities and crucial differences among real-world cases much more easily. Ideal types are heuristic devices – research tools that sociologists use to devise hypotheses and make comparisons.

An ideal type is akin to a standpoint from which we can observe the social world, a reference point that enables the researcher to begin to formulate some realistic questions about the phenomena in question. Hence, ideal types can never be said to be true or false, and it was not Weber's intention that they should be tested against empirical cases in the same way that might be the situation with scientific hypotheses, and then falsified if negative instances are found. Their value lies in the research that flows from them and the contribution they make to our understanding. If ideal types fail to give us any better grasp of reality or just do not work in generating further research questions and studies, they will simply be abandoned as, simply and literally, useless.

Critical Points

Weber's critics see ideal types as being of limited use in sociology. Norbert Elias, for instance, caustically remarked that it was strange to think we should spend our time constructing ideal types when we can study 'real types' or empirical cases instead. This criticism seems a good one, though we have to remember that ideal types are meant to be part of the preliminary stages of research which will then develop into formal empirical studies.

A further problem with ideal types lies more in the way they are used than in the concept itself. In particular, what starts out as a heuristic device to aid understanding can quickly become a real characterization that needs to be defended. In short, a fictitious ideal type comes to be treated as though it represents a real social phenomenon and, instead of aiding understanding, becomes an obstacle to it. Talcott Parsons observed this slippage even in Weber's own work on 'capitalism', in which he moves between the construct and the unique historical form. In Parsons's view, the ideal type is useful when identifying general aspects of social phenomena for comparative studies, but much less so when investigating unique historical periods and **cultures**, which demand detailed empirical investigation.

Continuing Relevance

Ideal types continue to be used in sociology, especially when apparently new phenomena emerge. Sociologists researching 'new' **social movements** (NSMs), the 'new' terrorism or 'new' wars have all constructed ideal types of the phenomena they want to study, which they then use to guide their research into specific cases. For instance, theories of NSMs in the 1980s portrayed them as relatively loosely organized, involving mainly the new middle classes, which employed symbolic direct actions to bring new issues, such as the environment, to public attention. This ideal typical model was then subject to merciless critique, as historical sociologists such as Craig Calhoun (1993) had little difficulty finding 'new social movements' back in the nineteenth century. However, without the initial ideal type to guide the later research effort, we may not have arrived at the present more realistic understanding of the new movements. This is a good example of the continuing value of the ideal type as a heuristic tool that stimulates research and helps us gain a better understanding of social phenomena.

In a critique of the type of **class** analysis conducted by researchers looking to explore the Goldthorpe class scheme, Prandy (2002) notices some similarities with Weberian ideal types and their problems. Many empirical studies of social class necessarily have to summarize a whole series of characteristics into ideal-typical class categories. In a sense this is a similar procedure to the generation of stereotypes in social life: in both cases, the resulting types are inevitably oversimplifications that are not intended to represent real-world class groups accurately. Because of this, Prandy's concern is that theories built on this kind of analysis are effectively insulated from empirical falsification. His article explores a potential alternative to this standard method.

References and Further Reading

Calhoun, C. (1993) '"New Social Movements" of the Early Nineteenth Century', *Social Science History*, 17(3): 385–427.

Hekman, S. J. ([1983] 2006) *Weber, the Ideal Type and Contemporary Social Theory* (Notre Dame, IN: University of Notre Dame Press).

Lister, C. R. (2015) *The Islamic State: A Brief Introduction* (Washington, DC: Brookings Institution Press).

Parkin, F. (2009) *Max Weber* (rev. edn, London: Routledge), esp. chapter 1.

Prandy, K. (2002) 'Ideal Types, Stereotypes and Classes', *British Journal of Sociology*, 53(4): 583–601.

Weber, M. ([1904] 1949) 'Objectivity in Social Science and Social Policy', in E. A. Shils and H. A. Finch (eds), *The Methodology of the Social Sciences* (New York: Free Press), pp. 50–112.

Qualitative/Quantitative Methods

Working Definition

A basic distinction between those approaches to research that look for in-depth knowledge by tapping into the subject's reasoning and decision-making processes (qualitative) and those that make extensive use of measurement to quantify social phenomena (quantitative).

Origins of the Concept

Quantitative research was central to sociology from the discipline's inception. Durkheim's use of official statistics to quantify suicide rates and make comparisons across societies is typical of the kind of technique sociologists adopted. Given the desire in the nineteenth century to establish sociology as the '**science of society**', it is not surprising that sociologists turned to quantitative methods, which held out the promise of accurate and reliable measurement. Such methods also offered the potential for comparative and historical studies which could yield insights into the extent of social changes, both geographically and over time.

Qualitative research began as a more specialized form, acting as a kind of under-labourer to supposedly more significant, large-scale quantitative studies. Qualitative work was often seen as an important prerequisite which took the form of small pilot studies aimed at clarifying meanings. From the 1970s, though, this situation began to change, and qualitative research gradually came to be seen as a method of inquiry in its own right. For a growing number of sociologists today, qualitative research is actually superior to quantitative methods, being a more appropriate, object-adequate type for the study of human beings and social life.

Meaning and Interpretation

Quantitative studies typically produce numerical information in the form of, say, numbers or percentages, in order to assess the size of a social problem or the percentage of a given population sharing similar attitudes. Descriptive statistical information is extremely useful in helping us to create an accurate picture of society. What proportion of the population is working class? What is the proportion of married women in paid employment? How many people believe that global warming is real? All these questions demand quantitative research, which is typically carried out by selecting a representative population sample from which general conclusions can be drawn. Quantitative samples tend to be much larger than those used in qualitative research in order to enable statistical testing.

Quantitative methods can be taken a stage further using inferential statistical analysis, which tries to arrive at general conclusions about data – for example, on the probability that an identified difference between groups within a sample is reliable and has not occurred simply by chance. Inferential statistics are widely used in variable analysis, when sociologists try to pick their way through several variables that are found to be correlated in order to establish relationships of cause and effect. This has been made somewhat easier over recent years with the advent of computer-based software programs such as the ubiquitous SPSS, which simplify the manipulation of raw data and enable automated calculations. Ironically, perhaps, this development has coincided with a turn towards qualitative methods in sociology.

Qualitative research includes all of the following methods: focus groups, ethnography, semi-structured or unstructured questionnaires, face-to-face interviews, participant observation, biographical research, oral histories, narrative studies, grounded theory and life histories. In all of these, sociologists try to understand how social life is lived and how people interpret and make sense of their social position. In short, the aim is to tap into the quality of people's social lives, not to measure the shape and size of society as a whole. One area in which qualitative inquiry has had success is in giving a voice to under-represented or disadvantaged social groups. Studies of homelessness, self-harm, domestic violence, children's experiences and many more have benefited enormously from qualitative research methods designed to allow marginalized groups to speak freely.

One further benefit of qualitative methods is the possibility of enhancing the validity of research conclusions. Within interviews or ethnographies, researchers can tell participants how they are interpreting their responses and ask if that understanding is correct. After interview, a debriefing session can be held which allows any possible misunderstandings to be ironed out. In the approach known as grounded theory, the traditional deductive method involving the construction of hypotheses which are then empirically tested is turned on its head, as researchers collect data in the form of interview transcripts before exploring these in systematic ways, using sorting, coding and categorizing, before moving on to the creation of concepts and theories which are said to 'emerge' from the data. All of these interactions mean the involvement of research participants in the research process rather than maintaining a strict division between researcher and subject.

Critical Points

The increasing use of qualitative research methods has produced many useful and insightful studies, but some sociologists are concerned that quantitative methods may be falling out of favour. In a national survey of British sociology students' attitudes to quantitative methods, Williams et al. (2008) found that many students had anxieties about working with numbers and learning statistical techniques. More worrying is that a majority of the authors' sample just had little or no interest in quantitative methods because their perception of sociology was of a discipline that lies closer to the humanities than to the sciences. This apparent generational shift in attitudes may pose a danger to the status of sociology as a scientific discipline and consequently to its funding streams and, ultimately, student recruitment.

In spite of the apparently clear distinction between qualitative and quantitative methods, some sociologists argue that the divide is not as firm as previously thought. Some qualitative methods also involve numerical measurement and, conversely, some ostensibly quantitative methods analyse meaningful statements (Bryman 2015). Qualitative researchers use software packages to analyse large amounts of text and interview material by codifying, categorizing and quantifying it, while some quantitative studies are conducted via semi-structured interviews that allow participants to go beyond the fixed frame of researchers' questionnaires. Survey research is also interested in people's attitudes and opinions, which suggests a concern with meanings and interpretation, while the conclusions drawn in many observational studies of social **interaction** implicitly assume a more general application.

Continuing Relevance

Some qualitative researchers take the view that measurement and statistical testing are not appropriate for the study of meaning-making humans, while some quantitative researchers see many of the methods adopted by qualitative sociologists as too subjective to be reliable and hopelessly individualistic. But an increasing number of projects now adopt 'mixed-methods' approaches, which use both quantitative and qualitative methods. Findings that are consistent across quantitative and qualitative methods are likely to be more valid and reliable than those arrived at using just one. In mixed-methods studies, the choice of research method tends to be driven by research questions and practical considerations.

A good example of the productive use of mixed methods can be found in the study of cultural capital – as outlined by Bourdieu (1986) – and social exclusion over a three-year period (2003–6) by Silva and her colleagues (2009). The project made use of a survey, household interviews and focus groups, thus mixing quantitative with qualitative methods. The authors describe their approach as 'methodological eclecticism', arguing that this not only allows a way of corroborating facts but also enables the plausibility of interpretations to be checked.

Mixed-methods approaches are not without problems. Giddings and Grant (2007) suspect that many mixed-methods studies favour the kind of evidence that is characteristic of a positivist orientation at the expense of alternative forms of inquiry. The pragmatic, apparently 'post-positivist' methodology then becomes a Trojan horse for a resurgent positivism. This is visible, according to Giddings and Grant, in the kinds of studies now popular in health, education and applied social science, particularly those studies reliant on government research funds. Positivistic experimental designs – those based on methods derived from the natural sciences – have become the 'gold standard' for government-funded research, and many pragmatic mixed-methods approaches promote this idea at the expense of all alternative avenues of research. However, it is not mixed-methods approaches per se that form the target here, but those versions which reinforce positivist experimental design as the best or only way to scientific truth.

References and Further Reading

Bryman, A. (2015) *Social Research Methods* (5th edn, Oxford: Oxford University Press), esp. parts 2, 3 and 4.
Giddings, L. S., and Grant, B. M. (2007) 'A Trojan Horse for Positivism? A Critique of Mixed Methods Research', *Advances in Nursing Science*, 30(1): 52–60.
Silva, E., Warde, A., and Wright, D. (2009) 'Using Mixed Methods for Analysing Culture: The Cultural Capital and Social Exclusion Project', *Cultural Sociology*, 3(2): 299–316.
Williams, M., Payne, G., Hodgkinson, L., and Poade, D. (2008) 'Does British Sociology Count?', *Sociology*, 42(5): 1003–21.

Realism

Working Definition

An approach to social research that insists on the existence of an objective external reality, the underlying causes of which are amenable to scientific investigation.

Origins of the Concept

Though the term 'realism' has been in use since ancient times, it entered social science via the sixteenth- and seventeenth-century philosophical debates between proponents of realism and idealism in the study of knowledge. Philosophical realists argued that there is a real world out there which can be known only through sense experience and observation. The task of **science** is to represent the real world in its descriptions and explanations so that, as these improve, we get closer and closer to the truth. Philosophical idealists saw knowledge as starting from the human mind rather than from an external world, so that the structures of our thinking effectively determine what can be known about that world. There is, then, no 'direct', unmediated access to an external world 'out there'.

In the 1970s there emerged a reinvigorated 'critical' form of realism associated with the ideas of Roy Bhaskar ([1975] 2008), Andrew Sayer (1999) and others. Critical realism has come to be seen as an alternative to social constructionist approaches in sociology, thus mirroring the old philosophical debate between idealism and realism. Critical realism looks to preserve the scientific credentials of sociology but without the drawbacks associated with positivism, and it has developed into a tradition of inquiry that is particularly influential within British sociology. Critical realism provides a method which can be used to study social phenomena of all kinds, though it has been more widely adopted in some fields, such as **environmental** sociology, than others.

Meaning and Interpretation

Critical realism is not just a philosophy of science but also a research method that, its advocates argue, is capable of getting below the surface of observable events to gain access to the underlying causes or 'generative mechanisms' of real-world phenomena. It is a serious attempt to maintain the social sciences as 'sciences', and those who endorse it claim it is the task of scientists to uncover the underlying social processes that produce the world we experience and observe. The realists' starting point is that human societies are part of nature and that both should be studied together using the same method. But this does not mean importing natural science methods into sociology. Instead, the realist method is said to be appropriate for both natural and social sciences.

A fundamental tenet of critical realism is that knowledge is stratified, and realists work with both abstract and concrete levels of knowledge. Abstract knowledge consists of high-level theories, such as natural science 'laws' or general theories of society, while concrete knowledge refers to that which is contingent in historically specific circumstances. The study of specific historical situations or 'conjunctions' is then required, along with detailed empirical research, in order to sort out how contingent factors interact with necessary relations to produce specific conjunctural outcomes that can be observed. In a simple example, Dickens (2004) says that gunpowder has an unstable chemical structure giving it the causal **power** to explode. But whether this power is triggered depends on other contingent factors – how it has been stored, whether it is linked to an ignition source and how much of it there is. Similarly, human beings have certain powers and capacities (human nature), but whether they are able to exercise these depends on historically contingent factors too: are they enabled or constrained by existing social relations, and does society provide enough opportunities for their abilities to be used?

Clearly critical realism approaches knowledge production in a different way than does **social constructionism**. Constructionist studies very often adopt an 'agnostic' stance towards the reality of a social problem such as global warming, leaving such assessments to environmental scientists and others. But realists want to bring together natural and social scientific knowledge, which should produce a better and more comprehensive understanding of global warming and its underlying causes or 'generative mechanisms'. Some critical realists see Marx's theory of **alienation** as an early realist social theory, as it links a theory of human nature to contingent factors such as the emergence of capitalist social relations, which effectively prevent humans from fully realizing their 'species being'.

Critical Points

One problem with critical realism is its willingness to make use of natural science knowledge. Given that they are not routinely trained in the natural sciences and are not in a position to enter debates on, say, the physics and chemistry of climate change processes, on what basis can sociologists assess this evidence? If we simply accept natural scientific knowledge, this appears to many social constructionists as rather naïve. This is especially the case as there is a long tradition within the sociology of scientific knowledge of studying the processes through which scientific consensus is arrived at. For sociologists of science, it is absolutely necessary to adopt an agnostic stance in order to maintain the relative detachment required to get under the skin of experimental procedures and other scientific methods.

There is also an internal debate within critical realism regarding the extent to which the natural and social sciences can be studied using the same method. Bhaskar himself, for instance, has argued that there are fundamental differences between social and natural sciences. He sees social structures as different from natural structures. Social structures do not endure over long periods of time and are not independent of people's perceptions of their actions. Hence, it may be necessary to use different methods for studying social and natural phenomena. But, if this is true, then critical realism may not offer the kind of unifying approach which makes it so attractive as an alternative to postmodernism and other 'decorative sociologies'.

Continuing Relevance

In spite of criticisms, it can be argued that all sociological studies in practice adopt some form of 'simple' realism regardless of theoretical and methodological perspective. What would be the point of carrying out research if we did not think there was a real social world out there worth studying? Critical realism is seen as a way of moving sociology away from some of the strict social constructionist arguments which deny the reality of the natural world. For many sociologists who see strict constructionism as an abdication of professional responsibility, critical realism offers perhaps the most attractive, non-positivist alternative currently available.

Probably the best way to grasp critical realism is to look at some specific examples. For instance, Suzanne Fitzpatrick (2005) shows how a critical realist approach to social problems analysis can generate more rigorous and causally adequate analyses. Fitzpatrick explored the problem of homelessness, arguing that currently dominant approaches to the problem combine individual and structural factors into what is thought to be more comprehensive explanations. However, many of these also present structural factors – such as **poverty** – as most significant. A realist approach allows for the fact that explanations are always contingent, so, while unemployment may be more significant in rising youth unemployment, personal factors such as bereavement could affect older people more. The balance between individual and structural causes will differ across social groups and particular types of homelessness, and a realist approach is arguably more attuned to this complexity.

Critical realism has also been applied to the study of crime and is seen as holding out the possibility of reinvigorating the policy relevance of criminology. Matthews (2009) argues that much contemporary criminology is pessimistic about intervening to reduce crime and recidivism, as nothing seems to work. But he suggests that realism requires interventions to be more than simply strategies or practices. Interventions embody theories about what might work in particular contexts, and an important aspect is not just the intervention but evaluating it to identify the points at which the intervention fails. Because all interventions target active human agents, their aim is to change or shape the potential criminal's reasoning process. For Matthews (2009: 357), even if such interventions do not have a radical transformative impact, 'even small gains are gains' that may lead to further reforms.

References and Further Reading

Bhaskar, R. A. ([1975] 2008) *A Realist Theory of Science* (London: Verso).

Carter, B. (2000) *Realism and Racism: Concepts of Race in Sociological Research* (London: Routledge).

Dickens, P. (2004) *Society and Nature: Changing our Environment, Changing Ourselves* (Cambridge: Polity), esp. pp. 1–24.

Fitzpatrick, S. (2005) 'Explaining Homelessness: A Critical Realist Perspective', *Housing, Theory and Society*, 22(1): 1–17.

Matthews, R. (2009) 'Beyond "So What?" Criminology', *Theoretical Criminology*, 13(3): 341–62.

Sayer, A. (1999) *Realism and Social Science* (London: Sage).

Reflexivity

Working Definition

A characterization of the relationship between knowledge and **society** and/or researcher and subject, focusing on the continuous reflection of social actors on themselves and their social context.

Origins of the Concept

Reflexivity is related to ideas of reflection or self-reflection, and therefore it has a very long history. However, its usage in the social **sciences** can be traced back to the ideas of George Herbert Mead (1934) and Charles H. Cooley (1902) on the **social self**, W. I. Thomas's **social constructionist** approach, and some early work on self-fulfilling and self-defeating prophecies. Cooley and Mead rejected the notion that the individual self is innate. Instead, Cooley argued that the self is created through social **interaction** with others as people come to see themselves in the way others see them. In Mead's theory, this continuous interaction between the biological human organism and the social environment of other people produces a two-part self consisting of an 'I' and a 'me', which are in constant internal conversation within the individual person. This individual reflexivity forms the backdrop to meaningful social interaction.

However, individual and social reflexivity have become more central to social theory from the late twentieth century. In particular, the theoretical ideas of Ulrich Beck (1994) and Anthony Giddens (1984) have extended the concept of reflexivity from the individual to the social level, while a renewed emphasis on **qualitative** research methods has drawn attention to the fundamentally reflexive nature of social life per se. The existence of both individual and social reflexivity has been seen as fatally undermining any vestiges of positivism in sociology.

Meaning and Interpretation

For Cooley, Mead and the symbolic interactionist tradition more generally, the process of 'self' construction makes human beings 'reflexive' – actively engaged in social life and, at the same time, able to reflect on it. This individual reflexivity means that active human agents can confound scientists' predictions of how they will or should behave, and it also shows that the thing called 'society' is a continuous social construction rather than a fixed, objective entity that is set apart from individuals. Self-fulfilling prophecies can illustrate some of the consequences of reflexivity as well. Rumours of trouble at a solidly solvent bank can lead to investors rushing to withdraw their money, which in turn fulfils the false prophecy by putting the bank into trouble (Merton [1949] 1957). Knowledge and information of all kinds have the potential to alter people's decision-making processes and lead to unpredictable actions.

In the work of Anthony Giddens, Ulrich Beck and others, reflexivity is a key concept for understanding contemporary societies. Giddens and Beck argue that 'late' **modernity** is a 'de-traditionalized' social context in which individuals are cut adrift from the social structure and, hence, forced to be continuously reflexive in relation to their own lives and identities. Beck calls this emergent form of society 'reflexive modernization', a 'second modernity' or a '**risk** society' beyond the industrial form. The consequences of this heightened reflexivity for research practice are said to be profound. Sociological research findings become part of society's stock of knowledge, which individuals carry around with them and which underpins their decision-making. The kind of recursive effects evident in self-fulfilling and self-defeating prophecies become part and parcel of social life as such. In this way a simple positivistic approach based on the objective study of an external world 'out there' appears misguided, as the gap between researcher and research subject is eroded. Similarly, the methods adopted by sociologists have to reflect this, which may be why qualitative methods such as biographical research, oral histories and the inclusion of the researcher's own biography in the research process are growing in popularity. The concept of reflexivity has become central to both social theorizing and sociological research methods, pointing up the inevitable connections between the two.

Critical Points

The theory of reflexive modernization and the heightened individualization that is assumed by it is open to criticism on empirical grounds. While some of the social changes described by the theory are indisputable – the diversification of **family** life, shifting marriage and divorce rates, for example – the idea that the industrial society has given way to a new form of reflexive modernity is contentious. Has handling risk really become the new organizing principle of contemporary societies? Industrial production processes are now global in scope, with most manufacturing taking place in the developing countries, and it can be argued that industrial **capitalism** remains the best characterization of societies today. The thesis of individualization and enhanced reflexivity can also be exaggerated. Though people may not consciously identify with social **class**, for instance, in quite the same way that they did in the first half of the twentieth century, it does not follow that their lives and life chances are no longer shaped by class position. Indeed, there has been a backlash against the individualization thesis as sociologists have shown the continuing salience of class.

The adoption of reflexivity in sociological research has also had a mixed reception. For some, the rush to include the researcher's own biography within the research process can all too easily tip over into self-indulgence and an irrelevant listing of personal details. In addition, a focus on reflexivity can lead into a never-ending process of reflecting on reflection and interpretation layered on interpretation, which risks paralysing researchers who get caught up in their own practice at the expense of what many consider to be the real task of sociology, namely to produce valid and reliable knowledge of social life in order better to understand and explain it. It is also unclear how reflexive research practice could apply to the large-scale social and attitude surveys that are still necessary if we are to uncover the patterns and regularities that form the basis of societies.

Continuing Relevance

Not all of those who adopt more reflexive research methods in their work would subscribe to Beck's reflexive modernization theory or Giddens's thesis of de-traditionalization. For many, reflexivity is simply part of the way they approach the job of studying society which helps them to be more aware of their own biases and theoretical assumptions. Certainly a dose of reflexivity can be very healthy for researchers who might otherwise not be in the habit of reflecting on their longstanding habits and practices.

To get a sense of what it means for the researcher to bring their self into the research process, try Kim Etherington's *Becoming a Reflexive Researcher* (2004), which is a very hands-on, practical guide to doing reflexive research. However, not all sociologists are in favour of researchers laying out their personal and biographical details as part of their studies, which can seem self-indulgent and perhaps irrelevant. Nevertheless, in the present period it does seem likely that we will see younger researchers increasingly looking to build reflexivity into their research designs.

References and Further Reading

Beck, U. (1994) 'The Reinvention of Politics: Towards a Theory of Reflexive Modernization', in U. Beck, A. Giddens and S. Lash, *Reflexive Modernization: Politics, Tradition and Aesthetics in the Modern Social Order* (Cambridge: Polity), pp. 1–55.

Buttel, F. H. (2002) 'Classical Theory and Contemporary Environmental Sociology: Some Reflections on the Antecedents and Prospects for Reflexive Modernization Theories in the Study of Environment and Society', in G. Spaargaren, A. P. J. Mol and F. H. Buttel (eds), *Environment and Global Modernity* (London: Sage), pp. 17–40.

Cooley, C. H. (1902) *Human Nature and the Social Order* (New York: Scribner's).

Etherington, K. (2004) *Becoming a Reflexive Researcher: Using Our Selves in Research* (London: Jessica Kingsley).

Finlay, L., and Gough, B. (eds) (2003) *Reflexivity: A Practical Guide for Researchers in Health and Social Sciences* (Chichester: Wiley-Blackwell).

Giddens, A. (1984) *The Constitution of Society* (Cambridge: Polity).

Mead, G. H. (1934) *Mind, Self and Society*, ed. C. W. Morris (Chicago: University of Chicago Press).

Merton, R. H. ([1949] 1957) *Social Theory and Social Structure* (rev. edn, Glencoe, IL: Free Press).

Science

Working Definition

A method of gaining valid and reliable knowledge of the world based on testing theories against collected evidence.

Origins of the Concept

The concept of science originated as a description of knowledge as such, but, by the fourteenth century in Europe, science or 'natural philosophy' was used in a more limited way to describe knowledge that was written down and recorded. During the seventeenth-century 'scientific revolution', which included many breakthroughs, such as Newton's discovery of the force of gravity, science came to be seen more as a method of inquiry. By the nineteenth century the term came to be used only in relation to the physical world and the disciplines which studied it, among them astronomy, physics and chemistry. At the end of that century, debates in the philosophy of science focused on what kind of methods were 'scientific', how scientific knowledge could be verified as true, and, eventually, whether the emerging social subjects could match the kinds of evidence produced in the natural sciences.

In the twentieth century, various schools of positivism argued the relative merits of deduction or induction and verification or falsification as principles to which all sciences, not just the natural science disciplines, should adhere. However, gradually sociologists came to see their discipline as scientific but in a different way to the natural sciences, on account of the intentional actions of humans and the **reflexivity** that exists between **society** and sociological knowledge. Today sociology is divided between those who continue to see themselves as scientists of society and those who are happier with the idea that they engage in social studies, rendering questions of scientific method and **status** obsolete.

Meaning and Interpretation

Arguably, the key issue for sociology since Auguste Comte's positivism has been whether or not sociology is a science. How does the discipline relate to other acknowledged sciences such as astronomy, physics, chemistry and biology? And what is it that makes them so unproblematically 'scientific' anyway? Many people believe that scientific research involves the use of systematic methods, the gathering of empirical evidence, the analysis of data and the development of theoretical explanations for that data. Over time, the sciences can then build a significant body of reliable knowledge. If we accept this characterization, then sociology is a science, as it does involve systematic methods of empirical investigation, the analysis of data and the assessment of theories in the light of evidence and logical argument. However, a growing number of sociologists are uneasy about discussing their discipline as scientific and may be more comfortable seeing it as closer to the humanities than to the natural sciences.

Studying human beings is clearly different in some ways from observing events in the natural world, so maybe sociology and the natural sciences can never be identical. Human beings do not merely act on instinct or through some biological imperative but interact with each other in meaningful ways. This means that, in order to describe and explain social life, sociologists need to find ways of understanding *why* people act in the ways that they do. People generally behave according to intentions, and sociologists will often reconstruct the meanings individuals attached to their own actions. To grasp the behaviour of frogs involves no such reconstruction of complex mental reasoning. The meaningful nature of human action is both an advantage and a problem. Sociologists cannot simply adopt the methods of successful natural sciences such as biology or chemistry but must devise their own methods that are adequate for their specific subject matter – human beings and social life. One important advantage is that sociologists can speak directly with their research participants and understand the responses they get. This opportunity to converse with the participants of research studies and to confirm one's interpretations means that sociological findings are, at least potentially, even more reliable (different researchers would arrive at the same results) and valid (the research actually measures what it is supposed to) than those from the natural sciences. Max Weber saw such gains as crucial to the scientific status of sociology. Even though its methods are necessarily different, they are no less systematic, rigorous and theoretically informed than those of any other science.

Yet sociologists face some problems that natural scientists do not. Self-aware individuals may subtly alter their usual behaviour when they know it is being studied, thereby invalidating the researcher's findings. For instance, in daily life people constantly attempt to manage the presentation of their self to others, and this process of 'impression management' may occur during sociological research. Sociologists must be aware of the distinct possibility that, during interviews and questionnaires, respondents may offer the answers they believe the researchers are looking for. These various issues illustrate a key feature of studying human beings – the problem of reflexivity.

Sociological knowledge filters back into society and becomes part of the very same social context being studied, potentially altering that social context. Social reflexivity has no counterpart in the natural sciences, which means that, if it is a science, sociology cannot simply adopt the same methods as natural science but must develop its own 'object-adequate' methods.

Critical Points

A fundamental problem with the notion that sociology should be scientific is that it presumes agreement on what constitutes science. Although this used to mean simply looking at what the natural sciences do, this is no longer the case. Several important studies by historians of science have eroded the certainty which used to exist in relation to science. Thomas Kuhn (1970) studied breakthroughs in science – scientific revolutions – which we might expect would occur as a result of knowledge accumulation over long periods. In fact, Kuhn saw natural science operating through 'paradigms' – ways of doing science based on particular theories. 'Normal' science was essentially a continual testing and retesting of the paradigm, which did not lead to major advances. Breakthrough moments happened when someone went beyond the paradigm to resolve an anomalous finding which then led to a new paradigm.

A further blow to the **ideal type** of science came from historical studies of scientific methods by Paul Feyerabend (1975). He argued that many revolutionary discoveries in science had nothing to do with scientific method. Instead, they came about through simple trial and error or even by mistakes and chance occurrences which simply cannot be taught. Feyerabend's conclusion was that there is only one important principle of scientific method – 'anything goes'. Only by encouraging **deviance** from the scientific model could innovation be safeguarded. Sticking rigidly to one method was merely a recipe for stagnation and a lack of progress. Hence, after many decades of trying to work out how sociology could mimic the methods of the natural sciences, by the 1980s it no longer seemed a worthwhile exercise.

Continuing Relevance

Science is still viewed by many as a superior form of knowledge compared to theological knowledge or common-sense ideas, though the basis of this superiority may be based on awareness of the practical successes of science rather than on a widespread understanding of the scientific method. Even those sociologists who do not view their discipline as scientific generally see their own systematic and methodologically rigorous studies as the best way of producing reality-congruent knowledge. For example, in social welfare, health and government there has been a strong trend towards 'evidence-based policy-making', which suggests that some of the principles of scientific work continue to inform public policy. Sociologists also have to pay heed to more prosaic matters, such as the demands of funding agencies, which require clear evidence of scientific rigour and innovation before funding research studies. In addition, the development of critical **realism** and its adoption in many recent research studies testifies to the desire among many sociologists to hang onto their scientific credentials in a 'post-positivist' age.

References and Further Reading

Benton, T., and Craib, I. (2010) *Philosophy of Social Science: The Philosophical Foundations of Social Thought* (2nd edn, Basingstoke: Palgrave Macmillan).

Chalmers, A. F. (2013) *What is this Thing Called Science?* (4th edn, Maidenhead: Open University Press).

Feyerabend, P. (1975) *Against Method* (London: New Left Books).

Fuller, S. (1998) *Science* (Buckingham: Open University Press).

Kuhn, T. (1970) *The Structure of Scientific Revolutions* (Chicago: University of Chicago Press).

Social Constructionism

Working Definition

An approach to sociology which is agnostic towards the reality of social phenomena, preferring to investigate the way that these are produced within social relationships.

Origins of the Concept

The origins of social constructionism can be traced back to the 'social problems' perspective of the early 1970s, which saw social problems as claims on people's attention and the state's resources. In a competitive claims **environment** where there are always too many claims for the available resources, this perspective analysed how some claims are able to rise to prominence while others are neglected. However, constructionism today also draws on ideas from the sociology of scientific knowledge (known as SSK), which studies the social processes underlying knowledge production. SSK sees **science** as itself a form of social activity which must therefore be amenable to sociological investigation. Scientific theories are products of their **society**, and SSK has often questioned their apparently 'universal' validity.

The coming together of these two strands has led to a general and widespread social constructionism in sociology. This general perspective has been used to analyse a variety of phenomena, from the social construction of Europe to serial homicide, dementia, **sexuality** and even the ocean. The common theme in all of these studies is an attempt to raise questions about the 'natural' or 'objective' **status** of their objects of inquiry. Social constructionist arguments have also been useful for **social movements**, such as feminism and disabled people's movements, which challenge the seemingly 'natural' status quo that disadvantages women and disabled people respectively.

Meaning and Interpretation

Social constructionism is very widely adopted in sociology and involves piecing together all the elements which have brought about a specific social phenomenon, such as **gender** or crime. Constructionism challenges conventional wisdom and common-sense ideas in so far as these accept the existence of, say, gender and crime as natural or normal. For social constructionists, gender and crime are created through historical social processes and social **interactions**. Of course, this means that gender and crime are not fixed and can be shown to have changed, in both meaning and form, over time and across societies. In this way, social constructionism is rooted in the idea that society and its institutions are always in process, and the task of sociology is to investigate this constant process.

Not all constructionist approaches are the same, and a basic distinction has been made between 'strong' and 'weak' forms, a distinction lifted from SSK. However, recently this distinction has been reframed as a contrast between 'strict' and 'contextual' constructionism, which appears to be more neutral. Strict constructionists argue that neither nature nor society presents itself in unmediated form. All phenomena are accessible only through human concepts and theories, and these are open to change – sometimes quite radical change. Strict constructionists are a small minority of constructionists. The vast majority of constructionist studies are happy to acknowledge that there is a reality that is external to sociologists' **discourse**, but what is at issue is how we gain access to it. Contextual constructionists have much to say about social and environmental problems and the claims that social groups make about them, pointing out that what cannot be accepted at face value is the existing hierarchy of social problems. Some problems seem very urgent and in need of attention, but others appear relatively trivial and can be safely ignored. Contextual constructionists take the present ordering of social problems as the starting point. Does this ordering actually reflect the seriousness of society's problems? Sociology can perform a useful role in investigating the arguments made by 'claims-makers' and 'claims-deniers', and sociologists can thereby ensure that all the information needed for a rational evaluation can be put into the public domain.

A good example of how constructionists work is Hannigan's (2014) study of the environmental problem of biodiversity loss, which rose rapidly to prominence in the 1980s. Biodiversity loss had been known about since at least 1911, evidenced by numerous legislative attempts to protect threatened birds and animals. But no international institutions existed to give such concerns a political focus. What changed in the 1980s was the involvement of multinational business looking to patent genetic resources – such as species within rainforests – the creation of a new 'crisis' discipline of conservation biology, the establishment of a United Nations infrastructure that gave the necessary political focus, and a range of legislation to preserve species. In short, a much more effective range of 'claims-makers' had an interest in making this demand, and their combination brought the subject to the top of the environmental problems agenda. Of course, there were also some claims-deniers, but on this occasion the claims-makers proved too strong and well organized. Only a constructionist account which pays attention to the historical construction of this claim is able to show clearly how and why it was successful.

Critical Points

Interesting though many constructionist accounts may be, critics object to their 'agnosticism'. Hannigan's study of biodiversity, for instance, is missing something important. Is biodiversity loss an increasingly serious social and environmental problem? This question is not addressed and cannot be addressed by social constructionism. To do this we need the expert knowledge of biologists, natural historians and environmental scientists. Very few sociologists have the expert knowledge required to engage in detailed debates about biodiversity or many other problems. For some, such as critical realists, without including this expertise in the analysis, sociology gets reduced to a series of discourse studies looking at statements, documents and texts without ever getting to the bottom of the real issue at hand.

One further criticism is that social constructionism seems to prioritize the politics of claims-making and sometimes appears more useful to political and social movements than to scientific sociology. Demonstrating how relatively powerful social groups are able to shape and dominate political debates is a useful function, but constructionism very often seems to take the side of the underdog. In that sense it has been argued that the perspective is politically biased. For example, women's movements used constructionist arguments to show that there was no 'natural place' for women in the private, domestic sphere, and that child-bearing and child-rearing did not present 'natural' barriers to gender equality. The criticism here is not that such arguments are illegitimate, but that constructionism is closer to political strategy than scientific research methods.

Continuing Relevance

Social constructionism has been enormously successful in sociology and probably accounts for the majority of research studies today. There is no doubt that it has produced many new insights into social life. Social constructionism points to the inexorably social nature of all known phenomena, which puts human societies at the heart of the analysis, thus giving sociologists a central place. It can be extremely valuable as it gives sociologists a clearly defined task, which is to lay bare the processes of social construction and thus enable better informed public debate about major issues rather than leaving these to 'experts'.

A fair number of social constructionist studies analyse media reports and contributions to public debates. A recent example of this is the examination by Wanda Siu (2009) of American newspapers' framing of the dangers of tobacco use in relation to a critical surgeon general's report in 1964 and a 1998 trial involving the tobacco industry in Minnesota. Siu compared the coverage in the *New York Times*, a national 'liberal' newspaper, and the *Wall Street Journal*, a financial paper lying closer to the business community. On both occasions, she found that the *Wall Street Journal* tended to frame the issue in a manner more sympathetic to the tobacco industry – for example, by downplaying the surgeon general's findings and blaming lawyers in the Minnesota case for withholding scientific evidence. What this study illustrates is that newspapers did not just report on the conflict around the social construction of tobacco use in the USA but were actively involved in those processes of construction.

Given that all social phenomena are potentially amenable to a social constructionist analysis, it was only a matter of time before social constructionism was itself seen as socially constructed – hence, Motyl's (2010) caustic discussion and dismissal of radical constructionism. His paper is concerned with nationalism and **identity** formation but should be read for its critique of social constructionism, which the author sees as 'run-of-the-mill' but, in its strong variants, is 'unusual, exciting and wrong'.

References and Further Reading

Goode, E., and Ben-Yehuda, N. (2009) *Moral Panics: The Social Construction of Deviance* (2nd edn, Chichester: Wiley-Blackwell).

Hannigan, J. (2014) *Environmental Sociology* (3rd edn, London: Routledge), esp. chapter 5.

Motyl, A. J. (2010) 'The Social Construction of Social Construction: Implications for Theories of Nationalism and Identity Formation', *Nationalities Papers*, 38(1): 59–71.

Siu, W. (2009) 'Social Construction of Reality: The Tobacco Issue', *Critical Public Health*, 19(1): 23–44.

3   Environment and Urbanism

Alienation

Working Definition

The separation or estrangement of human beings from some essential aspect of their nature or from **society**, often resulting in feelings of powerlessness and helplessness.

Origins of the Concept

Sociological usage of the term 'alienation' stems from the early ideas of Marx relating to the impact of **capitalism** on social relations and the lack of control of humans over their lives. However, Marx was influenced by Ludwig Feuerbach's philosophical critique of Christianity. Christianity, with its religious notion of an all-powerful, all-knowing God, was a projection of what were really human powers onto a spiritual being, with human salvation achievable only after death, not in this world. Feuerbach saw this as a form of alienation or estrangement and a mystification of human powers which needed to be exposed and eliminated.

Marx ([1844] 2007) took the concept of alienation out of this essentially religious context and used it to analyse the conditions of work and life in secular industrial-capitalist societies. For Marx, human 'salvation' lay in wresting collective control over all aspects of society away from a small, dominating ruling **class** which exploited the mass of workers. Certain religious beliefs were part of the ideological control that encouraged workers to accept their lot in lieu of genuine salvation in the afterlife. In the twentieth century, industrial sociologists used the concept of alienation to inform empirical studies of workplace relations under different management systems. This later body of research tended to be much more social-psychological than the earlier Marxist studies.

Meaning and Interpretation

Alienation is a concept that has slipped out of sociological **discourse** and into media commentary and everyday language. We may be told that a whole generation is becoming 'alienated from society', for instance, or that youth subcultures represent the alienation of young people from mainstream values. Clearly the idea of distancing or separation is evident here, but in sociology alienation is associated with the inequalities of capitalist societies. Marx's historical materialist approach began with the way that people organize their affairs together to produce goods and survive. For Marx, to be alienated is to be in an objective condition which has real consequences, and the key to changing that situation is a matter of changing not what we think or believe but the way we live, in order to gain more control over our circumstances. In previous times, working lives may appear to us to have been more physically demanding, unstinting and exhausting, but for many social groups, such as peasant farmers and craftsmen, their labour was skilled and satisfying in itself, allowing for more control over work tasks than we might find in modern manufacturing plants, large office environments, call centres or fast-food restaurants. Work today may in many ways be less physically demanding than in the past, but it does not offer any more control and therefore continues to generate high levels of alienation.

Marx's theory suggests that capitalist production creates alienation in four main areas. Workers are alienated from their own *labour power*: they have to work as and when required and perform tasks that are set for them by employers. They are alienated from the *products* of their labour, which are successfully claimed by capitalists to be sold in the marketplace for profit, while workers receive only a fraction as wages. Workers are also alienated from *one another*, as capitalism forces workers to compete for jobs and factories and regions to compete for market share. Finally, Marx argues that, because labour is an essential and defining feature of human nature, the alienation of people from work in the above ways means they have become alienated from their own '*species being*'. Labour is no longer satisfying in itself but has become merely a means to an end – earning wages to survive. This is represented in the negative connotations attached to the very idea of 'work' and its separation from the much more pleasant sphere of 'leisure'. The solution Marx looks forward to is an end to exploitative capitalist relations and the movement to communism, in which collective control of the production process is established and alienation abolished.

Critical Points

Marx's thesis has been influential, though it is very general and abstract and is intimately connected to his general social theory, with its revolutionary conclusions. In order to make the concept useful for empirical research studies, sociologists stripped it of these connections, and as a result it became possible to compare levels of alienation in differing working environments and under differing management regimes. During the twentieth century there were several attempts to operationalize the concept. One example is Robert Blauner's *Alienation and Freedom* (1964), which compared the alienating effects of working conditions in four industries. Blauner was interested in how workers themselves experienced the key aspects of alienation: powerlessness, meaninglessness, isolation and self-estrangement. He reasoned that it was possible to measure each of these aspects in a range of employment situations in order to assess which types of work generate the highest and lowest levels of alienation. His conclusion was that routine factory work, especially on production assembly lines, produced the highest levels of alienation. Yet, when production lines were automated, levels of alienation reduced as this method offered workers more control over their work process. This finding ran contrary to standard Marxist theories of the inexorable deskilling of the workforce as technology took over from humans. Blauner's introduction of subjective perceptions into the theory of alienation was innovative and empirically productive, and it brought the perceptions and views of workers into theories of alienation. It also suggested that alienation could be reduced without destroying capitalism.

Continuing Relevance

The concept of alienation appears inextricably linked with Marxist theory, notwithstanding attempts to broaden it for more general sociological use. As nominally Marxist regimes collapsed after 1989 and revolutionary Marxist theory lost ground, the concept of alienation seems to be less relevant to the future of the discipline. However, studies of Japanese management practices have implicitly assumed that the adoption of workgroups and team decision-making lessens worker alienation and improve workplace relations. There have also been attempts to use the concept in other fields, and these may revive the concept for a new century.

Smith and Bohm (2008) take issue with the extensive use of the Durkheimian concept of **anomie** in criminology, arguing that alienation offers a more rounded and useful perspective. The authors contend that central to anomie theory is the notion of 'normlessness', but this is just one of five dimensions within the theory of alienation. Hence, the other four dimensions – powerlessness, meaninglessness, isolation and self-estrangement – have been largely ignored. This has tended to produce a criminology that remains too close to crime control policy and fails to explain criminal behaviour. Smith and Bohm argue that alienation is a more integrative concept which holds out the possibility of finding effective ways to reduce the alienating effects of a capitalist social structure.

In a similar vein, Yuill (2005) looks at alienation theory in relation to health, which, he maintains, has been largely neglected by medical sociologists. This is strange, given that Marx's original theory is rooted in the idea that the exploitative and alienating conditions of capitalist economies impact on and shape material, emotional and embodied human beings whose well-being and health is clearly affected. Yuill makes the case for Marx's version of the concept and looks at some examples of medical sociology through the lens of alienation.

References and Further Reading

Archibald, W. P. (2009) 'Marx, Globalization and Alienation: Received and Underappreciated Wisdoms', *Critical Sociology*, 35(2): 151–74.

Blauner, R. (1964) *Alienation and Freedom: The Factory Worker and his Industry* (Chicago: University of Chicago Press).

Marx, K. ([1844] 2007) *Economic and Philosophic Manuscripts of 1844*, ed. and trans. Martin Milligan (Mineola, NY: Dover).

Smith, H. P., and Bohm, R. M. (2008) 'Beyond Anomie: Alienation and Crime', *Critical Criminology*, 16(1): 1–15.

Yuill, C. (2005) 'Marx: Capitalism, Alienation and Health', *Social Theory and Health*, 3: 126–43.

Environment

Working Definition

In environmental sociology, the natural environment of planet Earth, rather than the economic environment, the business environment or other such human creations.

Origins of the Concept

If 'environment' means 'the natural environment', then it seems no different to the concept of 'nature'. 'Nature' is a very old and complex word with diverse meanings, but in sociology it has often been seen as the opposite of **culture** or **society**. The use of 'environment' to describe the natural world within which societies exist is much more recent. The contemporary concept of the environment is a mix of ideas of natural forces and natural things, such as plants, animals and ecosystems. This concept of environment began to take over from 'nature' in the post-war period and was in widespread use among 1960s environmental and green activists in the developed countries. However, this origin gave the environment a clear moral standing as something valuable that required protection against encroachment by human activity, especially **industrialization** and the spread of **urbanism**. In its widest sense the environment is planet Earth itself, and images relayed by satellite from space missions gave the concept a clear and widely circulated visible symbol. The environment entered sociology as matters such as acid rain, global warming and pollution rose to prominence as key issues demanding solutions. Today, 'environmental sociology' is a specialist field with a major presence in the USA, while in Europe a 'sociology of the environment' rooted in a broadly social constructionist perspective tends to dominate.

Meaning and Interpretation

Many sociologists have a deep suspicion of explanations that apply biological concepts to the study of social life, and this is one reason why the study of environmental problems took a long time to become accepted within the discipline. For some, environmental issues remain at the margins of sociology compared with longstanding social issues such as inequality, **poverty**, crime and health. For others, the environment is one of several new 'central problems', including **risk**, terrorism and **globalization**, that are reshaping sociology and the social sciences more generally. Studying the environment–society relationship involves understanding both social relations and natural phenomena, because environmental issues are hybrids of society and environment (Irwin 2001). This can be seen quite clearly when we think of oil and air pollution, the genetic modification of foods and global warming, all of which demand that sociologists get to grips with the natural scientific evidence. We cannot expect sociologists to have useful things to say on these subjects unless they appreciate why they are of concern and what consequences they have for people. Conversely, environmental issues can never be wholly 'natural', as their causes are often traced back to human activity. Hence, natural scientists also need to understand the social causes or 'manufactured' character of the environmental problems they seek to address. Indeed, the environmental issue identified by natural scientists as the most serious – global warming – is widely accepted as the result of large-scale industrial production and modern ways of life.

Sociologists exploring environmental issues tend to fall into one of two camps. Social constructionists do not take the 'natural' aspects of environmental issues for granted and tend to be agnostic about whether they really are as serious as campaigners and scientists say they are. There is good reason for this. Most sociologists are not trained in the natural sciences and do not have the expertise to engage in debates with natural scientists. Instead, constructionists investigate the history and sociology of environmental problems, opening up the issues for general public consideration.

In the second camp are environmental sociologists and critical realists. If environmental problems are real and pressing, then it must be possible to understand their social and natural causes and to intervene to solve them. Critical realists, especially those working in British sociology, have argued that sociologists should be involved in the task of getting beneath the surface appearance of reality to explain the mechanisms that are at work in generating environmental problems.

Once the amount of CO_2 in the atmosphere reaches levels that trap more of the sun's heat, causing planetary-wide warming of the Earth's surface, we begin to see how natural processes have been generated that can produce dangerous consequences. But those natural processes have been triggered by human activity over a long period of time, and we need properly to understand exactly which of those activities are causes and which are merely correlations or consequences. Realists argue that we cannot be agnostic in relation to these issues.

Critical Points

Introducing the environment into sociology has been seen as problematic. If sociologists have to defer to natural scientists for their knowledge of environmental problems, will that compromise the critical approach that sociology demands? Given the very different theories, methods and types of evidence that are used in the social and natural sciences, is it realistic to suppose that their practitioners will be able to work together? As many sociological researchers adopt a social constructionist approach that is at odds with the basic **realism** inherent in the natural sciences, it seems more likely at present that sociology will continue to study not just environmental issues as such but also the processes and social **interactions** that are involved in producing scientific knowledge of them.

Continuing Relevance

It has taken quite some time for sociologists to appreciate the significance of environmental issues, and they have lagged far behind green campaigners and environmental scientists. The environment is a contested concept, and it is unlikely that a single definition will ever be acceptable to all. Nonetheless, there is a growing body of sociological research and theorizing about the environment that has enriched our understanding of the society–environment relationship. Given the high profile of global climate change, **sustainable development** initiatives, and the growing interest in issues such as food production methods and energy security, sociologists need to make sure these are integrated into the discipline if it is to remain relevant to new generations of students.

Lever-Tracy (2008) claims that sociology has struggled to integrate environmental issues – especially global warming – into the discipline, largely because sociologists have a deep suspicion of 'naturalistic' arguments, preferring instead a more comfortable **social constructionism**. However, she suggests that it is time to make the issue of climate change central to the discipline and for sociologists to embrace multidisciplinarity. This is necessary since understanding global warming and working to mitigate its impact and reduce carbon emissions demands that natural and social scientists work together. However, in a response to Lever-Tracy's article, Grundmann and Stehr (2010) defend a constructionist approach to environmental issues and argue that constructionism both helps sociologists to avoid being drawn into essentially political debates and brings a balancing social perspective to scientific findings.

References and Further Reading

Bell, M. M. (2015) *An Invitation to Environmental Sociology* (5th edn, Thousand Oaks, CA: Sage).
Dunlap, R. E. (2002) 'Paradigms, Theories and Environmental Sociology', in F. H. Buttel, P. Dickens and A. Gijswijt (eds), *Sociological Theory and the Environment: Classical Foundations, Contemporary Insights* (Lanham, MD: Rowman & Littlefield), pp. 329–50.
Grundmann, R., and Stehr, N. (2010) 'Climate Change: What Role for Sociology? A Response to Constance Lever-Tracy', *Current Sociology*, 58(6): 897–910.
Irwin, A. (2001) *Sociology and the Environment: A Critical Introduction to Society, Nature and Knowledge* (Cambridge: Polity).
Lever-Tracy, C. (2008) 'Global Warming and Sociology', *Current Sociology*, 56(3): 445–66.
Sutton, P. W. (2007) *The Environment: A Sociological Introduction* (Cambridge: Polity).

Industrialization

Working Definition

The process, which began in mid-eighteenth-century Britain and Europe, of replacing human and animal labour with machinery, especially in the field of production and work.

Origins of the Concept

Before the modern period, the words 'industry' and 'industrious' were widely used to mean 'diligent'. By the late sixteenth century, 'industry' was also used to describe manufacture and trade. This meaning later became employed extensively to describe particular areas of manufacture, such as mining, electronics and even service industries. The concept of industrialization therefore suggests a long-term process of change, from a pre- or non-industrial **society** towards a society based primarily on manufacturing. In that sense, industrialization is perhaps the most significant aspect of the modernization process. The 'Industrial Revolution' in Europe and North America began in Britain between the mid-eighteenth and the first decades of the nineteenth century. This period saw the process start to take off and become self-perpetuating, with a series of connected developments such as coal mining, iron production and new technologies which facilitated the production of larger quantities of goods. More production meant population movements, as people left rural agricultural areas to find work in the growing towns and cities where the new workshops and factories were located.

By the late nineteenth century it had become possible to talk of an industrial society, based on continuous technological change in which manufacturing processes were dominant and the bulk of working people were employed in manufacturing rather than agriculture. Though many saw this as a positive development, the period also witnessed many critics who railed against the terrible living and working conditions in overcrowded towns and cities, as well as the damaging impact of machines on traditional craft skills. Early sociologists studied the radical expansion of the **division of labour**, an emerging **class conflict** and the increasingly secular ways of urban living. Since the 1970s, sociologists have argued that many previously industrial societies have gradually become post-industrialized, as fewer and fewer workers are directly engaged in manufacturing and more are employed in services such as **education**, health and finance.

Meaning and Interpretation

Industrialization refers to the replacement of animal and human labour by machines. Technological development in itself is not new and can be traced all the way back to very basic stone tool-making in ancient tribal societies, which enabled new social practices such as more effective hunting and house-building.

But the eighteenth-century Industrial Revolution is viewed as a revolutionary change similar in significance to that wrought by the Neolithic Revolution that began around 9000 BCE, which brought about settled communities and agricultural production. Industrialization transformed the way in which the mass of people lived their everyday lives and in all sorts of ways. An industrial society is therefore one in which technology mediates the relationship between human beings and the natural world.

Industrialization changes the relationship between people and nature, as the latter comes increasingly to be seen simply as the source of raw materials or resources for use in the production process. In the early nineteenth century, many social commentators wondered if industrialization was just a short-term process that might be stopped or reversed, but by the end of the century that prospect appeared impossible. Today de-industrialization seems not only unlikely but also impossible without huge reductions in the global population, which has expanded beyond anything forecast by social scientists. Global human population levels of over 7 billion are only sustainable with the industrialization of food production, transportation and a global division of labour.

Some theories of post-industrial change from the 1970s suggest that the latest wave of electronic development using microcircuits, computing, satellites and information technology represents a move beyond simple industrialization. However, all of these technologies are still produced in industrial settings where machinery rather than human and animal labour dominates. Computers still have to be produced in industrial factories and they work using electricity generated in power stations. The Internet is a wonderful global means of communication, but it cannot be accessed without the relevant technological devices and a power source. It is probably more accurate to describe the emergence of information technologies as a form of advanced industrialism rather than as a movement away from industrial principles.

One significant consequence of industrialization is the related movement of people known as urbanization, which accelerated very rapidly over the nineteenth century. Industrial production generated more raw materials for houses, factories and infrastructure, which speeded up the flight away from agriculture and a rural way of life. For large numbers of people, the new cities and towns seemed like a whole new society, with many industrial inventions such as gas, electricity and new machines along with higher wages. Many critics, including William Morris and John Ruskin in Britain, saw traditional ways of life and morality disappearing as new social problems were created. Early sociologists also complained about the loss of **community** and social solidarity and the growth of individualism and calculating self-interest (Tönnies [1887] 2001).

Critical Points

In many ways industrialization is a continuing process as more and more countries undergo their own development. However, since the 1970s, the theory of post-industrialization has alerted us to the way in which the advanced industrial societies are moving in a different direction. Manufacturing processes have been moved into developing countries where labour costs are cheaper and regulations are less rigidly enforced. This has led to less and less manufacturing in the developed countries and an expansion of service-sector employment in which people increasingly work with and for other people rather than with raw materials and machines in the production of goods. Service-sector work demands a very different set of skills, including 'emotional labour', and this has been seen as one important reason for the 'feminization' of the workforce as more women enter paid employment and higher education. Clearly, in these countries, industrialization is not what it used to be, though the concept still captures the experience of recently industrializing nations such as China, the Philippines and India.

Continuing Relevance

The post-industrial thesis describes the situation in countries such as England, the USA and France, but it is important to note that these countries cannot avoid the industrial pollution generated elsewhere in the world. The socio-economic changes experienced in the developed world do not mean the end of industrialization, only that the process now takes in the whole world. The scale of industrial change and the transformation of human life that it brought are just not matched by post-industrial changes – at least, not yet. Industrialization was a world-historical development which enabled the most rapid population growth ever seen, and industrial production continues to support that population.

Most developing countries have industrialized long after the developed world and in a period when environmental concerns are at the forefront of global political debate. What some scholars now argue for is an ecological form of modernization which avoids the damaging levels of pollution generated in earlier industrialization and allows the developing countries to modernize. Frijns and his colleagues (2000) look at this thesis in relation to development in Viet Nam along three dimensions: environmental awareness, state–market relations and technological development. On all three they find a significant divergence from the expectations of ecological modernization theory (EM), which was devised in European contexts. The theory therefore needs to be refined if it is to be useful in developing countries. However, reforms in Viet Nam in relation to democratization, internationalization and economic liberalization may offer possibilities for a different form of EM to that in Europe.

References and Further Reading

Clapp, B. W. (1994) *An Environmental History of Britain since the Industrial Revolution* (London: Longman).
Frijns, J., Phuong, P. T., and Mol, A. (2000) 'Ecological Modernization Theory and Industrialising Economies: The Case of Viet Nam', *Environmental Politics*, 9(1): 257–92.

Kumar, K. (2005) *From Post-Industrial to Post-Modern Society: New Theories of the Contemporary World* (2nd edn, Oxford: Blackwell).

Tönnies, F. ([1887] 2001) *Community and Society [Gemeinschaft und Gesellschaft]* (Cambridge and New York: Cambridge University Press).

Migration

Working Definition

The movement of people from one geographical region to another, especially across national societies, which became more widespread and commonplace over the twentieth century.

Origins of the Concept

People have moved from one region to another throughout recorded history, and large-scale migration is largely responsible for the global spread of the human species. In modern times, **industrialization** altered migration patterns within individual countries as new work opportunities drew rural migrants into urban areas, while the labour needs of employers and labour markets also generated much cross-country migration. During the Nazi persecution of minorities in the 1930s and 1940s, many Eastern European Jews were forced to flee to Western Europe for safety, showing that migration is often forced rather than freely chosen. Migration tends to produce a mixing of ethnic groups and create ethnically diverse societies. As part of European integration, many barriers to the free movement of people have been removed, leading to a large increase in regional migration. Large-scale migration can therefore have very different causes, and theories of migration need to take this into account.

Meaning and Interpretation

Immigration refers to the process of moving *into* a country in order to make a new life, while emigration is the opposite – moving *out of* a country to live elsewhere. Studying immigration and emigration involves identifying patterns of migration that connect 'countries of origin' to 'countries of destination' and how these patterns change over time. It also means examining the consequences of shifting migration patterns for the individuals, communities and societies involved in the process. The intensification of global migration since the Second World War, and particularly in more recent decades, has transformed migration into an important political issue across the world. Migration is not a new phenomenon, but it has significantly accelerated in modern times, speeding up the integrative process of **globalization**. This trend has led some to call the present period an 'age of migration'. For example, since the end of Eastern European communism from 1989, Europe has experienced a 'new migration'. The opening of borders led directly to the migration of several million people between 1989 and 1994, while war and ethnic **conflict** in the former Yugoslavia saw around 5 million refugees move to other European regions. Recent conflicts in Syria and Iraq have also led to large numbers of displaced people seeking refuge outside their country of origin, mainly in the nation states of the European Union. Migration patterns have also changed, since the line between countries of origin and countries of destination has been blurred as states break up.

Four models can be used to characterize global population movements since 1945 (Castles et al. 2013). The USA and Australia fit the '*classic model*' of migration. In these countries, the **society** has been shaped by actively encouraging immigration, with new migrants becoming full citizens. However, immigration is not unrestricted and, typically, limits are placed on the number of migrants allowed to relocate. An alternative, the '*colonial model*', can be seen in the UK, which at various times encouraged migration from its former colonies, mainly to fulfil the needs of the labour market. Immigration from Commonwealth countries such as India and Jamaica in the 1950s is perhaps the best example of this model. A third model, the '*guest workers model*', promotes short-term immigration strictly on the basis of labour market requirements. Germany and Belgium have adopted this model, which, unlike the colonial model, does not allow migrants to become citizens regardless of their length of residency. The fourth version covers all forms of '*illegal immigration*'. This form has been increasing over recent years as the migration policies in relatively wealthy countries have become more restrictive and globalization processes facilitate the more fluid movement of ideas, information and people.

Theories accounting for migratory patterns have been dominated by so-called push and pull factors. Push factors are those within a country which force or 'push' people to emigrate, such as conflicts, wars, famine or political oppression. 'Pull' factors are those which exist in destination countries and attract new immigrants, such as better labour markets, job opportunities, better living conditions and political encouragement. In recent times push–pull theories have been seen as too simple, particularly as migration patterns have become more fluid and global. An alternative is to link micro- and macro-level factors. For example, at the macro level we might look at changing legislation, the political situation, or the formation of regional blocs such as the EU, which give rise to a novel migration framework. We could then link these to micro-level factors such as people's own finances, their knowledge of other countries and their existing ties to **family** members. In this way more convincing and satisfactory accounts of specific migrations can be produced.

Critical Points

Critics of theories of migration argue that most have failed to break away from a very old, conventional perspective, which has not been able to engage with new and emerging theoretical work such as new studies of mobilities (Urry and Sheller 2004). Much of the research on migration patterns remains state-centred, exploring movements across countries rather than being able to take in regional patterns or movements within large urban areas. New migration patterns have also challenged conventional notions of **citizenship** and **identities** based on **nation-state** allegiances, resulting in problems for theories which stay wedded to established positions. However, as described above, some recent work in this field is beginning to address these potential flaws.

Continuing Relevance

Studies of migration look set to become a major area of sociology, mainly because of the size, speed and scope of contemporary migration. Hence, sociologists need to grasp the contours of new patterns, in contrast with earlier periods, such as the tendency towards the acceleration of migration across borders and diversification as most countries receive immigrants from many different places. There is also a tendency towards the globalization of migration, involving a much larger number of countries as both 'senders' and 'recipients' of migrants, and a feminization of migration, with growing numbers of female migrants, again contrasting with previous patterns (Castles et al. 2013). It seems likely that there will be more migration, much of it involving women, and that countries will experience a more diverse range of immigrant groups. Just as significantly, migration is becoming a 'normal' feature of our global world which governments and international bodies will have to find creative ways of managing.

A useful way into migration studies is with a case study of a single country, and Robert Winder's (2004) history of British immigration is as good as any. Offering a broad historical sweep, Winder tells the story of successive migrations to and emigrations from the country up to the beginning of the twenty-first century. He reminds us that the bulk of migrants are very often 'entrepreneurial risk-takers' with a strong sense of individual liberty and adventure, and that emigration from Britain is also a large part of the story. The overarching message of the book is that Britain (and this applies to many other countries) is settled 'at a deep level' by immigrants.

The idea of moving to another country for a better life is also pursued in Benson and O'Reilly's (2009) study of the so-called lifestyle migration among relatively wealthy individuals. Migration offers for some the promise of being able to live an alternative, simpler lifestyle, for others a chance to escape difficult personal histories or refocus on shaping the self anew. Although it is not typically part of migration studies, the authors examine lifestyle migration from the standpoint of the affluent, which allows them to set the decision into the context of the whole **life course**. This may be a productive move in the study of other types of migration.

Not all migration is voluntarily chosen. At the opposite end of the scale are human trafficking and modern slavery, which many thought had been wiped out for good some time ago. Yet Masci's (2010) chapter in the CQ Researcher volume shows that, today, the bulk of human trafficking dislocates people from some of the poorest parts of the world for forced labour, sex and prostitution, and much of this is closely tied to international organized crime. The brief historical sketch asks whether governments around the world are doing enough to control and prevent trafficking and covers debates in both the developing and developed countries, which students should find helpful.

References and Further Reading

Benson, M., and O'Reilly, K. (2009) 'Migration and the Search for a Better Way of Life: A Critical Exploration of Lifestyle Migration', *Sociological Review*, 57(4): 608–25.

Castles, S. (2007) 'Twenty-First Century Migration as a Challenge to Sociology', *Journal of Ethnic and Migration Studies*, 33(3): 351–71.

Castles, S., de Haas, H., and Miller, M. J. (2013) *The Age of Migration: International Population Movements in the Modern World* (5th edn, Basingstoke: Palgrave Macmillan).

Masci, D. (2010) 'Human Trafficking and Slavery: Are the World's Nations Doing Enough to Stamp it Out?', in *Issues in Race, Ethnicity, Gender and Class: Selections from CQ Researcher* (Thousand Oaks, CA: Pine Forge Press), pp. 25–46.

Urry, J., and Sheller, M. (eds) (2004) *Tourism Mobilities: Places to Play, Places in Play* (London: Routledge).

Winder, R. (2004) *Bloody Foreigners: The Story of Immigration to Britain* (London: Little, Brown).

Risk

Working Definition

According to Ulrich Beck, attempts to avoid or mitigate potential hazards, especially those 'manufactured risks' that are the product of human activity.

Origins of the Concept

'Risk' is a term that has been taken out of everyday usage and developed into a sociological concept as well as a more general theory of social change. Taking risks or engaging in pleasurable risky behaviour, such as extreme sports, is part of many people's normal lives and involves actions containing an element of danger. Most of these activities are calculated risks, as every attempt has been made to render them as safe as possible. The separate discipline of risk assessment is used by businesses, government and voluntary agencies to weigh up the pros and cons of a course of action, evaluate the possibility of success, and suggest ways of minimizing the financial and other dangers associated with it.

Once sociologists began using the concept of risk it became much more general, and it now refers to the social conditions prevailing as people in the industrial societies start to reflect on the more detrimental aspects of **modernity**. Ulrich Beck (1992) and Anthony Giddens (1991) have been influential in establishing theories of risk (and trust) as highly relevant to our understanding of contemporary societies. However, the general concept of risk has been introduced into a wide variety of subject areas, including health, crime and **deviance**, **environment** and social theory.

Meaning and Interpretation

Risks are nothing new. The risk of being personally attacked, being involved in an accident or becoming caught up in a natural disaster is longstanding in human affairs. However, sociologists of risk argue that today's 'high-consequence' risks, such as those of global warming or nuclear weapons proliferation, are not 'natural' or beyond human control. Rather, they are *'manufactured risks'*, the products of scientific knowledge applied to production and the unplanned impacts of continuous technological advancement.

Numerous decisions in everyday life have also become infused with risk and uncertainty. Many working lives are subject to short-term contracts, casualization and insecurity, while self-identities are no longer rooted in or underpinned by traditional sources of **identity** such as the **family** and **community**. The resulting uncertainties present both real opportunities and risks, as, much more than previously, individuals have to draw on their own resources and make their own decisions from the welter of information available to them. For example, marriage used to be quite straightforward, a stage in the **life course** and a stabilization of adult **sexuality**. Today, many people cohabit without getting married, divorce rates are high, remarriage rates are also high, and people must make a risk assessment in an increasingly uncertain situation. This is typical of the way the concept of risk has entered sociological **discourse** as well as people's everyday lives (Arnoldi 2009).

The last twenty years or so have seen numerous terrorist attacks that have also changed people's views of how safe their communities are from threats of violence and how governments can protect their citizens. Boarding a plane for an internal flight may now involve a whole raft of security measures, including full body scanners, intended to reduce the risk of passengers becoming victims. Because they are products of our modern way of life, such risks present us with new choices, challenges and decisions. Even seemingly simple decisions about what to eat are now made in the context of conflicting information and opinions about the food's merits and drawbacks.

For Ulrich Beck, the concept of risk has even greater significance. He argues that we are currently living through the slow death of the industrial **society** as a new type of 'risk society' emerges, in which risk consciousness and risk avoidance are becoming central features and environmental issues rise to prominence. During the nineteenth and twentieth centuries, politics was dominated by the major **conflict** of interest between workers and employers played out through left- and right-wing parties, focusing on wealth distribution. According to Beck (2002), this industrial **class** conflict has lost significance as people realize that fighting for a better share of the 'wealth cake' is futile if the cake itself is poisoned as a result of pollution and environmental damage. We are entering a 'world risk society' where even the relatively rich countries are not immune from industrial pollution, climate change or ozone depletion. Managing risks will be the key feature of the new global order, but single **nation states** are not able to cope in a world of global risks. Hence transnational cooperation between governments, such as the international agreement in the Kyoto Protocol to tackle global warming by reducing carbon emissions, is likely to become more commonplace.

Critical Points

One of the main criticisms of risk theory is that it is exaggerated. For example, there is not enough empirical research and concrete evidence to support Beck's thesis of the transition to a 'risk society', even though there is more awareness of environmental issues and risks. Green political parties have not made the kind of electoral breakthroughs we might expect if the old class-based politics really was dying out, and the older Labour, Conservative and Liberal parties of the 'left–right' spectrum continue to dominate national politics. At the global level, the issue of wealth creation and distribution remains the dominant one, as developing countries are desperately trying to close the gap between rich and poor. Solving the enormous problem of absolute **poverty** in the developing world is still the focus of international politics. Some critics see risk theory as rather naïve about the concept of risk and how this varies across **cultures**. What may be defined as 'risks' in some societies may not be considered as such in others, in the same way that what is defined as pollution in the wealthy industrialized societies is often seen as a sign of healthy economic development in poorer developing countries. What counts as a risk is culturally variable, which makes international agreement on tackling risks very difficult.

Continuing Relevance

Although some of the larger claims of risk theory may be overblown, there is no doubt that recent social changes have led to more uncertainties and less reliance on traditional and habitual ways of life. In this changed context, sensitivity to risk does seem to be increasing, along with the need for individuals to make their own decisions on a much wider range of issues with which they are now presented. Global health scares such as swine flu or the national controversy over the safety of the MMR jab in the UK, as well as continuing debates on the dangers of the Internet to children, show that what might have been seen as non-political matters are moving into the sphere of 'risk politics'.

Judith Green (2009) acknowledges that the concept of risk has been very productive in her field of medical sociology, particularly in understanding how people make sense of illness and map out their actions in relation to health risks. But she argues that 'risk' is now much less useful in this field, especially for those carrying out empirical studies. This is because risk research has become much narrower in focus, circumscribing research into a few themes of risk assessments, rational decision-making and technical calculation. Framing research studies in terms of risk may now be unnecessarily restrictive.

References and Further Reading

Arnoldi, J. (2009) *Risk* (Cambridge: Polity).

Beck, U. (1992) *Risk Society: Towards a New Modernity* (London: Sage).

— (2002) *Ecological Politics in an Age of Risk* (Cambridge: Polity).

— (2008) *World at Risk* (Cambridge: Polity).

Giddens, A. (1991) *Modernity and Self-Identity: Self and Society in the Late Modern Age* (Cambridge: Polity).

Green, J. (2009) 'Is it Time for the Sociology of Health to Abandon "Risk"?', *Health, Risk and Society*, 11(6): 493–508.

Tulloch, J., and Lupton, D. (2003) *Risk and Everyday Life* (London: Sage).

Sustainable Development

Working Definition

An approach combining the long-term conservation of the global natural **environment** with economic development for the developing countries.

Origins of the Concept

The concept of sustainable development has a definite origin in the 1987 United Nations Brundtland Commission report, though some much earlier precursors have also been found. In the late eighteenth century, Malthus wrote about the dangers of continuous population growth, arguing that population growth always tended to outstrip the capacity of the Earth to feed it. Unless population was stabilized at a safe level, the result could be mass starvation, famine and social breakdown. John Stuart Mill ([1848] 1999) argued that indefinite economic growth would damage the quality of life and the environment. What both Malthus and Mill were seeking was, in modern language, a form of sustainable development.

In the 1970s, the *Limits to Growth* report (Meadows et al. 1972) took five global trends – accelerating **industrialization**, rapid population growth, widespread malnutrition, depletion of non-renewable resources and a deteriorating environment – and manipulated them to create future scenarios. It concluded that continuous economic growth was unsustainable and would grind to a halt before 2100, despite new technologies and a doubling of available resources. The Brundtland report followed, offering a political platform to marry economic development and natural conservation by reducing global inequality.

Meaning and Interpretation

The seminal report *Our Common Future* (1987) (known, after its president, Gro Harlem Brundtland, as the Brundtland report) was produced by the World Commission on Environment and Development. It was here that the famous definition of sustainable development was introduced: 'development which meets the needs of the present without compromising the ability of future generations to meet their own needs'. This concept is politically contested, very flexible and thus open to conflicting interpretations. However, some version of it is used by environmentalists, governments and international agencies trying to find ways of dealing with serious environmental problems and global inequalities. The definition asks today's people to find ways of creating enough wealth to meet their needs without damaging the natural environment on which we all depend, so that future generations will not be compromised.

Combining *sustainability* and *development* makes this concept appealing to environmentalists and governments in the relatively rich northern hemisphere and to all those working to improve the economies of the relatively poor global South. It has led to many targets covering a wide range of social indicators, such as **education** and literacy, health, provision of services and **community** participation. At the same time, environmental indicators such as corporate and governmental environmental audits, urban air quality, recycling and many more are aimed at reducing the human impact on the environment. So far, the results of sustainable development initiatives have been rather mixed, with lots of small-scale community initiatives and progress on some but not all indicators.

An overall assessment was provided by the report of the UN Millennium Ecosystem Assessment Board (2005), which concluded that humanity was still living beyond its means, putting an unsustainable strain on the global environment. In particular, it noted that the commitment to leaving a planet fit for future generations to meet their own needs could not be assured and that the millennium targets of halving global **poverty** and malnutrition by 2015 would not be met. In fact, global inequality was increasing, environmental damage was worsening, and some 1.8 million people per year were dying through inadequate hygiene, sanitation or water supplies – hardly a ringing endorsement of the concept and practice of sustainable development.

Critical Points

The inclusivity of sustainable development is a possible strength, as it enables everyone to participate in it. But it can also make the public **discourse** of sustainability seem incoherent, meaning 'all things to all people' but ultimately making little impact. After almost twenty-five years of sustainable development initiatives, real progress on the most urgent and pressing issues remains elusive. Perhaps one reason why sustainable development has not yet fulfilled its initial promise is that the concept has been emptied of radical content and used as an **ideological** smokescreen to promote unsustainable projects. In short, what passes for sustainable development in practice is 'neither sustainable nor development' (Luke 2005).

Other critics take issue with the concept itself. As it originated within Western conservationism and environmental politics, there is an inherent bias in favour of the industrialized world's main issue of environmental protection rather than the developing world's central concern with eliminating material poverty. This leads to the unedifying spectacle of Western governments chastising developing countries for their failure to protect rainforests and coral reefs, while the West continues to be profligate with resources. Conversely, developing countries have complained that proposed curbs on greenhouse gas emissions take no account of the fact that, for the rich countries, most of these are 'luxury emissions' (such as those produced by car ownership), while for poorer countries they are 'survival emissions' for much-needed economic development. Disputes such as these may show that sustainability and development are incompatible goals.

Continuing Relevance

Sustainable development is a very easy concept to criticize. It is ambitious to the point of utopian, an attempt to solve the most insoluble problems of modern times. However, sustainable development is best seen as a continuous process, and it is this process which really matters. There are also few if any serious alternatives that would appeal to such a wide range of people, governments and NGOs. It is further the case that some of the most biting criticisms have come from within rather than without. The Millennium Ecosystem report *Living Beyond our Means* (2005) is a good example, admitting the poor progress to date and shaming national governments to do more. As long as this kind of hard-nosed self-criticism continues, then sustainable development will probably retain its current pre-eminent position for some while yet.

One form of economic development that might also be sustainable is tourism, particularly when compared to industrial production with the pollution that entails. However, tourism has its own environmental impacts, and Mbaiwa and Stronza (2009) explore the possibility of 'ecotourism' in developing countries. Ecotourism is based on three principles: economic efficiency, social equity and ecological sustainability. Yet many tourist businesses are foreign-owned and revenue flows outwards rather than being used for development. The authors note that, in the Okavanga Delta region of Botswana, tourism is foreign-dominated, with 71 per cent of revenues repatriated to developed countries. Local workers tend to get low-paid jobs, while expatriates dominate management positions, residents may lose their sense of home and place as their environment is transformed for tourists, and local authorities lose control over resources. Clearly the challenges of meeting the basic principles of ecotourism are huge, and Mbaiwa and Stronza's article explores how they might be met.

References and Further Reading

Baker, S. (2015) *Sustainable Development* (2nd edn, London and New York: Routledge).

Luke, T. (2005) 'Neither Sustainable, Nor Development: Reconsidering Sustainability in Development', *Sustainable Development*, 13(4): 228–38.

Mbaiwa, J. E., and Stronza, A. L. (2009) 'The Challenges and Prospects for Sustainable Tourism and Ecotourism in Developing Countries', in T. Jamal and M. Robinson (eds), *The Sage Handbook of Tourism Studies* (London: Sage), pp. 333–53.

Meadows, D. H., et al. (1972) *The Limits to Growth* (New York: Universe Books).

Mill, J. S. ([1848] 1999) *Principles of Political Economy with Some of their Applications to Social Philosophy* (Oxford: Oxford University Press).

UN Millennium Ecosystem Assessment Board (2005) *Living Beyond our Means: Natural Assets and Human Well-Being* (Washington, DC: Island Press); available at www.millenniumassessment.org/en/BoardStatement.aspx.

World Commission on Environment and Development (1987) *Our Common Future* (Oxford: Oxford University Press) [Bruntland report].

Urbanism

Working Definition

The distinctive character of life in modern cities and urban areas and the impact of this on surrounding suburban and rural areas.

Origins of the Concept

Cities are large types of human settlement, often centres of **power** in relation to outlying areas and smaller settlements. Although the existence of recognizable cities can be traced back to ancient times, the idea that cities and urban living take on a distinctive character or form of life is a sociological thesis traceable to the late nineteenth century. At that time the process of urbanization was leading to very rapid population growth and increasing density, which seemed to many to mark a new stage of civilization. Ferdinand Tönnies ([1887] 2001) and Georg Simmel ([1903] 2005) explored the contrast with previous settlements, showing how individuals developed new psychic and social strategies to survive in the new **environment**. However, urban studies came of age with the work of the Chicago School in the 1920s and 1930s. Robert Park, Ernest Burgess, Louis Wirth and others using the distinctive Chicago approach known as 'urban ecology' effectively launched the sub-discipline of urban studies. More recent work in this field has looked at the role of **social movements** and processes of **globalization** in both shaping and being shaped by urban life.

Meaning and Interpretation

Ferdinand Tönnies was an important forerunner of urban studies. In the 1880s he observed that traditional social bonds of *Gemeinschaft* (**community**), which were close and long-lasting, were giving way to looser, more transitory *Gesellschaft*, or mere association. Tönnies saw this as inevitable but that, in the process of change, something vital was being lost, as the resulting individuality easily tipped over into a more selfish and instrumental individualism. Another forerunner, Georg Simmel, tried to grasp the experience and quality of urban life, focusing on how people coped with the city. Simmel suggested that urbanites adapt by adopting a blasé attitude, a 'seen-it-all-before' mentality that dulls and negates the draining effect of city life on the senses. Without such coping mechanisms, the urban environment would become unbearable.

Louis Wirth (1938) firmed up the previous impressionistic accounts of urban experience in his now famous phrase that urbanism was 'a way of life'. The emergence of modern urbanism marked a new form of human existence characterized by loose, short-term interactions aimed at achieving particular outcomes. Buying a bus ticket, fuelling a car, discussing savings accounts at a bank – all such routine interactions are typical of what Wirth calls 'secondary contacts'. What distinguishes these from the 'primary contacts' of **family** and community is that people are involved only with a part of their self – just enough to complete the **interaction** successfully. These interactions are merely the means to other ends. Secondary contacts are, of course, essential, but Wirth's argument is that urbanism demands they become the dominant type, and, in turn, social bonds – the glue that holds society together – inevitably become weaker.

The Chicago School provided the basic tools which helped to build urban studies in sociology. Its members developed a perspective known as 'urban ecology' which analysed the process in which cities became internally socially differentiated. As Robert Park argued, the city is 'a great sorting mechanism'. Using concepts derived from the biological sub-discipline of ecology – competition, invasion and succession – it was possible to show that cities developed as a series of concentric rings. Businesses gravitated to the city centre alongside deteriorating private housing stock. The next ring contained established localities, while the next was marked by suburbs inhabited by wealthier social groups. As in ecology, processes of invasion and succession generate constant movement across the concentric rings so that cities retain their distinctively dynamic, mobile character. The ecological approach has stimulated much empirical research, though the biological analogy has generally fallen out of favour.

More recent trends in urban studies have explored the continual restructuring of space in urban environments as businesses relocate, investors buy up land and property, and government and councils act to encourage employment but also seek to protect green spaces. The restructuring of urban space is a continuous process as capitalist firms move around to gain a competitive advantage, and the process has now become a global one. This leads to urban degeneration in some areas and rapid regeneration in others. It also means that the form of urbanism changes with the business environment, in recent times from manufacturing plants to office blocks and redeveloped industrial sites which have been turned into private housing.

Critical Points

A problem with the concept of urbanism is its use as a general characterization of life in all urban areas when it was distilled from early studies only in the USA and Europe. Are wealthy Western cities such as London, New York or Paris really similar to those in developing countries such as Nairobi, Mumbai or Dhaka? Apart from a large concentration of population, the differences seem more striking, such as the impoverished, makeshift shanty towns that surround the central city area of many cities in developing countries, for which there is no spatial equivalent in the developed world. Similarly, the urban condition even within a single city is diverse and varied, meaning that the picture painted by Simmel or Wirth may really apply only to the central business district and main shopping areas.

The negative tone of the characterization of urbanism which emerges from many urban studies can also be questioned. It is entirely possible that many urbanites experience impersonality as liberating, enjoying the freedom which comes with it. In this sense, urbanism could be interpreted as an improvement on previous tightly knit communities which stifled individuality. The formation of 'communities of choice' such as friendship groups and associations of like-minded people also gives the lie to exaggerated notions of urbanism as promoting excessive individualism. Herbert Gans (1962) noted that urban villages were common among immigrant groups in American cities, showing that urbanism can generate rather than destroy community life. Generally, the ecological perspective underemphasizes the importance of conscious urban design and planning which may mitigate the problems they describe.

Continuing Relevance

Urbanism alerts us to the distinctive character of densely populated urban environments, which are historically unique. Simmel's account of mental life in cities may be impressionistic, but it did capture something of what it feels like to live in cities, and he is credited with showing us that the city is as much a sociological phenomenon as a spatial one. Urban studies have not stood still since the Chicago School introduced its urban ecological approach. The separate studies of urban social movements and their impact on shaping urban life by Manuel Castells (1983) and Alberto Melucci (1989) have added a new dimension to our understanding, as has David Harvey's (2006) geographical exploration of the shifting city landscape and urban forms.

Urbanism today may be more diverse than the early theorists allowed for, and the emergence of 'world cities' shows that the external forces and pressures of globalization must also be taken into account. However, in more recent years, design of the built environment has been influenced by ideas of **sustainable development**. For example, Douglas Farr (2008) argues that the USA (and, by extension, other developed countries) is on the wrong course and needs a 'comprehensive reform of the built environment' in order to embed human societies within nature. To do so means embracing 'the precautionary principle', which states that the onus lies with developers to demonstrate that their projects will not harm the environment before they are allowed to go ahead. Farr's book includes many case studies and examples of how an ecological design approach may change the look and experience of urban life in the future.

An interesting take on the experience of urbanism is provided by Sharon Zukin's *Naked City* (2010), a personal journey into urban regeneration in America in the 1980s – a period that saw the redevelopment of many run-down buildings and areas but which also led some to argue that the city had lost a certain feeling of authenticity. Zukin writes that, in New York, the influx of private finance has led to an overconcentration on shopping and security. And, though she does not suggest that people should bemoan the loss of slum dwellings, high levels of street crime and hard drugs, the kind of homogenizing redevelopment experienced in the 1980s also swept away with them much of the diversity, creativity and vibrancy of the city. This is a personal account, but one which avoids nostalgia and contains many sociological insights into the challenges for contemporary urban planners.

References and Further Reading

Abrahamson, M. (2014) *Urban Sociology: A Global Introduction* (New York: Cambridge University Press).

Castells, M. (1983) *The City and the Grass Roots: A Cross-Cultural Theory of Urban Social Movements* (London: Edward Arnold).

Farr, D. (2008) *Sustainable Urbanism: Urban Design with Nature* (New York: John Wiley).

Gans, H. J. (1962) *The Urban Villagers: Group and Class in the Life of Italian-Americans* (2nd edn, New York: Free Press).

Harvey, D. (2006) *Spaces of Global Capitalism: Towards a Theory of Uneven Geographical Development* (London: Verso).

Melucci, A. (1989) *Nomads of the Present: Social Movements and Individual Needs in Contemporary Society* (London: Hutchinson Radius).

Simmel, G. ([1903] 2005) 'The Metropolis and Mental Life', in J. Lin and C. Mele (eds), *The Urban Sociology Reader* (London: Routledge), pp. 23–31.

Tönnies, F. ([1887] 2001) *Community and Society [Gemeinschaft und Gesellschaft]* (Cambridge and New York: Cambridge University Press).

Wirth, L. (1938) 'Urbanism as a Way of Life', *American Journal of Sociology*, 44(1): 1–24.

Zukin, S. (2010) *Naked City: The Death and Life of Authentic Urban Places* (Oxford and New York: Oxford University Press).

4 Structures of Society

Bureaucracy

Working Definition

A type of organization based on written rules, contracts and a hierarchy of positions that is very widely adopted in modern industrial societies.

Origins of the Concept

'Bureaucracy' derives from the combination of the French *bureau* (office or writing table) and the Greek *kratos* ('to rule'). The modern concept of bureaucracy as 'the rule of officials' dates from the mid-eighteenth century, when it referred purely to government officials. Gradually the concept spread outwards to many other types of organization and almost immediately was seen in negative ways. There are many fictional works which critique bureaucratic **power**, such as Franz Kafka's novel *The Trial*, with its nightmarish depiction of an impersonal and unintelligible officialdom. This negative view continues in popular **culture**, with bureaucracies seen as tying people in 'red tape' and also being inefficient and wasteful.

Sociological studies of bureaucracy have been dominated by the ideas of Max Weber, who created a classic **'ideal type'** bureaucracy which has formed the basis for much research. In contrast to previous views which saw bureaucracy as inefficient, Weber argued that, in fact, modern bureaucracy was ultimately so widespread because it was the most efficient form of organization yet devised. However, he also recognized that bureaucratic forms of domination tended to stifle creativity and nullify enterprise, producing many irrational outcomes and conflicting with the principle of **democracy**. In that sense, his view, in part, continued the tradition which portrays bureaucracies as, on balance, a negative force in **society**.

Meaning and Interpretation

Modern life is complex and needs some kind of organization to run smoothly. Weber saw bureaucracy as the dominant model of formal organization, and his characterization continues to inform sociological studies. Although bureaucratic organizations existed in large, traditional civilizations such as imperial China, only with the advent of industrial capitalism have bureaucracies been used across all areas of society. For Weber, this extension and expansion was inevitable and the only way of coping with the demands of **modernity**. A modern welfare system or national health system without written records, archived files and written rules would be almost impossible to imagine. Weber constructed an ideal or 'pure' type of bureaucracy by accentuating certain common features from real cases in order to highlight the definitive aspects of modern bureaucracies.

Weber's ideal type included all of the following features:

1 a clear hierarchy of authority, where power resides at the top. Within this over-all structure, an office controls and monitors the office immediately below it in the hierarchy;
2 the conduct of officials being governed by written rules, which makes for pre-dictability and order;
3 employees who are salaried, permanent and generally work full time. People can make lifetime careers within the organization;
4 a clear separation between the work of officials and their personal life – these are not mixed;
5 all resources (including desks, computers, pens, paper, etc.) being the prop-erty of the organization; workers are not permitted to own their 'means of pro-duction'.

Although this pure type probably never could exist, the more that real cases approach it, the more efficient should be the organization in achieving its objectives.

Weber argued that, as it becomes dominated by bureaucratic organizations, society begins to feel more like a 'steel-hard cage', trapping people within. Many people do believe bureaucracies are obstructive to their individual needs when they come into contact with them personally, but this is because personal con-siderations and emotional appeals cannot be catered for, as bureaucracies are designed for peak efficiency when dealing with thousands or even millions of cases. Hence, the very principle of equal treatment helps to produce much indi-vidual dissatisfaction. A more serious problem is that bureaucratic domination could oppose democracy. As the permanent machinery of government becomes the real power broker, democratic processes and elections could be undermined.

Critical Points

Critics of Weber's arguments see his perspective as essentially a *partial* one that largely ignores the informal relationships and small-group dynamics that help make organizational life 'work'. Blau's 1963 study of an American government tax agency found that procedural rules were routinely broken in the interests of 'getting the work done', and group loyalties were generated at lower levels of the hierarchy as an informal system of mutual help and advice had grown up.

For others, Weber's concerns about bureaucracy do not go far enough.

Zygmunt Bauman (1989) argues that the German National Socialists' mass murder of Jewish populations during the Second World War was only made possible by using the bureaucratic machinery of the modern state. The vast organization involved in moving millions of people across Europe to concentration camps and recording a myriad of personal details – all during wartime conditions – required systematic, meticulous bureaucratic planning and execution. It was precisely the impersonality of bureaucracies that enabled officials to avoid personal, moral responsibility. For Bauman, the Holocaust was not an aberration in a normally civilized modernity; rather, it was one consequence of its central organizing feature – bureaucracy.

Conversely, some see Weber's perspective as *too negative*. Paul du Gay (2000) makes a strong case in favour of bureaucracy and the traditional bureaucratic ethos, arguing that many of the problems commonly attributed to 'bureaucracy' are really caused by attempts to *bypass* the rules and guidelines of procedure. Indeed, he argues that Bauman's study ignores the real causes of the Holocaust, which lie in racist attitudes and ideologies and the use of intimidation and coercion. The bureaucratic ethos is one of equal treatment for all, and bureaucracies contain some important safeguards which prevent, rather than facilitate, abuses of power by political leaders.

Continuing Relevance

Weber could not have foreseen all of the consequences of bureaucratization, and some of the criticisms of his original analysis may be conceded. The fact that sociologists are still engaged in 'debates with Weber' shows that he managed to put his finger on a crucial aspect of the modern world. Weber was also clear that bureaucracy was one important contributor to the ongoing **rationalization** of society, which was spreading to more and more areas of social life. Although we may quibble with parts of his analysis, the global spread of **capitalism** and modern bureaucracies means that the general thrust of Weber's argument remains pertinent and must be taken seriously.

In contrast to some recent studies suggesting that loose **networks** may be replacing the rigid hierarchies characteristic of bureaucracies, Casey (2004) argues that bureaucracies have begun to allow or build into workplace life some novel activities. If this becomes widespread, then it may challenge our existing understanding of what constitutes a 'bureaucracy' in the first place. Casey focuses on the trend for bureaucratic organizations to allow and enable the expression of spirituality at work. Many individuals pursue New Age and other 'spiritual' activities in the workplace, while some large corporations – Ford, IBM and Apple among others – support and even encourage 'spirituality at work' programmes, making the literature and seminars available to managers. Casey argues that, rather than ossifying, bureaucracies are adapting to and evolving within changing societies.

A growing body of research suggests that bureaucratic procedures may actually prove beneficial for women within organizations, as they ensure that career promotions are based on capabilities and qualifications rather than on the personal ties and social networking that have long been part of the exclusionary devices used by men to protect their privileges. DeHart-Davis (2009) extends this argument by exploring men's and women's *perceptions* of their bureaucratic workplace. Using a mixed-methods approach, the study found some clear gender differences. Women were more likely to emphasize the efficiency, legitimacy and equity of bureaucracy, while men were focused on what they saw as the excessive controls and rules. The author's conclusion is that women emphasized those elements that empowered them and enabled their participation and career progression on equal terms. This challenges some feminist theories which portray bureaucracies as male dominance in organizational form.

References and Further Reading

Bauman, Z. (1989) *Modernity and the Holocaust* (Cambridge: Polity).

Blau, P. M. (1963) *The Dynamics of Bureaucracy* (Chicago: University of Chicago Press).

Casey, C. (2004) 'Bureaucracy Re-enchanted? Spirit, Experts and Authority in Organizations', *Organization*, 11(1): 59–79.

DeHart-Davis, L. (2009) 'Can Bureaucracy Benefit Organizational Women?', *Administration and Society*, 41(3): 340–63.

Du Gay, P. (2000) *In Praise of Bureaucracy: Weber, Organization, Ethics* (London: Sage).

Capitalism

Working Definition

An economic system, which originated in the West, based on market exchange and the production of profit for reinvestment and business growth.

Origins of the Concept

Eighteenth-century political economists discussed markets, exchange, prices and the production of goods, while Adam Smith argued that a certain social order and economic equilibrium was produced as if by the 'hidden hand' of the free exchange in the market (Ingham 2008). However, the term 'capitalism' did not appear until the mid-nineteenth century, when Marx and Engels discussed the capitalist mode of production. For Marx, capitalism is an exploitative economic system based on the production of goods for exchange in the marketplace in order to produce profits for a bourgeois or capitalist **class**. In Marxist theory, capitalism is the final stage of social development before communism, which would finally end the grossly unequal class societies that preceded it.

An alternative conception was provided by Max Weber, whose study of the origins of capitalism in the interpretation of Calvinistic religious beliefs contrasted with Marx's grand historical scheme. For Weber, capitalism was not the product of revolutionary change, nor was it likely to give way to communism in the future. Instead, the future of the working class lay in the development, not the ending, of capitalism. He argued that the long-term process of **rationalization** and the spread of bureaucratic organizations were the keys to understanding **modernity**. Capitalism at least encouraged competition and innovation, which helped to mitigate the stultifying effects of bureaucratic domination, thus allowing the freedom to experiment with new ideas.

Meaning and Interpretation

The most influential theory of capitalism remains the Marxist perspective, which sees capitalism emerging out of feudal society as the latest stage in the overall history of human societies. Marx outlined progressive stages that began with primitive communist societies of hunters and gatherers and passed through ancient slave-owning systems and feudal systems based on the division between landowners and serfs. The emergence of merchants and craftspeople marked the beginning of a commercial or capitalist class that came to displace the landed nobility. Marx identified two main elements in capitalism: capital – any asset, including money, machines or even factories, which can be used or invested to make future assets – and wage-labour – a pool of workers who do not own the means of production and must find paid employment. Those who own capital form a ruling class, while the majority make up the working class or proletariat. Capitalists and workers were mutually dependent, but, as the relationship is exploitative, class **conflict** would become more acute. Marx argued that, over time, all other classes would shrink, leaving the two main classes whose interests were in direct conflict.

Nonetheless, Marx was not just a critic; he saw clearly that capitalism was enormously productive, freeing people from the unnecessary yoke of religious **authority** and 'the idiocy of rural life'. It also demonstrated the immense **power** of humanity to shape its own future rather than being at the mercy of natural forces. The problem was that competitive capitalist social relations would become an obstacle to the cooperation that was necessary if people were to take control of their destiny. The contradiction between immense productive forces and their competitive rather than cooperative use could only be resolved by revolution. More than 150 years after Marx forecast that revolution, it has patently not occurred.

There have been major changes in the development of capitalism, from the '**family** capitalism' of Marx's time, through the managerial capitalism which developed as firms outgrew control by family members, to the welfare capitalism of the twentieth century, when large firms provided services for their employees such as child care, paid holidays and life insurance. The peak of welfare capitalism was before 1930, after which trade unions became the main source of workers' attempts to gain benefits from the system. The latest stage is 'institutional capitalism', based on the widespread practice of corporations holding shares in other firms. In effect, interlocking boards of directors control much of the corporate world, thus reversing the process of managerial control, since the managers' shareholdings are dwarfed by large blocks of shares owned by other corporations. With the intensification of **globalization**, most large corporations operate in an international economic context.

Critical Points

The debate between Weberian and Marxist positions has always involved moral and normative judgements. For Marxists, capitalism is an economic system that produces and thrives on inequality which deserves to be consigned to the 'dustbin of history'. For Weberians, however, capitalism may be exploitative, but all alternatives have turned out to be less productive and more authoritarian, providing less scope for **democracy** and the exercise of personal freedom. Today there is still no agreement among sociologists regarding an overall assessment of capitalist economies.

However, most sociologists consider that Marx's forecast of revolution and the overthrow of capitalism has been proved decisively wrong. Where revolutions did occur – as in Russia (1917) or China (1949) – they tended not to follow Marx's model, since they involved peasants and agricultural workers rather than a developed industrial proletariat. The late twentieth-century collapse of Soviet communism is also seen as marking the end of an era, as globalization and the tighter integration of the global capitalist system seem to preclude any movement towards socialism or communism. Many Marxists still hold that Marx's analysis of the central mechanisms of capitalism and its tendency to veer towards crisis is sound, though he clearly underestimated the adaptive capacity of capitalist economies.

Continuing Relevance

There is no serious disagreement that capitalist economic systems dominate the global economy, though this is a relatively recent development following the collapse of rival communist systems in the former Soviet Union, Eastern Europe and other parts of the world. After the fall of the Berlin Wall in 1989 and the reunification of Germany, the break-up of the Soviet Union and the abandonment of communism in Eastern Europe, existing communism/socialism was all but dead. Today's opposition seems to be taking the form of post-socialist movements such as the anti-globalization and anti-capitalist mobilizations of recent years, as well as anarchist and environmentalist campaigns.

In more recent scholarship, there has been much interest in the differences across national capitalist economies, and Campbell and Pedersen's (2007) comparison of capitalism in Denmark and the USA is a useful way into the 'varieties of capitalism' debate. Capitalist economies have often been thought to 'work' more effectively with minimal economic regulation, low tax regimes and a small welfare state. However, Denmark defies this prediction. The Danish version of capitalism is built on relatively high taxes, a large state budget, high levels of regulation and an open economy, yet it still competes effectively against other variants that fit the low-regulation model much more closely. The study argues that Denmark is successful because companies gain advantages from the country's institutions, which coordinate labour markets, manage vocational and skills training, and pursue industrial policy. It is this set of institutions that enables Denmark to compete, showing that there is more than one way to succeed in global markets.

Given the current concern with global warming, the question of whether capitalism can ever become 'sustainable' is a serious one. Markandya (2009) thinks that it could, but only if market-based measures are made to work strongly in favour of carbon reduction. He argues that environmental problems, particularly climate change, demand state regulation and concerted action if carbon emissions are to be reduced and stabilized. However, any carbon reduction scheme must be perceived as fair if it is to have a chance of succeeding. Hence, Markandya proposes that a global per capita allowance of carbon emissions should be introduced over time. In addition, if a carbon trading system is to be successful, the price would need to be around US$420 per tonne of CO_2. The 2009 market price was just €15 per tonne! The radical disparity in market price clearly raises serious doubts about the feasibility of such capitalist, market-oriented measures to tackle global warming.

References and Further Reading

Campbell, J. L., and Pedersen, O. K. (2007) 'Institutional Competitiveness in the Global Economy: Denmark, the United States and the Varieties of Capitalism', *Regulation and Governance*, 1(3): 230–46.
Ingham, G. (2008) *Capitalism* (Cambridge: Polity).
Markandya, A. (2009) 'Can Climate Change be Reversed under Capitalism?', *Development and Change*, 40(6): 1139–52.
Marx, K., and Engels, F. ([1848] 2005) *The Communist Manifesto* (London: Longman).

Consumerism

Working Definition

The way of life common to the relatively rich societies, which promotes the continual purchase of consumer goods as beneficial for both the economy and personal fulfilment.

Origins of the Concept

Arguably, consumerism can be traced to the Industrial Revolution of the early nineteenth century, when the sheer amount of material goods being produced rose enormously and cheaper prices enabled many more social groups to engage in their consumption. The first groups to emerge as modern consumers were the upper classes and aristocracy, which formed the largest market for the new luxury goods. Over the course of the nineteenth and twentieth centuries, conspicuous consumption spread to many more social groups, and by the mid-twentieth century consumerism as a way of life characterized the developed economies.

One important development stimulating the growth of consumerism was the easier availability of credit from the early twentieth century. By the end of the century, living with large amounts of debt had become normalized and social **status** competition was increasingly based on patterns of consumption. Since the 1960s, sociologists have argued that capitalist societies have become reliant on consumerism, which encourages high material lifestyles and the desire for and use of purchased goods. These changes are said to have led to a 'consumer society'. Environmental activists argue that the shift towards high-consumption societies has produced disastrous environmental damage, unnecessary waste and unsustainable practices.

Meaning and Interpretation

Industrial capitalist societies are based on a system of mass production, but this must therefore mean there is also mass consumption. Goods and services must be bought and consumed, though the producing and consuming may well take place in very different geographical locations. Goods will be produced wherever it is cheapest but consumed wherever the best price can be gained, and the two are likely to be in different places. Over the twentieth century the central orientation of industrial capitalist societies shifted away from a 'production paradigm' towards a 'consumerist' one, and it is now commonplace in sociology to see the relatively rich societies characterized as 'consumer societies' or 'consumer **capitalism**'.

Work is becoming less important in the process of **identity** formation. Instead, consumption provides people with the opportunity to construct a personal identity by purchasing the various elements, giving at least the perception of more free choice and individuality. The central focus on consumption and the **ideology** of consumerism promote a rapid turnover of products based on fashionable shifts in the exchange value of commodities and, as a result, more waste. Consumer identification with products and brands makes consumption central to the routines of everyday life. Secondly, corporations are more concerned to tap into and produce for a more flexible and differentiated consumer demand rather than putting the needs of production first and worrying about customers later. Typically this shift is represented as the demise of uniform 'Fordist' production methods and a move to more flexible 'post-Fordist' methods catering for niche markets. The consumer, not the worker, becomes the main actor. Thirdly, the construction of personal identities enabled by consumer societies serves to decentre production-based social conflicts, engaging more social groups in the competitive process of status competition through symbolic exchanges. The shift towards consumerism and the consumer society therefore marks significant changes in the economic, political and cultural spheres.

Consumerism is also a way of thinking, a mentality or even an ideology that works to produce the *desire* to consume continuously. Sociologists of consumption argue that the pleasure of consuming lies not in the *use* of products but in the *anticipation* of purchasing things. People spend time browsing magazines, shop windows and the worldwide web looking for products and desiring them before making a purchase. Campbell (2005) argues this is because the most pleasurable and addictive part of modern consumerism is the wanting, the longing after, the seeking out and the desiring of products, not the use of them. This is a 'romantic ethic' of consumption based on the desire and longing encouraged by the advertising industry, which explains why people are never truly satisfied.

Critical Points

Although the concept of consumerism has added a new dimension to our understanding of capitalism, it is not clear that it is the *cause* of capitalist expansion. The idea that consumption is driving production gives much weight to the demands of consumers, but some find this highly implausible, pointing to the very large marketing and branding budgets of companies aimed at creating desires and demands, turning people into active consumers. The issue at stake here is who really wields power in this system – the producer or the consumer? Are large transnational capitalist corporations really at the mercy of consumer demand?

Other criticisms are of consumerism itself, which is seen as destructive of social relations and the natural **environment**. Consumerism 'works' by turning wants into 'needs' and then encouraging people that they can and should realize them. In this way there is a potentially endless stream of fashions, new products and services for us to consume. This conflation of needs and wants has been seen as dangerous, leading to the false belief that happiness can be bought and that consuming products is natural. Instead, we should separate wants from needs and cut back on the former in order to ensure that the real needs of people all over the world can be met. The problem is that all attempts to define 'needs' have floundered. Needs are culturally specific, and no firm criteria have been agreed for making the distinction.

Continuing Relevance

The concept of consumerism and its corollary, the consumer society, have been very productive for sociologists. A better balanced understanding of capitalism has become possible by linking production processes with consumption patterns. For example, an approach that has brought the two elements together successfully is the theory of a 'treadmill of production and consumption'. This combines **industrialization**, capitalist economics and mass consumerism to understand how **modernity** has transformed the relationship between human society and the natural environment. The image of the treadmill shows that, once the system of mass production and consumption has started up, it becomes impossible to get off again.

Consumerism has become not just a lifestyle but also a feature of the whole **life course**, including the extended period of later life that has become commonplace in the developed world. Jones and his colleagues (2008) note that this is especially the case, as many older people today, in Britain and elsewhere, have higher incomes than did previous generations, and some are choosing to retire fully or partially at an earlier age. The current generation of older people is also the one which helped to generate a post-1945 consumer culture. They are among the first 'consumer-citizens' and, as such, are continuing actively to consume well into old age rather than settling into the 'passive consumption' of services. This empirical study explores in detail the diverse ways in which older people are both affected by and drive forward consumerism.

A growing trend is 'green' consumption, though this is quite a broad catch-all concept that is hard to pin down. In a questionnaire survey of 1,600 households in Devon, England, Gilg and his colleagues (2005) explored what motivates green consumers to try and adopt more sustainable lifestyles. The research identified four main groups. *Committed environmentalists* were most likely to engage in sustainable consumption – buying local, organic or fair-trade produce and composting waste. *Mainstream environmentalists* engaged in very similar behaviours with the exception of composting waste, while *occasional environmentalists* only rarely or never undertook the same actions. *Non-environmentalists* were not inclined to perform any of the actions described. There was a connection between sustainable consumption and pro-environmental values, suggesting that governments may struggle to encourage a move from green consumption to sustainable lifestyles.

References and Further Reading

Aldridge, A. (2003) *Consumption* (Cambridge: Polity).

Campbell, C. (2005) *The Romantic Ethic and the Spirit of Modern Consumerism* (Oxford: Blackwell).

Gilg, A., Barr, S., and Ford, N. (2005) 'Green Consumption or Sustainable Lifestyles? Identifying the Sustainable Consumer', *Futures*, 37(6): 481–504.

Jones, I. R., Hyde, M., Higgs, P., and Victor, C. R. (2008) *Ageing in a Consumer Society: From Passive to Active Consumption in Britain* (Bristol: Policy Press), esp. chapter 5.

Division of Labour

Working Definition

The separation of work tasks and occupations in a production process, which creates extended economic interdependence.

Origins of the Concept

One of the first systematic explorations of the division of labour is Adam Smith's *The Wealth of Nations* ([1776] 1991), in which the division of labour in a pin-making factory is described. Smith argued that one person working alone could make twenty pins per day but, by breaking down the task into several simple actions, collective production could produce 48,000 pins per day. This is a classic instance of the enormous benefits to be gained in a planned, systematic division of labour. Émile Durkheim ([1893] 1984) theorized that the industrial division of labour, in its widest sense, was leading to fundamental changes in the type of social solidarity that binds **society** together. He saw traditional forms of solidarity based on similarities giving way to the modern form rooted in differences and cooperation. For Durkheim, the division of labour was not simply an economic phenomenon but a transformation of the whole society.

Meaning and Interpretation

Modern societies are underpinned by a division of labour that is constituted by a very large number of occupational categories and increasing specialization. This has become such a normal feature of life that we hardly notice its world-historical significance any more. Yet, in most previous forms of agrarian society, many of those who did not work directly in agriculture were craft workers who served a long period of apprenticeship. This was necessary as craft workers were involved in all aspects of their tasks rather than one specific aspect of it. **Industrialization** gradually eliminated most traditional crafts by producing the same goods much more quickly, efficiently and cheaply using machinery and an extended division of labour. Manufacturing workers typically learn just one part of the production process, which allows them to become proficient very rapidly without having to undergo a long training period. This principle also extends to most other forms of work. One consequence is specialization, with many thousands of occupations, roles and job titles, which is completely different to the thirty or so major crafts and roles available in traditional societies.

Émile Durkheim saw the extended division of labour as hugely significant, and, though it brought some serious problems, such as a potential **conflict** between owners and workers, it also had many long-term advantages. In traditional societies, the collective was dominant over the individual and individualism was minimized. The type of solidarity that held society together was a 'mechanical solidarity' rooted in similarities, stable and relatively unchanging institutions, shared lifestyles and deference to authorities. Solidarity was not something that had to be consciously worked at but arose 'mechanically' through the continuous patterns of life.

With **capitalism**, industrialization and urbanization, traditional life and, with it, mechanical solidarity broke down. Many commentators were fearful that the destruction of social solidarity and the promotion of individualism would lead to more conflict as well as social and moral breakdown. However, Durkheim disagreed. He argued that a new form of 'organic solidarity' was emerging as a result of the extensive division of labour. The specialization of roles would strengthen social solidarity within larger communities and, rather than living a relatively isolated, self-sufficient communal life, people would be linked together through their mutual dependency. We are all dependent on an immense number of other people – today stretching right across the world – for the products and services that sustain our lives. With few exceptions, the vast majority of people in modern societies do not produce the food they eat, the houses in which they live or the material goods they consume. In fact, organic solidarity tends to produce stronger bonds of mutual interdependence and, in addition, a better balance between individual differences and collective goals.

Critical Points

The division of labour has led to a global economic interdependence among nations, and, in that sense, Durkheim was right to argue that it would bring the peoples of the world into closer contact and cooperation. However, many critics have argued that this continues to be bought at the expense of deskilling workers and the degradation of work. Scientific management principles linked to the advent of factory-based mass production created what industrial sociologists call 'low-trust' systems – production methods in which management have control of the process while workers have very little, if any, autonomy in the workplace. Workers tend to experience low-trust systems as lacking job satisfaction, which means that they do not identify with the company. High levels of **alienation** and absence from work have often been the result, and for much of the twentieth century employees had to endure low-trust systems. While many still do so today, the majority of these are now in the developing countries, where highly exploitative sweatshops are commonplace. The global division of labour may have many advantages for consumers in the West, but it is also the source of much misery and exploitation.

Continuing Relevance

Since the 1970s and 1980s, there has been a growing interest in the breakdown of an older model based on the mass production of uniform goods in large plants and the movement towards production that tailors items to target niche markets. This shift has been theorized as a move away from Fordism to post-Fordist flexibility. Flexibility occurs in almost every aspect of the production process, from methods of production, warehousing practices, and management-worker relations to the marketing of products. Factory production has seen the introduction of problem-solving teams with the autonomy to find solutions to problems, while specific commodities are targeted at small niche markets rather than uniform products being aimed at a mass market. The aftermath of the global financial crisis of 2008 has had many more consequences for corporate and government decision-making and the global division of labour.

Since the late twentieth century there has been a significant growth in service occupations in the developed countries. However, the next stage may be 'offshoring' – the systematic movement of more and more work tasks abroad (Blinder 2006). Indeed, Blinder argues that offshoring could have revolutionary consequences for the developed economies that are service-based. Many office and service tasks can easily be moved offshore and, as these tend to be stable and relatively well paid, the shock of losing such employment may be felt most keenly by middle-class and professional groups. For example, university courses can be delivered over the Internet from anywhere in the world, banking and most customer service roles likewise. So the question is: what kinds of work will remain in the 'post-industrial' economies? Blinder suggests that those jobs which require contact – caring and transport, for example – should be safe. But whether the extent of offshoring will be quite this radical is not yet clear.

Using the case of London, Jane Wills et al. (2010) show how modern cities have become dependent on migrant labour drawn from around the world to fill many of the taken-for-granted jobs such as bar work, cleaning, caring and catering. Although major cities have always drawn migrants looking for work, this study argues that something has changed over the last twenty years. The neo-liberal, free-market model of economic development has encouraged the normalization of subcontracting and a reduction in wages and conditions, resulting in London becoming almost entirely dependent on foreign-born workers who do the necessary jobs that keep the city moving. This raises policy issues to do with **poverty** and social cohesion, and the book by Wills and her colleagues outlines these together with some possible solutions.

References and Further Reading

Blinder, S. (2006) 'Offshoring: The Next Industrial Revolution?', *Foreign Affairs*, March/April: 113–28.
Durkheim, É. ([1893] 1984) *The Division of Labour in Society* (London: Macmillan).
Morrison, K. (2006) *Marx, Durkheim, Weber: Formations of Modern Social Thought* (2nd edn, London: Sage), chapter 3.
Smith, A. ([1776] 1991) *The Wealth of Nations* (London: Everyman's Library).
Wills, J., Datta, K., Evans, Y., Herbert, J., May, J., and McIlwaine, C. (2010) *Global Cities at Work: New Migrant Divisions of Labour* (London: Pluto Press).

Education

Working Definition

A social institution which promotes and enables the transmission of knowledge and skills across generations, most commonly through compulsory schooling.

Origins of the Concept

Education is the passing on of knowledge, skills and norms of behaviour so that new members can become part of their **society**. Education today is widely seen as 'a good thing', and most people who have been through an education system and emerged literate, numerate and reasonably knowledgeable would agree that it has clear benefits. However, sociologists make a distinction between education and schooling. Education can be defined as a social institution, which enables and promotes the acquisition of skills, knowledge and the broadening of personal horizons and can take place in many settings. Schooling, though, is the formal process through which certain types of knowledge and skill are delivered via a pre-designed curriculum and is usually compulsory up to a certain age. Increasingly mandatory education in the developed countries is being extended to college and even university level.

Before the late eighteenth century, education in schools was a private matter, and only the wealthiest families could afford an education for their children. Throughout the nineteenth and into the twentieth century, compulsory state education systems were introduced as the need for literacy and numeracy among workers grew in industrial workplaces and offices. While functionalist theories see the formal function of schools as the production of an educated and skilled population, many Marxist and radical critics argue that there is a hidden curriculum that subtly conveys the values and norms which support a grossly unequal capitalist society. More recent research has tended to focus on the role of education and schooling in cultural reproduction, the generational transmission of cultural values, norms and experience, and all of the mechanisms and processes through which this is achieved.

Meaning and Interpretation

Émile Durkheim argued that education is a key agency of **socialization**, inculcating in children society's common values which sustain social solidarity. Durkheim was concerned particularly with moral guidelines and mutual responsibility, as these helped to mitigate the kind of competitive individualism that many thought would destroy solidarity. But in industrial societies, Durkheim argued, education also has another function in teaching the skills needed to take up increasingly specialized occupational roles which could no longer be learned within the family. Talcott Parsons took this basically functionalist approach further. He maintained that one of the key functions of education is to instil the central value of individual achievement, often via competitive examinations and assessment. This is crucial because exams are based on universal, meritocratic standards in contrast to the particularistic standards of the **family**, and in the wider society people generally achieve their positions on the basis of ability and merit rather than on their **class**, **gender** or **ethnicity**.

However, many research studies have found that education and schooling reproduce social inequalities rather than helping to equalize life chances. Paul Willis's (1977) UK study, based on fieldwork in a Birmingham school, asked how it happens that working-class kids generally get working-class jobs. This is a pertinent question in a meritocratic education system. Willis found anti-school subcultures in which young boys had no interest in exams or a 'career' but simply wanted to get out and earn money. He argued that these were very similar to the blue-collar work cultures, and, in that way, failing in school did, unintentionally, prepare such children for working-class work.

Critical Points

Functionalist theory is correct to point out the formal functions of education systems, but is there really a single set of society-wide values, especially in the multicultural societies of today? Marxists agree that schools socialize children, but they do so to ensure that capitalist companies get the kind of workforce they need, not because they are committed to equality of opportunity. The structures of school life correspond to the structures of working life: conforming leads to success, teachers and managers dictate tasks, pupils and workers perform them, school and work staff are organized hierarchically, and this is taught as inevitable (Bowles and Gintis 1976).

This idea of a 'hidden curriculum' has also had a major influence on the sociology of education. Illich (1971) argued that schools are custodial organizations designed to keep young people occupied and off the streets until they enter work. They promote an uncritical acceptance of the social order and teach children to know their class position. Illich advocated the 'deschooling' of society in favour of making educational resources available to everyone at whatever time they need them and to study whatever they want rather than being forced to learn a standardized curriculum. Resources could be stored in libraries and information storage banks (today probably online) and made available to any student. These ideas seemed hopelessly idealistic at the time, but, with today's new focus on lifelong learning and distance learning over the Internet, they no longer seem quite so far-fetched.

Continuing Relevance

How can we square the positive functions of education with the serious critiques? Schooling is part of the reproduction of structural inequalities, but, at one and the same time, it also equips people with some of the skills and knowledge that enable them to understand and challenge those inequalities. And, in addition, it is the case that many teachers who fully appreciate the structural role of the education system work to improve and change it from the inside. Any theory which offers no prospect of change perhaps gives too much weight to the **power** of social structure and not enough to creative human agency. Education is an important site for a whole range of debates that are not just about what happens within schools but also about the direction of society itself.

In recent years many developed societies have seen girls 'overtake' boys in achieving school and college qualifications, and a debate has emerged as to why boys are 'underachieving' and what can be done about it. This implies that girls must have overcome the previous obstacles to their doing well. However, an empirical study in the UK found that a sample of twelve- and thirteen-year-old high-achieving girls continue to face identity problems caused by trying to 'be clever' within the existing norms of acceptable femininity (Skelton et al. 2010). The girls faced particular problems in their relations with classmates but also struggled to gain the attention of their teachers. The reality of life for increasingly successful young girls and women is clearly more complex than is illustrated in the bald statistics of academic achievement.

References and Further Reading

Bartlett, S., and Burton, D. M. (2016) *Introduction to Education Studies* (4th edn, London: Sage), esp. chapter 2.
Bowles, S., and Gintis, H. (1976) *Schooling in Capitalist America: Educational Reform and Contradictions of Economic Life* (New York: Basic Books).
Gatto, J. T. (2002) *Dumbing us Down: The Hidden Curriculum of Compulsory Schooling* (2nd edn, New York: New Society).
Illich, I. D. (1971) *Deschooling Society* (Harmondsworth: Penguin).
Skelton, C., Francis, B., and Read, B. (2010) 'Brains before Beauty? High Achieving Girls, School and Gender Identities', *Educational Studies*, 36(2): 185–94.
Willis, P. (1977) *Learning to Labour: How Working-Class Kids Get Working-Class Jobs* (London: Saxon House).
Zamudio, M. M., Russell, C., Rios, F. A., and Bridgeman, J. L. (eds) (2011) *Critical Race Theory Matters: Education and Ideology* (New York: Routledge).

Organization

Working Definition

A social group or collective entity that is internally structured to meet a social need or to pursue specific aims.

Origins of the Concept

Organizations are as old as the first human groups that banded together for security, food and shelter. However, in sociology, the concept of the organization is much more recent. Max Weber's study of **bureaucracy** as a fundamental feature of **capitalism** and modern life more generally is often used as the starting point for organization studies. Weber acknowledged that bureaucracies were just one form of organization, but their modern, rational form was the most efficient yet devised, hence all organizations were destined to become bureaucratic. Much of the theory and research after Weber has expanded on or critiqued this basic interpretation. Over time the sociology of organizations has moved from theories of organizational structure and functions to informal relations, the **culture** of organizations, the operation of **power** and **gender** relations, and the growth of **networks**.

Meaning and Interpretation

Organizations (sometimes called 'formal' organizations) range from small groups of people to transnational corporations and multinational non-governmental organizations (NGOs), though most studies are concerned with relatively large national organizations such as government departments, universities, schools, hospitals, religious bodies, companies, trade unions and charities. Organizations can be contrasted to institutions, as the latter may be defined as all those established norms, values and patterns of behaviour which make up cultures, such as the **family**, **education** and marriage. Organizations are intentionally designed units geared to achieve certain objectives, usually through a set of written rules, regulations and procedures and housed in physical settings. Such formal organization rests partly on legal requirements. Universities, for instance, have to satisfy laws governing everything from assessment policies to health and safety and equality at work. Such formal organizations remain the dominant type across the world.

Organizations are involved in the lives of everyone: 'We are born in organizations, educated by organizations, and most of us spend much of our lives working for organizations' (Etzioni 1964: ix). Organizations also perform the bulk of the coordination needed for modern life today. However, **conflicts** of interest as well as cooperation are central to organizations. The outcome of power struggles between workers and employers or different groups of workers can shape the overall functioning and even the goals of organizations. Acknowledging such conflicts marked a move away from functionalist perspectives which portrayed organizations as smooth running machines (Silverman 1994). Although not entirely inaccurate, the latter separated the organization from the people who constitute it. A more contemporary 'social action' perspective sees the organization as an 'ongoing and ever-changing coalition of people with quite different and often conflicting interests and purposes who are willing, within rather closely defined limits, to carry out tasks which help to meet the requirements of those in charge' (Watson 2008: 110). This helps us to understand how the internal structure of organizations changes over time and draws attention to changing relationships between organizations and external groups.

In their research into electronics companies in Scotland, Burns and Stalker (1966) found two types of organization: mechanistic and organic. Mechanistic organizations are bureaucratic, while organic organizations are characterized by a looser structure, and the overall aims of the organization take precedence over narrowly defined responsibilities. More recently, Sine et al. (2006) used this contrast between mechanical and organic structures to study Internet companies which started up between 1996 and 2001. It might be assumed that such businesses may be less formally organized and would routinely adopt a loose, organic structure, but this is not necessarily the case. In the early stages, firms with a mechanical structure performed well, as the specialized roles of founding members reduced uncertainty and ambiguity, increasing organizational efficiency at a crucial stage. Therefore the mechanical/organic contrast may not be absolute, but which form is most effective depends on an organization's stage of development.

Organizations operate in specially designed physical settings which reflect their internal structure. For example, managers and executives are often located closer to the 'top' of a building in a system of vertical classification. The arrangement of rooms, hallways and open spaces can also be linked to the system of **authority**, enabling supervisors to observe workers' actions at all times, such as in call centres and open-plan offices. Michel Foucault (1973, 1978) argued that the level of visibility determines how easily workers are subject to surveillance. Self-surveillance also operates through uncertainty about when or if workers are being monitored, which forces them to control their behaviour at all times, 'just in case'.

Critical Points

A longstanding criticism of mainstream conceptualizations of organizations is that, although formal rules and processes clearly do exist, it is a mistake to take these at face value as constitutive. In practice, organizations function due to the routine avoidance or bypassing of rules. For example, factories may have extensive health and safety rules, but in practice workers will ignore many of these in order to 'get the job done' in timely fashion. Meyer and Rowan (1977) saw formal rules essentially as 'myths', which have a ceremonial or ritual character but tell us very little about the reality of organizational life.

Similarly, the impersonal vertical hierarchies said to characterize organizations may also be misleading, particularly at the higher levels. This is because only a few people at the top actually make key decisions, and this small group can be tightly knit with close personal relationships. This leaves boards of directors and shareholders with the task of 'rubber stamping' decisions made by a small number of people at the top of organizations. Similarly, business executives from many different companies may know each other socially, as they tend to gravitate towards the same set of clubs and social venues. Such personal connections lead to informal discussions, consultations and information sharing among a network of high-level individuals that some characterize as a 'business elite'. This situation was anticipated by Robert Michels ([1911] 1967), who argued that power and control in large organizations inevitably coalesces in a small elite. He called this the 'iron law of oligarchy' (rule by the few) and saw that it prevented genuine democratization both within organizations and, as a result, in **society** at large.

Feminist scholarship since the 1970s has focused on the imbalance of gender roles in organizations. Organizations have been characterized by occupational gender segregation, with women segregated into low-paid, routinized occupations and used as a source of cheap, reliable labour and not granted the same opportunities as men to build careers. Women serviced the needs of the male bureaucrat, allowing him to work long hours, travel and focus solely on his job. Thus, modern organizations are male-dominated environments in which women are excluded from power (Kanter 1977; Ferguson 1984).

Continuing Relevance

There were some key differences between the conventional organizational models and the large companies that emerged in Japan during the country's post-war industrialization. Japanese companies have a less obvious hierarchy: workers at all levels are consulted about policies, employees specialize much less than those in the West, and corporations are committed to 'lifetime employment'. However, economic problems have led to changes in the Japanese model, which has come to be seen as too inflexible and costly. Many analysts in Japan looked for a more competitive, individualistic model of business organization, closer to that pertaining in the West (Freedman 2001). The rise of networks and a networked model of the organization has been much discussed in recent years, though the extent of this shift is far from clear (Castells 2009). While there has been some informalization within the traditional organization, it seems unlikely that the modern world can be successfully coordinated without formal organizations.

More women now work within organizations, and we might expect one of the first places to observe this shift to be within 'progressive' political organizations such as labour parties and trade unions committed to equality. Guillaume and Pochic (2011) used biographical methods to examine this assumption in British and French trade unions. The research found that women were now well represented among new union members and activists, which in the UK was largely due to the proactive, targeted actions of unions themselves. However, even in the most feminized unions, women were still under-represented in leadership positions. It seems that, despite policy changes aimed at encouraging more women into higher positions, the 'masculine organizational culture', informal male networks and issues of work–life balance continue to postpone real gender equality.

References and Further Reading

Burns, T., and Stalker, G. M. (1966) *The Management of Innovation* (London: Tavistock).
Castells, M. (2009) *The Rise of the Network Society* (2nd edn, Oxford: Wiley Blackwell).
Etzioni, A. (1964) *Modern Organizations* (Englewood Cliffs, NJ: Prentice Hall).
Ferguson, K. E. (1984) *The Feminist Case against Bureaucracy* (Philadelphia: Temple University Press).
Foucault, M. (1973) *The Birth of the Clinic: An Archaeology of Medical Perception* (London: Tavistock).
— (1978) *The History of Sexuality* (London: Penguin).

Freedman, C. (ed.) (2001) *Economic Reform in Japan: Can the Japanese Change?* (Cheltenham: Edward Elgar).

Godwyn, M., and Gittell, J. H. (eds) (2012) *Sociology of Organizations: Structures and Relationships* (Thousand Oaks, CA: Pine Forge Press).

Guillaume, C., and Pochic, S. (2011) 'The Gendered Nature of Union Careers: The Touchstone of Equality Policies? Comparing France and the UK', *European Societies*, 13(4): 607–31.

Kanter, R. M. (1977) *Men and Women of the Corporation* (New York: Basic Books).

Lune, H. (2010) *Understanding Organizations* (Cambridge: Polity).

Meyer, J. W., and Rowan, B. (1977) 'Institutional Organizations: Formal Structure as Myth and Ceremony', *American Journal of Sociology*, 83: 340–63.

Michels, R. ([1911] 1967) *Political Parties* (New York: Free Press).

Silverman, D. (1994) 'On Throwing Away Ladders: Re-writing the Theory of Organizations', in J. Hassard and M. Parker (eds), *Towards a New Theory of Organizations* (London: Routledge), pp. 1–23.

Sine, W. D., Mitsuhashi, H., and Kirsch, D. A. (2006) 'Revisiting Burns and Stalker: Formal Structure and New Venture Performance in Emerging Economic Sectors', *Academy of Management Journal*, 49(1): 121–32.

Watson, T. J. (2008) *Sociology, Work and Industry* (5th edn, London: Routledge).

Religion

Working Definition

Following Émile Durkheim, 'a unified system of beliefs and practices relative to sacred things which unite the people who adhere to them into a community'.

Origins of the Concept

In one form or another, religion is found in all known human societies. The earliest recorded societies show clear traces of religious symbols and ceremonies. Cave drawings suggest that religious beliefs and practices existed more than 40,000 years ago, and since that time religion has continued to be a central part of human experience. The earliest European religions involved beliefs and practices that were deeply embedded within and thus constitutive of daily life rather than forming distinct social institutions. This is still true in other parts of the world today. In modern industrial societies, though, religions have become established in organizations separate from other spheres of life such as economics and politics. The central debate within the sociology of religion in the twentieth century was over the theory of secularization, with some arguing that religion is slowly losing its hold and others that religious beliefs are increasing, even though formal membership of religious organizations may be in decline.

Meaning and Interpretation

Marx saw religion as a haven for the masses from the harsh reality of life in **class**-divided societies. Christianity, for instance, long promised its believers a life after death while at the same time teaching that their material life in the here and now may be necessarily difficult, painful and riddled with suffering. For Marx, this demonstrates that religions are not immune from the ideological elements found in political theories. Indeed, the promise of a happier afterlife actually supports the continuing exploitation of the mass of workers. Max Weber's extensive studies of the 'world religions' arrived at a different conclusion. He found that religion may be a conservative force but that this is by no means inevitable. For example, religion inhibited social change for a very long period in India, where Hinduism stresses escaping the toils of the material world rather than controlling or shaping it. But in the West, Christianity, with its constant battles against sin and sinners, generated a tension and emotional dynamism that challenged the existing order. Similarly, the Catholic Church played an important role in legitimizing the Polish Solidarity movement which overthrew the communist regime in the 1980s. Hence, religions can promote social change.

Émile Durkheim saw the persistence of religion as its main feature. He argued that all religions divide the world into sacred and profane spheres, with sacred objects and symbols treated very differently from the rest of the routine aspects of existence, the 'profane'. The reason why religions have endured over very long periods is because they are the main avenue through which social bonds are created and strengthened. Ceremony and ritual are essential in binding people together, which is why they are found in the various life crises and transitions of birth, marriage and death. Collective ceremonials reaffirm group solidarity at times when people are forced to adjust to major change. Ceremonial occasions create 'collective effervescence' – the heightened feelings and energy generated at collective gatherings which take people outside of their mundane concerns and temporarily into an elevated state. Durkheim points out that people's religious experience cannot be dismissed as mere self-delusion or **ideology**. It is in fact the real experience of genuine social forces.

The sociology of religion is concerned with how religious institutions and organizations function, particularly in relation to the creation of social solidarity. Where there are numerous competing religions, differences may spill over into destabilizing **conflicts**. There are numerous examples of this in conflicts between Protestants and Catholics in Northern Ireland and between Sikhs, Hindus and Muslims in India, in clashes between Muslims and Christians in Bosnia and the former Yugoslavia, and in 'hate crimes' against Jews, Muslims and religious minorities in the United States.

Critical Points

Secularization describes the process whereby religion loses its influence over the various spheres of social life; if we lived in an entirely secular society, the concept of religion would be redundant. In Western Europe, the pattern has been described as one of 'believing without belonging', as surveys show a majority of people still believe in God or gods, but church attendance is in steady decline (Davie 1994). In the USA, though, both religious belief and church attendance remain high. The problem of arriving at an overall conclusion is compounded by disagreement as to how secularization should or can be measured.

Many people have religious beliefs but do not go to services, but, conversely, many others attend church regularly out of habit or to meet with friends, while their personal beliefs are not so strong. Even taking an historical approach is not conclusive. It may be thought that, before **industrialization**, church attendance was higher, ministers had high social **status**, and the mass of people had strong religious beliefs, but all of these assumptions have been challenged by historical research. In medieval Europe most people were, at best, lukewarm in their beliefs and attended church services through a sense of duty rather than religious commitment. On the other hand, most people today have less of a sense that everyday life is populated with divine or spiritual entities.

Critics of Durkheim's thesis argue that it is not possible to understand the essential character of *all* religions by generalizing from a few small-scale societies. Over the course of the twentieth century, many of the world's societies became more multicultural, with a diverse range of religions within the various nations. Durkheim's thesis of religion as a source of social solidarity may be less persuasive in multi-faith societies and does not properly account for intra-society conflicts around different religious beliefs. We might also take issue with the idea that religion is essentially the worship of society rather than of deities or spirits. This can be seen as a reductionist argument – that religious experience can be reduced to social phenomena, thus rejecting even the possibility of a 'spiritual' level of reality.

Continuing Relevance

As traditional religions lose their hold, religiosity seems to be channelled in new directions in various new religious movements. There is also little evidence of secularization in much of the developing world. In many parts of the Middle East, Asia, Africa and India, a vital and dynamic Islamic fundamentalism exists. Similarly, millions of Catholics attend papal visits to developing countries, while Eastern Orthodox religion has been enthusiastically embraced in parts of the former Soviet Union after decades of repression under communism. Even in the USA, religion exerts a strong hold and has taken on new forms such as the popular evangelical movement and 'televangelism'.

Michel Maffesoli (1995) theorized that we now live in the 'time of the tribes', as the rapid growth of small groups of people who band together on the basis of shared musical tastes, ideas, consumer preferences and leisure pursuits shows. Their commitment to these 'neo-tribes' may be quite weak and short-lived, but they show a strong human need for sociability, which is, in Durkheim's terms, still a 'religious' need. As traditional religions struggle to maintain their memberships, some sociologists argue that 'secular' ideas can take on a 'religious' role. One example of this is the secular focus on human rights, which connects the particular and the universal, looking forward to a democracy in the future. This

discourse has similarities with the Christian tradition and may be seen as representing a kind of 'secular religion' (Reader 2003). However, if so, then it is one with the individual rather than the community or society at the centre.

An interesting case study of one new religious movement is Carlo Barone's (2007) account of Soka Gakkai in Italy. Soka Gakkai began more than seventy-five years ago but is a fast-growing religious movement, and particularly successful in Italy. The author discusses why it should have been so successful. Soka Gakkai has around 8 million members in Japan and is closely tied to a political party – Komeito – which has played an important role in Japanese governing coalitions since the 1990s. Yet many, perhaps most, of the non-Japanese members are probably not aware of this political connection, seeing their religion as a private, individual matter. A key reason for the success of Soka Gakkai appears to be its organizational methods. Members join a small group (part of a **network**) and are encouraged to share experiences, which creates a strong sense of solidarity, while the group's attention is focused on sacred objects in an emotionally charged environment. In short, the groups create a (Durkheimian) collective effervescence that serves to integrate members relatively quickly and securely.

References and Further Reading

Aldridge, A. (2013) *Religion in the Contemporary World: A Sociological Introduction* (3rd edn, Cambridge: Polity).

Barone, C. (2007) 'A Neo-Durkheimian Analysis of a New Religious Movement: The Case of Soka Gakkai in Italy', *Theory and Society*, 36(2): 117–40.

Davie, G. (1994) *Religion in Britain since 1945: Believing without Belonging* (Oxford: Blackwell).

Fenn, R. K. (2009) *Key Thinkers in the Sociology of Religion* (New York: Continuum).

Jones, R. P., Cox, D., and Navarro-Rivera, J. (2012) *The 2012 American Values Survey: How Catholics and the Religiously Unaffiliated Will Shape the 2012 Election and Beyond* (Washington, DC: Public Religion Research Institute).

Maffesoli, M. (1995) *The Time of the Tribes: The Decline of Individualism in Mass Society* (London: Sage).

Reader, R. (2003) 'The Discourse of Human Rights – A Secular Religion?', *Implicit Religion*, 6(1): 41–51.

5 Unequal Life Chances

Class

Working Definition

The relative economic position of large social groups, defined in relation to occupation, ownership of property and wealth or lifestyle choices.

Origins of the Concept

Sociologists have long disagreed over social class since the rather different theories and approaches of Marx and Weber. Marx argues that a social class is a group, all of whom share a common relationship to the means of production in a society – bluntly, they are either owners or non-owners – and class systems therefore cover most of human history. In pre-industrial societies, the two main classes were landowners (aristocrats, gentry or slave-holders) and those who worked the land (serfs, slaves and free peasantry). But, in capitalist societies, factories, offices, machinery and the capital needed to buy them have become more important than land. In contemporary **capitalism** the basic class antagonism is between capitalists, who are owners of the means of production, and workers (Marx calls them 'the proletariat'), who have to work for capitalists in order to survive.

Weber also saw class as based on objectively given economic conditions, but he considered a variety of economic factors as important. Class divisions derive not just from ownership and non-ownership but also from skills and qualifications, which affect the types of work that people are able to get. Position within the labour market strongly influences people's life chances. Those with skills are relatively well paid in comparison with the unskilled labour force, while people in the professions, such as doctors, lawyers and those in high managerial positions, enjoy better pay, rewards (such as shares and bonuses) and overall conditions of employment than most other workers. Class position is therefore determined by quite a complex range of factors and cannot be reduced to simple ownership of means of production. Weber also distinguished class from **status**, the latter being formed from the perceptions of other people rather than an individual's objective economic situation. In recent years debate has focused on whether class is declining in practical significance and whether class schemes should also integrate consumer preferences and other cultural factors.

Meaning and Interpretation

Most sociologists today would agree that social class is a form of social stratification which characterizes the modern, industrialized countries of the world, though it has also spread into other societies with the advance of **capitalism**. Classes are large groups of people who share common economic resources, and these strongly influence the type of lifestyle they are able to lead. The ownership of wealth and occupation are the main bases of class differences. Sociologists generally agree that class is the most fluid form of stratification, as classes are not legal entities, the boundaries between them are not fixed, and there are no restrictions on intermarriage across them. Even so, research has shown that class position at birth constrains but does not preclude individual movement across class systems.

Studies of **social mobility** show that people can and do achieve their class position, and this contrasts sharply with, say, the traditional Indian caste system, which does not allow for such movement. Class systems are impersonal, and an individual's class position is an objective one unrelated to their personal relationships, which typically form quite a separate area of life. Theoretical and empirical studies have investigated the links between class position and other dimensions of social life, such as voting patterns, educational attainment and health. Sociologists have tried to map the class structure of modern societies by devising schemes which capture as much of the occupational structure as possible within as few categories as are necessary. Sociologists tend to use occupation as a broad indicator of social class because research shows that individuals in the same occupation tend to experience comparable lifestyles and similar life chances.

'Relational' class schemes are favoured by many class analysts, as they bring out some of the shifting tensions and inequalities within **society** as well as changing categories of employment and new occupational trends. John Goldthorpe has worked on class analysis for many years and created a Weberian scheme for use in empirical research. The Goldthorpe class scheme was designed not as a hierarchy but as a representation of the 'relational' nature of the contemporary class structure. His original scheme identified class location on the basis of market situation and work situation. Market situation concerns levels of pay, job security and prospects for advancement, while work situation focuses on issues of control, power and authority. More recently Goldthorpe (2000) emphasized employment relations rather than 'work situation', drawing attention to different types of employment contract.

Critical Points

Class theory and analysis have a long history in sociology, but they have faced criticisms since the 1980s from sociologists who think that class is of declining significance. Pakulski and Waters (1996) argued that **globalization** has produced a global **division of labour** in which the major inequalities exist across rather than within **nation states** and that the developed countries have become post-industrial societies based on service occupations and a growing individualization. This has led, they say, to the emergence of status conventionalism, a system of inequality based on **consumerism** and lifestyle choices rather than on social class.

Others see the expansion of higher **education** and the widening of opportunity it brings, along with many more successful entrepreneurs, some of them using modern technologies such as the Internet, making their way through the class system as evidence of more social mobility and a fluid movement across classes. Again, the result is a weakening of class-based communities and class identification. Class is just less important to people as it loses ground to **gender**, **ethnicity**, **sexuality** and political affiliations as a source of **identity**.

A further issue in class analysis has been its inability to deal properly with gender, relying on class status derived from the 'head of household', usually taken to be the breadwinning male. Thus, women's class position has been read off from that of their partner, a situation that may have worked in the early twentieth century but, as more and more married women move into paid employment, is now very unreliable. It has also proved very difficult to assimilate groups such as students, retired people, the unemployed, and so on, into class categories, which means the scheme is incomplete and partial.

Continuing Relevance

A lessening of class identification can be conceded, but this does not mean that class has also become irrelevant in shaping people's life chances. Subjectively, individuals may not perceive themselves to be working class, middle class, and so on, but a vast body of sociological research continues to show that the class we are born into is a strong determinant of our life chances (Crompton 2008). Both Marxist and Weberian approaches are right to maintain a focus on the objective character of social class if we are to understand how and why inequalities are reproduced. In fact, inequalities between rich and poor have actually expanded in many developed countries over the last thirty years or so even as their economies have grown.

Returning to Weber's original distinction between class and status, Chan and Goldthorpe (2007) explain that these are two related forms of stratification but with distinct outcomes. In the UK, economic position and life chances continue to be stratified by social class, as do left–right political attitudes and voter preferences for the two main political parties (Conservative and Labour). However, the study suggests that patterns of cultural consumption and the likelihood of holding libertarian or authoritarian attitudes are shaped more by social status than by class. Nonetheless, class and status are related in quite complex ways. For instance, class remains the best predictor of political values and basic voter preferences on material issues, but status strongly influences people's attitudes on 'ideal issues' such as censorship, surveillance and ethical matters. Therefore, combining the effects of class and status offers greater explanatory potential than dealing with each type of stratification separately.

Given more recent theories suggesting a declining significance of class, some studies have explored the experience of class in specific locations. Vincent and her colleagues (2008) used **qualitative** methods in an empirical study of 'working classness' in inner London, focusing specifically on child care and the resources available to people to cope with life. A key contrast the authors identified was between those who were 'struggling to cope' and the majority who were 'managing to cope'. The latter had good social capital (supportive friends and family), cultural capital (educational credentials) and economic capital (employment, albeit unstable). Although the working-class people in this survey were quite a heterogeneous sample, it seems that social class remains an important objective indicator of life chances.

References and Further Reading

Chan, T. W., and Goldthorpe, J. H. (2007) 'Class and Status: The Conceptual Distinction and its Empirical Relevance', *American Sociological Review*, 72(4): 512–32.
Crompton, R. (2008) *Class and Stratification* (3rd edn, Cambridge: Polity).
Edgell, S. (1993) *Class* (London: Routledge).
Goldthorpe, J. H. (2000) *On Sociology: Numbers, Narratives and the Integration of Research and Theory* (Oxford: Oxford University Press).
Pakulski, J., and Waters, M. (1996) *The Death of Class* (London: Sage).
Vincent, C., Ball, S. J., and Braun, A. (2008) '"It's Like Saying "Coloured"': Understanding and Analysing the Urban Working Classes', *Sociological Review*, 56(1): 61–77.

Gender

Working Definition

Expectations of the social, cultural and psychological traits and behaviour regarded as appropriate for the members of a particular **society**.

Origins of the Concept

Gender was a largely neglected subject in sociology until a body of empirical and theoretical feminist studies from the 1960s onwards drew attention to gross inequalities between men and women, even in modern societies. Classical sociology took the existing, male-dominated gender order very much for granted, with functionalism, for instance, theorizing that gender differences were rooted in the functional needs of society, such as the 'expressive' roles played by women in the household compared to the 'instrumental' ones played by men in the formal economy. Feminist studies challenged this apparently natural inequality, showing that male dominance was much more akin to **class** domination. Nonetheless, some theorists used existing sociological concepts and theories to explain gender inequality, such as **socialization** and a version of **conflict** theory. In recent years the very concept of gender has been seen as too rigid, with some suggesting that 'gender' is a highly unstable concept that is always in the process of change.

Meaning and Interpretation

In sociology, there has long been a distinction between sex (anatomical and physiological differences between male and female bodies) and gender (the social and cultural differences between the expected behaviour of men and women). Most sociologists argue that there is no evidence of the mechanisms which would link biological forces with the complex and diverse social behaviour exhibited by humans, which means that gender is a complex social construction.

Some sociologists see gender socialization – learning gender roles through social agencies such as **family**, school and **mass media** – as helping to explain observed gender differences. Socialization processes in the family, peer groups and schools tend to promote gendered forms of self-identity which children internalize, and in this way gender differences are culturally reproduced and men and women socialized into different roles. Gender-differentiated toys and clothes and stereotypical roles in TV, film and video games are all examples of the cultural encouragement to conform to gender expectations. More recent studies argue that gender socialization is not a simple or one-way process, as people actively engage with it and can reject or modify expectations, which makes socialization inherently unstable and open to challenge.

The basic distinction between gender and sex is also rejected by some sociologists as misleading, implying that there is a biological core which culture then overlays with gender differences. Rather than seeing sex as biologically determined and gender as culturally learned, some now see *both* sex *and* gender as **social constructions**. It is not just gender identity, but the human body itself, that is the subject of shaping and altering social forces. People choose to construct and reconstruct their bodies almost as they please, from exercise, dieting, piercing and personal fashions to plastic surgery and sex-change operations. Gender identities and sex differences are inextricably linked within individual human bodies, and it has become almost impossible to extricate biology from **culture**.

Connell (2005) set out one of the most complete theoretical accounts of gender, integrating **patriarchy** and masculinity into a theory of gender relations. Connell argues that labour, **power** and cathexis (personal/sexual relationships) are distinct but interrelated parts of society that work together and change in relation to one another. Labour refers to the sexual **division of labour** both within the home and in the labour market. Power operates through social relations such as **authority**, violence and **ideology** in institutions, the state, the military and domestic life.

Cathexis concerns dynamics within intimate, emotional and personal relationships, including marriage, **sexuality** and child-rearing. At the top of the gender order is hegemonic masculinity, exercised through culture, which extends into private life and social realms. Hegemonic masculinity is associated primarily with heterosexuality and marriage, but also with authority, paid work, strength and physical toughness. Though only a few men live up to this stylized image, a very large number gain advantages from it. In a gender order dominated by hegemonic masculinity, the homosexual is seen as the opposite of the 'real man'. Homosexual masculinity is stigmatized and ranks at the bottom of the gender hierarchy for men. Femininities are all formed in positions of subordination to hegemonic masculinity. Women who have developed non-subordinated identities and lifestyles include feminists, lesbians, spinsters, midwives, witches, prostitutes and manual workers, but the experiences of these resistant femininities are largely 'hidden from history'.

Critical Points

Several critics have argued that, although hegemonic masculinity appears fairly obvious, Connell does not really present a satisfactory account of it. This is because she does not specify what would count as 'counter hegemonic'. For example, with more men now involved in child care and parenting, is this part of the continuation of or a trend against hegemonic masculinity? Unless we know what actions would challenge hegemonic masculinity, how can we know what actions constitute it in the first place? Some social psychologists also wonder how men come to 'embody' complicit masculinity. If they themselves do not live up to the hegemonic masculine ideal, what does this failure mean for them? In short, what would resistance look like in practical terms?

Continuing Relevance

The concept of gender has become increasingly important in sociology, partly as a result of feminist research, but more recent research on sexuality, including so-called queer theory, has also made extensive use of the concept and in the process transformed it. Butler (2004) argued that gender is 'performative' – that is, people's gender is not thing-like, something inhering within the body, but is more like a continuous performance or a work in progress. This means that gender is an unstable social category that can accommodate many variations and can change quite radically. Take, for example, the new performances of transgender, bisexuality and lesbianism that emerged in the gay liberation movement. What gender is and how we understand it is dependent on how people perform their gender, and this can change quite rapidly.

Gender inequality is an established fact in most societies, though the extent of that inequality differs. Hadas Mandel (2009) looked at the gender order and public policies in fourteen developed countries to compare the impact of different state interventions aimed at reducing gender inequality. She argues that some regimes paid women to mother children while others provided benefits to ease work and family tensions. However, both were rooted in traditional gender roles and did not end women's economic disadvantage. Policies aimed at enabling more women to move into paid work appear to have more to offer, but Mandel suggests that these cannot work in isolation and require changes to the ideology which places the burden of care on women. Hence, the introduction of parental leave policies may be the first practical steps in shifting the burden of care onto a more equal basis.

References and Further Reading

Bradley, H. G. (2012) *Gender* (2nd edn, Cambridge: Polity).

Butler, J. (2004) *Undoing Gender* (London: Routledge).

Connell, R. W. (2005) *Masculinities* (2nd edn, Cambridge: Polity).

Holmes, M. (2007) *What is Gender? Sociological Approaches* (London: Sage).

Mandel, H. (2009) 'Configurations of Gender Inequality: The Consequences of Ideology and Public Policy', *British Journal of Sociology*, 60(4): 693–719.

Intersectionality

Working Definition

The interweaving of social inequalities, including **class**, **'race'/ethnicity**, **gender**, disability and **sexuality**, which produces more complex patterns of discrimination than allowed for by single-dimensional conceptualizations.

Origins of the Concept

Sociology after Marx theorized social class as the primary form of inequality which shaped the life chances of individuals. Gradually over the twentieth century other dimensions of inequality came to be recognized as increasingly significant, and by the 1970s sources of inequality in modern societies were seen as diverse. Despite the attempt in some studies to theorize how, say, class and gender reinforce each other, there was no systematic way of doing so. As sociological studies shifted away from an exclusive focus on class, it became increasingly clear that existing class theories were not readily transferable to other forms of inequality. The first use of the concept of intersectionality is thought to be in Kimberlé Crenshaw's (1989) paper on the intersection of 'race and sex' in the USA (see Taylor et al. 2010). This was quickly followed by Andersen and Collins's ([1990] 2016) anthology exploring the ways in which intersections of class, 'race', gender and sexuality shape people's identities and life chances. Black feminist scholarship was instrumental in the development of intersectional theories, and intersectionality theory grew from, and has, so far, been dominated by, American scholars, though this is slowly changing (Crenshaw 1991).

Meaning and Interpretation

The gradual movement away from an exclusive concern with social class has led sociologists to suggest that, if we are to understand the lives of people today, ways have to be found to connect class with other inequalities (Andersen and Collins [1990] 2016; Rothman 2005). To date, intersectionality theory is arguably the most influential perspective which tries to do this, beginning from the fact of social and cultural diversity. This is not a trivial recognition. It suggests that all sociological studies and theories which discuss generic categories such as 'black people', 'the working class', 'women', 'disabled people', 'gay men', and so on, are overgeneralized. When sociologists discuss and debate the experience of 'the working class' or 'women', what does that mean? Class position may not be the primary identification of a majority of working-class people. The lives of white heterosexual working-class men may be very different from those of black homosexual working-class men, and only empirical research can tell us which of these forms of identity is more important.

Intersectional research examines the ways in which the varied forms of difference intertwine in specific cases, and it can lead to highly complex analyses of real lives as they are lived. This body of work is not simply descriptive, however, as it seeks to understand how **power** relations operate in society to produce inequality and discrimination (Berger and Guidroz 2009). Intersectional research is more than just, for example, class + race + gender. Instead, it insists that each category informs the other, and taken together they produce ways of experiencing the world as 'sometimes oppressed and marginalized and sometimes privileged and advantaged depending on the context' (Smooth 2010: 34). In short, intersecting categories produce social positions that cannot be separated out into their apparently discrete elements; they are more than simply the sum of the parts.

Intersectional research favours **qualitative** methods that are able to tap into people's real life experiences and biographical methods that reconstruct the impact of inequality across the **life course**. This marks a significant difference from mainstream class research, which has conventionally been dominated by the survey method and **quantitative** analyses. Intersectionality, then, is a description of the diversity in social life and a theory of that diversity, but it can also be seen as a methodology – a way of bringing into sharp focus the interplay between social positions – designed to deliver more comprehensive and valid accounts of divergent experiences.

Critical Points

There are some problems with intersectional theory and research. How many inequality and identity categories are out there to be included in the analysis? This issue is often called the 'et cetera' problem. That is, some studies add 'etc.' onto class, gender and 'race' to indicate there are many other sources (Lykke 2011). But, if this is so, how do researchers know that they have covered them all in order to validate their findings? A second issue is the relative weight afforded to the different categories in use. Should we theorize them all as being broadly similar, or are there reasons to suppose that one is in some way more important in shaping people's lives? Marxist theory, for instance, argues that, in what remain capitalist societies, it is not unreasonable to suggest that class position continues to be the driving force in shaping opportunities and life chances. Analysing the ways in which the varied elements of individual identities intersect has become more commonplace, but it is important to remember that, in the UK and elsewhere, there is a large body of reliable sociological work which continues to find structured patterns of disadvantage, involving large social groups – such as class fractions and minority ethnic groups – that influence the life chances of similarly positioned individuals.

Continuing Relevance

The concept of intersectionality has become more important in attempts to understand the differentiated experience not just of poverty but also of social life as a whole. And, as more studies are conducted, the character of social life appears ever more complex, with increasingly fine-grained distinctions. Barnard and Turner (2011: 4) argue that 'The experience of a middle class, third generation, Indian, Hindu woman with a degree, living in Milton Keynes, may have little in common with a second generation, Indian, Muslim woman, with a level three qualification, living in Bradford with a disabled husband and two children.'

In recent years it has been suggested that social policy must take heed of intersectionality if equality legislation is to be successful (Hancock 2007). Alonso (2012) explores this idea in relation to Portugal, a country with a history of involving groups within civil society in drawing up equality policy. Portugal's solution is to encourage the development of a coordinated model using existing equality bodies rather than moving directly to a new integrated body. Although this may appear limiting, the author argues that this intermediate approach may allow the expertise that exists within the present arrangements to be retained. It also offers the potential to work on intersecting inequalities across agencies as well as on single-group issues. Although short of a fully integrated intersectional regime, it paves the way for this to be established in the future.

References and Further Reading

Alonso, A. (2012) 'Intersectionality by Other Means? New Equality Policies in Portugal', *Social Politics*, 19(4): 596–621.

Andersen, M. L., and Collins, P. H. (eds) ([1990] 2016) *Race, Class, and Gender: An Anthology* (9th edn, Boston, MA: Cengage Learning).

Barnard, H., and Turner, C. (2011) *Poverty and Ethnicity: A Review of the Evidence* (York: Joseph Rowntree Foundation).

Berger, M. T., and Guidroz, K. (eds) (2009) *The Intersectional Approach: Transforming the Academy through Race, Class, and Gender* (Chapel Hill: University of North Carolina Press).

Crenshaw, K. W. (1991) 'Mapping the Margins: Intersectionality, Identity Politics and Violence against Women of Color', *Stanford Law Review*, 43(6): 1241–99.

Hancock, A.-M. (2007) 'Intersectionality as a Normative and Empirical Paradigm', *Politics and Gender*, 3(2): 248–54.

Lykke, N. (2011) 'Intersectional Invisibility: Inquiries into a Concept of Intersectionality

Studies', in H. Lutz, M. T. H. Vivar and L. Supik (eds), *Framing Intersectionality: Debates on a Multifaceted Concept in Gender Studies* (Farnham: Ashgate), pp. 207–20.

Rothman, R. A. (2005) *Inequality and Stratification: Class, Race and Gender* (5th edn, Upper Saddle River, NJ: Prentice Hall).

Smooth, W. G. (2010) 'Intersectionalities of Race and Gender and Leadership', in K. O'Connor (ed.), *Gender and Women's Leadership: A Reference Handbook*, Vol. 1 (London: Sage), pp. 31–40.

Taylor, Y., Hines, S., and Casey, M. E. (eds) (2010) *Theorizing Intersectionality and Sexuality* (Basingstoke: Palgrave Macmillan).

Patriarchy

Working Definition

The systematic domination of women by men in some or all of society's spheres and institutions.

Origins of the Concept

Ideas of male dominance have a very long history, with many **religions** presenting it as both natural and necessary. In sociology, the first theoretical account of patriarchy is found in Engels's discussion of women's subservience to men under **capitalism**. Engels argued that capitalism concentrated **power** in the hands of a small number of men and, because the system produced more wealth than ever before, intensified **gender** as well as **class** inequality, as men passed on their wealth to their male heirs.

However, the main source of patriarchal theory today stems from feminism, especially since the 1960s, when the concept was developed and used to help explain the persistence of male dominance in modern societies. Feminist theorists disagree about the concept's usefulness, though, and several perspectives emerged, including liberal, socialist and radical feminist explanations. The feminist slogan 'the personal is political' pointed to the domestic sphere as a key site for the reproduction of male dominance – something that had not previously been accepted. The continued oppression of women is also seen in everyday sexist comments and assumptions, representations of women and girls in the media, and male violence and sexual assaults against women in both public and private settings. In the late twentieth century, empirical research studies served to ground the concept of patriarchy and locate its different forms within all of the varied spheres of **society**.

Meaning and Interpretation

The concept of patriarchy forms the basis of radical forms of feminism. Patriarchy is something of a catch-all concept covering a very wide range of instances where women are oppressed by male domination. For example, women struggle to attain positions of power in business, politics and other spheres of social life as men actively or passively deny them access. For many radical feminists the conventional **family** is a crucial element of patriarchy in which women perform domestic labour without pay, enabling men to enjoy the freedoms of the outside, public world. Women continue to do the majority of household chores today, even when both they and their male partners are in formal employment. Shulamith Firestone (1970) argued that men's domination is underpinned by a fundamental 'biological inequality'. As only women can carry babies and give birth, they are reliant on men afterwards. In capitalist societies the institutional basis of this 'biological inequality' is the nuclear family form, which must therefore be destroyed as a prerequisite to the emancipation of women.

For radical feminists, male violence and the threat of violence against women reinforces male dominance. Domestic violence and rape in the privacy of the home, rape and sexual harassment in the **public sphere**, and the aggressive nature of men's behaviour towards women in routine **interactions** all contribute to a pervasive and pernicious, yet often unacknowledged, male domination. This does not mean that all men are actively involved in such behaviour, but the radical feminist case is that all men benefit from patriarchy, which is underpinned by the violence of some men. In the wider culture, women are objectified in magazines, fashion, television and other **mass media**. Many media representations continue to focus on women primarily as sexual objects for men. Clearly patriarchy is embedded within all the institutions of modern societies, and feminist researchers have thrown these into sharp relief.

Sylvia Walby's (1990) reconceptualization of patriarchy opened up the concept to detailed empirical investigation. She argued that patriarchy has failed to account for growing gender *equality*. At the centre of Walby's analysis is the distinction between private and public forms of patriarchy. Private forms include domestic relations and intimate relations, while public forms involve paid employment, the state and politics. Over the twentieth century there was a major shift away from private forms towards public forms, as women moved into areas of society that were previously off limits. Just because women are now more visible in formal employment, for instance, does not mean that gender equality has been achieved. For example, women tend to receive lower pay than men at work, they face male violence in public areas, they continue to suffer the sexual double standard, and now they have to deal with sexualized representations of women in the mass media and via the worldwide web.

Critical Points

The concept of patriarchy has been criticized both from mainstream sociologists and from within feminist theory itself. Although many might accept patriarchy as a *description*, it has also been used as an inadequate and very abstract *explanation* for all women's oppression, but without the identification of a convincing mechanism. Some radical feminists also claim that patriarchy has existed throughout history and across cultures and is therefore a universal phenomenon, but such a broad conception leaves no room for historical and cultural variation and ignores the important influences of **race**, class and **ethnicity** on women's situation. In short, the argument that patriarchy is a universal phenomenon risks falling into biological reductionism.

Many black feminists, as well as those from developing countries, argue that ethnic divisions among women have been largely ignored by mainstream feminism, as this tended to be based on the experience of white, mainly middle-class women in the developed world (hooks 1981). It is not valid to generalize from this, as women's experience is varied according to class and ethnicity. The work of American black feminists emphasizes the powerful legacy of slavery, segregation and the civil rights movement on gender inequalities in the black community, pointing out that black women were discriminated against on the basis of both their ethnicity and their gender. Similarly, the institution of the family, long seen as crucial to sustaining patriarchal dominance by white middle-class feminists, may not be viewed in quite the same way by black women and black feminists, for whom family life also serves as a bulwark against white racism. Black feminist theory has developed in ways that are more keenly aware of intersecting inequalities and the multiple disadvantages faced by black working-class women.

Recent postmodern and social constructivist theory takes issue with the very idea that there is a unitary basis of identity and experience shared by all women. We should not assume that middle-class, working-class, white, black, metropolitan or rural women will all share a primary identification of being 'women'. Does it even make sense to discuss the categories of 'women' or 'men' in sociological research when these concepts imply a biological or essential basis that gender studies rejected many years ago? The postmodern turn is provocative, but it presents serious problems for feminist activists and scholars whose empirical research details the full scope and extent of the inequalities faced by women in male-dominated societies.

Continuing Relevance

Feminist theorists argue that patriarchal dominance is achieved through a variety of social forms, and one of these is through language and **discourse**. In a nicely balanced piece, Case and Lippard (2009) look at the ways in which jokes can perpetuate patriarchal relations but also how feminists have deconstructed these and produced their own subversive versions aimed at exposing and undermining sexism. The authors analysed over 1,900 feminist jokes in this study. The most common theme was 'men were useless' (25.7 per cent), and male stereotypes formed the bulk (62 per cent) of the concepts and categories used. However, Case and Lippard found that very few jokes (3.8 per cent) went beyond attempts to discredit men or to use stereotypical assumptions to critique gender itself. But they do accept that humour is a powerful ideological weapon in what remains a highly unequal society.

Despite legislative attempts to address male violence against women, some groups remain opposed to such change. Dragiewicz (2008) explored anti-feminist arguments within the fathers' rights discourse in the USA, which opposes the Violence Against Women Act (1994). Many of the objections to this Act are rooted in an argument that it does little to advance 'formal equality' of treatment and that legislation in this area should instead focus on ensuring a legal presumption of joint custody and shared parenting. However, Dragiewicz maintains that such arguments are aimed at limiting or circumventing considerations of domestic violence and harassment in individual cases. The backlash against gender-sensitive legislation seems to indicate that social change is not a linear process but is closer to an ongoing struggle, moving back and forth, over power, knowledge and **authority**.

References and Further Reading

Case, C. E., and Lippard, C. D. (2009) 'Humorous Assaults on Patriarchal Ideology', *Sociological Inquiry*, 79(2): 240–55.

Dragiewicz, M. (2008) 'Patriarchy Reasserted: Fathers' Rights and Anti-VAWA Activism', *Feminist Criminology*, 3(2): 121–44.

Firestone, S. (1970) *The Dialectic of Sex: The Case for Feminist Revolution* (London: Jonathan Cape).

hooks, b. (1981) *Ain't I a Woman? Black Women and Feminism* (Boston: South End Press).

Walby, S. (1990) *Theorizing Patriarchy* (Oxford: Blackwell), esp. chapter 8.

Poverty

Working Definition

The condition of not having access to those things considered 'basic' or 'normal' within a **society**.

Origins of the Concept

Although we can say that conditions of poverty have existed in the majority of human societies, use of the concept can be traced to the late nineteenth and the early part of the twentieth century. Seebohm Rowntree's ([1901] 2000) study of poverty in York set the tone for much later work which sought to establish the extent of poverty in society. This strand of research is important, as it is crucial to know how many people live in conditions of poverty if measures to reduce it are to be assessed. Since the work of Peter Townsend from the late 1950s onwards, an alternative method of assessing poverty has been widely used. Townsend (1979) developed a relational concept of poverty based on lifestyles, from which he distilled twelve recurring items, such as 'household does not have a refrigerator', into a poverty or deprivation index. This allowed him to produce an estimate of poverty levels which turned out to be much higher than previously thought. This is a relative rather than an absolute conception of poverty. Later studies have used questionnaires and interviews to ascertain from people themselves what *they* consider to be the necessities of life. Many national governments (and the EU) have also adopted a 'poverty line' based on household income level in relation to the national average income – usually 50 or 60 per cent – to identify those living in poverty.

Meaning and Interpretation

Sociologists recognize two basic concepts of poverty: absolute poverty and relative poverty. *Absolute poverty* is grounded in the idea of material subsistence – the basic conditions that must be met in order to sustain a reasonably healthy existence. People who lack sufficient food, shelter and clothing are said to be living in absolute poverty. On this definition, many developing countries still have large sections of their populations living in absolute poverty. More than one-third of the people in Bangladesh, Mozambique and Namibia, around two-thirds in Rwanda, and 70 per cent in Nigeria can be said to live in conditions of absolute poverty today. However, the existence of a universal standard of absolute poverty is contested, as definitions of need are culturally variable.

Most sociologists today use the alternative concept of *relative poverty*. This relates poverty to the overall standard of living in a society. The main reason for choosing this is that poverty is widely held to be culturally defined and cannot be measured on a universal standard. Things seen as essential in one society may be regarded as luxuries in another. In the developed countries, running tap water, flush toilets and the regular consumption of fruit and vegetables are regarded as basic necessities, yet in many developing countries these things are not part of normal life, and using their absence to measure poverty is not valid. Even definitions of 'absolute' poverty have changed over time as our knowledge has improved, so that even absolute poverty is 'relative'.

The concept of relative poverty is not a panacea. As societies develop, so does their understanding of poverty as criteria are adjusted upwards. At one time, refrigerators, central heating and telephones were considered to be luxury goods, but today most people regard them as necessities. Others see that the concept of relative poverty deflects attention away from the fact that the poorest members of society are much better off than in previous times, thus calling into question whether 'true' poverty even exists in the wealthy societies. Social groups that are more likely to be found living in poverty include children, older people, women and some ethnic minorities. In particular, people who are disadvantaged or discriminated against in other aspects of life have an increased chance of being poor.

Explanations of poverty focus on either the individual ('blame the victim') or the organization of society ('blame the system'). The idea that 'the poor will always be with us' has a long history and suggests that poor individuals are primarily responsible for their own situation. On this view, society offers many opportunities for advancement, and if some people do not succeed then it must be their own fault that they did not take advantage. In the nineteenth century, poorhouses and workhouses existed to house those who were deemed to have failed. Although these ideas later lost ground, they were revived in the 1980s, when neo-liberal political ideas explained poverty via the lifestyles and attitudes of poor people themselves. The American sociologist Charles Murray (1984) saw the emergence of a new 'underclass' with a dependency culture rooted in living on welfare benefits and avoiding entering work.

'Blame the system' approaches explore the ways in which socio-economic conditions generate certain levels of poverty. Periodic economic booms and slumps, changes in **education** policies and systems, and the major social divisions of **class**, **ethnicity**, **gender** and disability all contribute to shaping individual life chances and the probability that people will experience poverty. Such structural explanations reject the idea that individuals are primarily responsible for their own poverty. This view harks back to the 1930s, when R. H. Tawney theorized that poverty was in fact an aspect of social inequality, which led to extremes of wealth and poverty. The key to tackling the problem was therefore to reduce social inequality through social and economic policy, not by blaming individuals. Two recent examples of policy changes in this area in the UK are the introduction of a national minimum wage and the expansion of 'in-work' benefits, both of which are aimed at reducing levels of poverty. Economic restructuring can also lead to rising levels of poverty, and, in the 1980s, the decline of manufacturing industries, the 'suburbanization' of employment and a growing, low-wage service sector reduced job opportunities. In summary, poverty levels should be explained with reference to structural changes in society.

Critical Points

A number of criticisms have been levelled at the continuing use of the concept of poverty. Once we accept the cultural critique of absolute poverty, we are left with relative poverty. But critics see this as little more than an alternative description of social inequality, which adds nothing to our understanding. If standards of poverty shift along with affluence in social development, the original aim of the concept – to identify and raise awareness of severe deprivation – is lost. Can families with most of the technological trappings of modern life and access to welfare benefits really be defined as living in poverty?

Some sociologists have moved away from the concept in favour of the term *social exclusion*, which allows for the identification of processes that deny poorer people certain **citizenship** rights. Criticisms can also be made of attempts to measure poverty. The idea of a deprivation index based on the identification of a cluster of items is charged with an arbitrary selectivity. On what criteria do we choose which items are necessary or real needs and which are just wants? Some categories, such as a cooked breakfast or holidays away from home, may be more to do with choice and prioritization than with poverty. Such selectivity may divert attention away from the very real absolute poverty in developing countries.

Continuing Relevance

In spite of criticisms, the concept of poverty has remained popular in social research, especially that which aims to inform policy-makers working in this area. The concept of relative poverty has been very significant in dragging the debate on inequality into more sociological frameworks by drawing attention to the way in which underlying socio-economic processes can bring about increasing levels of deprivation that deny full citizenship to a range of social groups.

The old idea that 'the poor will always be with us' has also been challenged by more recent research studies, which show that a substantial proportion of people in poverty at any one time have either previously enjoyed superior conditions of life or can be expected to climb out of poverty at some time in the future (Jenkins 2011). A significant amount of mobility means that some people are successful in escaping poverty, but also that a larger number than previously realized live in poverty at some point during their lives. In this way, poverty has been 'humanized', and those living in such conditions do not seem so separate from mainstream society.

References and Further Reading

Alcock, P. (2006) *Understanding Poverty* (3rd edn, Basingstoke: Palgrave Macmillan).

Hulme, D. (ed.) (2010) *Global Poverty: How Global Governance is Failing the Poor* (London: Routledge).

Jenkins, S. P. (2011) *Changing Fortunes: Income Mobility and Poverty Dynamics in Britain* (Oxford: Oxford University Press).

Lister, R. (2004) *Poverty* (Cambridge: Polity).

Murray, C. A. (1984) *Losing Ground: American Social Policy 1950–1980* (New York: Basic Books).

Rowntree, B. S. ([1901] 2000) *Poverty: A Study of Town Life* (Bristol: Policy Press).

Townsend, P. (1979) *Poverty in the United Kingdom* (Harmondsworth: Penguin).

'Race' and Ethnicity

Working Definition

'Race' refers to various attributes or competencies assigned on the basis of biologically grounded features such as skin colour. Ethnicity refers to a social group whose members share a distinct awareness of common cultural identity, differentiating them as a social group.

Origins of the Concept

Distinctions between social groups based on skin colour were common in ancient civilizations, though it was more common for those between groups to be based on tribal lines or kinship. The bases of these distinctions were relatively unconnected to the modern idea of 'race'. Since the early nineteenth century, 'race' has had clear biological and, later, genetic connotations, which link the concept to scientific theories and classification schemes. Scientific theories of 'race' were developed in the late eighteenth and early nineteenth century and were used to justify the imperial ambitions of Britain and other European nations which ruled over territories in developing countries. These came to be described as examples of 'scientific racism', providing a 'scientific' gloss to the racist ideologies of the German National Socialists, South Africa's Apartheid system and other white supremacist groups, such as the Ku Klux Klan in the United States.

The concept of ethnicity in its modern sense, as referring to different cultural groups, is traced to the 1930s, with the connection to minority ethnic groups first emerging after 1945. As 'race' became thoroughly discredited as a useful concept for the social sciences, the concept of ethnicity, with its focus on group cultures, took its place. Studies of patterns of disadvantage and discrimination according to ethnicity have extended this idea to 'ethnic minorities' or 'minority ethnic groups', though 'minority' here does not have to mean a numerical minority. Some sociologists argue that the concept of 'race' should not be discounted altogether, as the term is in common usage in **society** at large. As such, sociologists need to consider how it is used and what meanings are attached to it.

Meaning and Interpretation

'Race' and ethnicity have been coupled together in this entry because they form a phrase that has become commonplace, implying that they are linked. Nonetheless, they are quite easily separable. 'Race' is a difficult concept today because, although its use as a scientific concept is discredited, it remains very widely used and, indeed, may still be the dominant conception. Yet, for biologists and social scientists, distinct 'races' cannot be found. Physical variations are clearly observable, of course, but these do not constitute genetically distinct racial types. Most sociologists argue that the concept of 'race' is nothing more than an ideological construct. For these reasons, many sociologists – particularly outside of North America – tend to put 'race' in scare quotes to indicate that its meaning is highly problematic.

When concepts of 'race' are adopted in order to categorize people into separate biological groups, sociologists call the process 'racialization'. As the examples of slavery in the USA and the Apartheid system in South Africa show, a racialized society is often based on extreme social inequalities covering unequal access to justice, healthcare, job opportunities, **education** and life chances more generally. 'Race' may be a thoroughly discredited scientific concept, but its material consequences throughout history form a telling illustration of W. I. Thomas's famous dictum that, 'if men [*sic*] define situations as real, they are real in their consequences.' If 'race' is rooted in ideas of biology, ethnicity is a concept which draws attention to **culture** – or, more accurately, cultures. Ethnic groups are often distinguished from each other by language, history, **religion** and various social norms and shared memories. But the crucial point is that there is nothing innate about ethnicity. It is purely a social phenomenon that is continually reproduced as young people assimilate the lifestyles, norms and beliefs of ethnic communities.

What marks out some ethnic groups is the use of exclusionary devices, such as the prohibiting of intermarriage, which serve to maintain culturally established boundaries. Ethnicity is a more useful concept for sociologists because it does not carry the biological baggage of 'race'. However, uses of the term 'ethnic' can also be problematic. For example, in Europe, 'ethnic' is often commonly employed to refer to cultures that differ from a supposed 'indigenous' (that is, non-ethnic) population. But ethnicity is an attribute of all members of a population, not just some segments of it.

The idea of ethnic minority groups is widely used in sociology, but it is more than just a matter of numbers. 'Minority groups' are defined by their relatively disadvantaged position in relation to other dominant groups, not necessarily because they are smaller in number. Minority ethnic groups tend to exhibit a strong sense of solidarity which stems from their members' shared experiences of discrimination, racism and prejudice. Being the subject of such victimization can heighten people's sense that they have common interests. Thus sociologists use the term 'minority' in a non-literal way to refer to a group's subordinate position within society rather than its numerical representation. There are many cases in which a 'minority' is in fact in the majority, such as under Apartheid in South Africa or in certain geographical regions of inner cities. Many minorities are both ethnically and physically distinct from the rest of the population. This is the case with West Indians and Asians in Britain or African Americans in the United States, though Britons and Americans of Italian or Polish descent are less likely to be considered ethnic minorities. Frequently, physical differences such as skin colour are the defining factor in designating an 'ethnic minority', which shows that ethnic distinctions are rarely neutral.

Critical Points

Quasi-racist attitudes have been known to exist for hundreds of years. But the notion of 'race' as a set of fixed traits emerged with the rise of 'race science'. Belief in the superiority of the white 'race', although completely without value factually, remains a key element of overt white racism. However, just as ideas of biological 'races' became discredited and fell out of favour, a more subtle 'new' or 'cultural' racism emerged. The 'new racism' uses cultural rather than biological arguments to justify the continued separation of ethnic groups. In particular, arguments tend to focus on the right of the majority culture to expect ethnic minorities to assimilate into it, and thus the new racism is antagonistic to pluralistic multiculturalism. Minority groups that seek to maintain their cultures are then likely to become marginalized or vilified for their refusal to assimilate. The fact that racism is increasingly exercised on cultural rather than biological grounds implies that there are multiple racisms where discrimination is experienced differently across segments of the population. Emergence of the new racism has blurred the previous distinction between 'race' and ethnicity, as this version of 'race' now includes cultural aspects. This may have the effect of making the concept of ethnicity less useful in sociology.

Continuing Relevance

As the shift from biological to cultural racism shows, racial ideas in **science** and society more generally appear to be persistent. Recent developments in genetic research, racial profiling in policing, and concerns about immigration levels have all kept the issue of ethnicity and ethnic relations at the forefront of politics. The concept of institutional racism, which was part of the civil rights struggles in late 1960s America and was accepted in an official report commissioned by the British government, also broadened issues of racism and racist practice from an individual to the institutional or organizational level.

Types of racism and, indeed, observed levels of racism differ across countries. However, Wieviorka (2010) finds both unity and diversity in patterns of racism across Europe. On the one hand, he argues, racism in its modern forms is clearly a product of **modernity**. **Industrialization**, mass **migration**, colonialism and its aftermath, and extended trading relations led to many tensions and **conflicts** both within and between countries, and one expression of this was racism. In that sense we could expect most European countries to exhibit similarities. However, Wieviorka claims that not all racisms are the same. He outlines four broad types which characterize different responses to modernity, noting that a 'universalist' type associated with the notion of inferior and superior races during the colonial period was for a long time the dominant form across Europe. However, today, racist attitudes have diversified and relate to concerns about downward mobility and a loss of national **identity**.

The idea of a 'clash of civilizations' – especially between Islam and 'the West' – was popularized by Samuel Huntington (1996) as one possible outcome as people increasingly identify with large-scale cultures in an era of **globalization**. Yet the empirical evidence for this thesis is weak. Chiozza (2002) approaches the thesis from the standpoint of observed international conflicts between 1946 and 1997, asking the key question: how many of these can be said to represent a clash of large-scale civilizations? This study brings some welcome empirical evidence to bear and finds no clear evidence of increased conflict or interaction across civilizational boundaries, which the thesis predicts. Countries in the same 'civilizational group' were just as likely to be in conflict as those across civilizations.

References and Further Reading

Ansell, A. (2012) *Race and Ethnicity: The Key Concepts* (2nd edn, London: Routledge).
Chiozza, G. (2002) 'Is There a Clash of Civilizations? Evidence from Patterns of International Conflict Involvement, 1946–97', *Journal of Peace Research*, 39(6): 711–34.
Huntington, S. P. (1996) *The Clash of Civilizations and the Remaking of World Order* (New York: Simon & Schuster).

Spencer, S. (2006) *Race and Ethnicity: Identity, Culture and Society* (London: Routledge).
Wieviorka, M. (2010) 'Racism in Europe: Unity and Diversity', in M. Guibernau and J. Rex (eds), *The Ethnicity Reader: Nationalism, Multiculturalism and Migration* (2nd edn, Cambridge: Polity), pp. 345–54.

Social Mobility

Working Definition

The movement of people or social groups upwards or downwards in a system of social stratification. In developed, modern societies, social mobility refers to movement within the social **class** system.

Origins of the Concept

Social mobility studies can be traced back to the post-1945 period, when sociologists tried to assess whether social inequality, usually class, was decreasing as societies grew wealthier. Some economists argued that, from low levels of inequality before **industrialization**, the take-off to continuous economic growth led to increased inequality but, over time, as social mobility increased, inequality would level off and go into reverse. In the late 1960s, studies in the USA found much vertical mobility, though the actual movement was quite small or short range. Long-range mobility from, say, working class to upper middle class was still very rare. Downward mobility was much less common, as white-collar and professional jobs grew more rapidly than blue-collar ones, enabling sons of blue-collar workers to move into white-collar work.

An important study was carried out by Lipset and Bendix (1959), who analysed data from nine countries – Britain, France, West Germany, Sweden, Switzerland, Japan, Denmark, Italy and the United States. Focusing on the mobility of men from blue-collar to white-collar work, they made some surprising findings. There was no evidence that the United States was more open than European societies, as total vertical mobility was 30 per cent in the USA and between 27 and 31 per cent in Europe. The authors concluded that all industrialized societies were experiencing a similar expansion of white-collar jobs which promoted upward mobility. Today mobility studies increasingly take in the dimensions of **gender** and **ethnicity** in attempts to assess whether overall social mobility is increasing or decreasing.

Meaning and Interpretation

Social mobility refers to the movement of individuals and groups between different socio-economic positions. Vertical mobility means moving up or down the socio-economic scale. Hence people whose income, capital or **status** improves are said to be upwardly mobile, while those whose economic or status position worsens are downwardly mobile. In modern societies there is also much geographical movement as people relocate to new regions to find work, and this is known as lateral mobility. The two can often go hand in hand, as individuals may gain a promotion that entails moving to a new branch of the same firm elsewhere, perhaps even abroad.

Sociologists study two main aspects of social mobility. Research into *intra*generational mobility looks at how far individuals move up or down the social scale over their lives. Studies of *inter*generational mobility explore whether and how far children move up or down the social scale compared to their parents or grandparents. Debates tend to focus on the relative fixity or fluidity of the class system and whether social mobility is becoming easier as industrial capitalist societies mature. If levels of upward social mobility remain low, then we may surmise that class continues to exert a strong hold on people's life chances, but if there is more social mobility today than previously, we may theorize that class is losing its grip and societies are becoming more meritocratic and less unequal.

Levels of mobility in Britain were extensively studied over the post-war period, and there is a wealth of empirical evidence and research studies. David Glass (1954) analysed intergenerational mobility over a long period up to the 1950s and concluded that Britain was not a particularly open society, though there was a good deal of short-range mobility. Upward mobility was more common than downward mobility, but those at the bottom tended to stay there. The Oxford Mobility Study by John Goldthorpe and his colleagues, *Social Mobility and Class Structure in Modern Britain* ([1980] 1987), sought to discover how far patterns of mobility had changed since Glass's study. It found that overall levels of male mobility were higher than in the previous period, with more long-range movement across the class system. But the occupational system had not become more equal: by the 1980s the chances of men from blue-collar backgrounds getting professional or managerial jobs had increased on account of changes in the occupational structure, not because of greater opportunity or reductions in inequality. Goldthorpe and Jackson (2007) used more recent datasets and concluded that there was no evidence of falling intergenerational mobility in an absolute sense, but that there were some indications of a decline in long-range mobility. They also found a less favourable balance between downward and upward mobility emerging for men, suggesting that a return to rising rates of upward mobility was very unlikely.

Critical Points

An important criticism of social mobility research is the fact that it has conventionally been based almost exclusively on the working lives of men. This was perhaps understandable in the 1950s and 1960s, when the **ideology** of males as breadwinners and women as homemakers was in force, but it has become untenable as more women have entered the sphere of formal paid employment. Indeed, increasing numbers of women are now effectively heads of household based on their incomes. Some recent studies suggest that women are experiencing much greater opportunity than in previous generations, with middle-class women benefiting the most. Mobility studies will need to take women's experience into account if they are to give us a realistic picture of changes in the openness or otherwise of society.

Some longstanding critics of the whole tradition of social mobility research argue that Britain and other developed societies *are* meritocratic, because rewards go to those who are best able to 'perform' and achieve. Thus ability and effort are the key factors in occupational success, not class background (Saunders 1996). Using empirical data from the National Child Development Study, Saunders showed that bright, hard-working British children succeed regardless of the social advantages or disadvantages they may experience. Britain is an unequal society, but it is also essentially a fair one, with the rewards going to those who have worked for and thus deserve them. Others see individual merit as one factor determining individuals' class positions, but that 'class of origin' remains a very powerful influence, which means that children from disadvantaged backgrounds have to show more merit than others to acquire similar class positions.

Continuing Relevance

The concept of social mobility is an important one for sociologists looking to establish trends in occupations and movement across class boundaries. Today many argue that **globalization** and the deregulation of economic markets are leading to a widening of the gap between rich and poor and a 'hardening' of class inequalities, resulting in fewer opportunities for mobility. However, it is important to remember that our activities are never completely determined by class divisions and that many people do experience social mobility.

Research has been dominated by large-scale surveys aimed at measuring the extent of social mobility. However, some studies have tried to redress the balance by using **qualitative** methods to gain a more detailed knowledge of people's experience of opportunities for mobility across the **life course**. In *Pathways to Social Class*, Bertaux and Thompson (2007) use life histories and case studies of families and communities to explore some of the qualitative aspects of social mobility, such as **family** dynamics, 'dreams of careers which never happened', and all of those **interactions** that surveys do not tap into. In this way, qualitative research offers the potential to fill out the subjective dimensions of social mobility (or lack of it) and therefore help to bridge the gap between micro and macro levels.

How does societal transition or revolution affect social mobility? This question is taken up by Hertz and his colleagues (2009) in the case of one post-socialist country, Bulgaria. This study documents the sharp decline in intergenerational social mobility in Bulgaria between 1995 and 2001, a time of radical change, economic depression and large public spending reductions, especially on **education**. In particular, children of less well-educated parents suffered an absolute decline in average educational attainment during the period and a concomitant reduction in intergenerational social mobility. Hertz et al. argue that the main reasons for this decline are large reductions in education spending and a fall in the number of schools, rising unemployment, and a shift in political orientation away from the former egalitarian position. We might not be too surprised that the transition of former socialist societies would cause much disruption, but it is conceivable that the worldwide financial crisis of 2008 may make it even harder to reverse the trend identified in this article.

References and Further Reading

Bertaux, D., and Thompson, P. (2007) *Pathways to Social Class: A Qualitative Approach to Social Mobility* (New York: Transaction).

Glass, D. (1954) *Social Mobility in Britain* (London: Routledge & Kegan Paul).

Goldthorpe, J. H. (2005) 'Progress in Sociology: The Case of Social Mobility Research', in S. Svallfors (ed.), *Analyzing Inequality: Life Chances and Social Mobility in Comparative Perspective* (Stanford, CA: Stanford University Press), pp. 56–82.

Goldthorpe, J. H., and Jackson, M. (2007) 'Intergenerational Class Mobility in Contemporary Britain: Political Concerns and Empirical Findings', *British Journal of Sociology*, 58(4): 525–46.

Goldthorpe, J. H., Llewellyn, C., and Payne, C. ([1980] 1987) *Social Mobility and Class Structure in Modern Britain* (2nd edn, Oxford: Clarendon Press).

Hertz, T., Meurs, M., and Selcuk, S. (2009) 'The Decline in Intergenerational Mobility in Post-Socialism: Evidence from the Bulgarian Case', *World Development*, 37(3): 739–52.

Lipset, S. M., and Bendix, R. (1959) *Social Mobility in Industrial Society* (Berkeley: University of California Press).

Platt, L. (2005) *Migration and Social Mobility: The Life Chances of Britain's Minority Ethnic Communities* (Bristol: Policy Press).

Saunders, P. (1996) *Unequal but Fair? A Study of Class Barriers in Britain* (London: IEA Health and Welfare Unit).

Status

Working Definition

People's standing in **society**, based on the esteem or prestige in which individuals or groups are held by other members of society.

Origins of the Concept

Social status is a basic concept in sociology which is associated particularly with the symbolic interactionist tradition. For Weber, status refers to the relative differences in esteem between social groups in the eyes of others. In traditional societies, status was often determined on the basis of first-hand knowledge of a person gained through face-to-face **interactions** in different contexts over a number of years. But with increasing population levels it became less and less likely that status could be accorded in this personal way. Weber argued that status gradually came to be expressed through the styles of life or what today we call lifestyles. Lifestyle symbols of status, such as housing and interior design, dress codes, manners of speech and occupation, all help to shape an individual's social standing in the eyes of other people, and those sharing the same status then form a community with a sense of shared **identity**.

Meaning and Interpretation

Max Weber saw societies as riven with competition and conflicts for **power** and material resources. However, unlike Marx, who saw **class** conflicts as the primary source of division in society, Weber viewed class as just one basis of **conflict**, and perhaps not even the main one. Stratified modern societies are multidimensional, and understanding them cannot be reduced to a simple matter of class but has to consider social status and 'party' affiliations (groups and associations that seek to influence society) as well. Because class, status and party combine and overlap, this produces a complex picture of the social structure, with many possible positions available within society. While Marx argued that status distinctions are generated by and run parallel to class divisions, Weber observed that status often varies independently of class. For example, as aristocratic families gradually lost their power and wealth, this did not inevitably lead to a loss of status. Some individuals from aristocratic families retained their high status in society on account of their continuing membership of powerful social **networks** (low economic capital, high status). Conversely, modern celebrities, who are widely seen as being 'famous for being famous', may be very wealthy but are also viewed with disdain (low status, high economic capital).

The social roles we adopt depend on our social status, and a person's social status can be different depending on the social context. As a student, for example, a person has a certain status and is expected to act in certain ways when in a classroom situation, but as a son or daughter a different status is effective, and others will have different expectations. Likewise, as a friend, an individual has an entirely different position in the social order, and the roles he or she adopts change accordingly. We all have many statuses in play at the same time, and this group of statuses is referred to as a 'status set'. Sociologists also distinguish between ascribed and achieved status. An ascribed status is one that is given, often based on biological factors such as sex or age, as in 'male' and 'teenager'. An achieved status is one that is attained through an individual's own effort, including, say, doctor, athlete or manager.

While we may like to believe that our achieved statuses are most important, others may not agree. In any society, some statuses have priority over all others, and this 'master status' generally determines a person's overall social position. **Gender** and **'race'** have commonly been seen as master statuses, though it is also not unusual for others, such as 'deviant', 'environmentalist' or 'Christian', to take on a master status for some people. The prestige attached to certain statuses also changes over time, and often this is due in no small measure to the direct actions of social groups. The status of 'black person' was at one time a negative status in Europe and North America according to its assignation by the white majority culture. To be black was to face prejudice, discrimination and social **stigma**. Over a long period, though, black civil rights movements and equal rights campaigns reclaimed the concept of 'black', turning it into a positive status and connecting it with a proud history and cultural tradition. The example shows that even ascribed statuses are subject to changing social definition and evaluation.

Critical Points

In spite of the strong case made by Weber and modern Weberians that status is as significant as social class in stratification systems, critics argue that this does not give enough weight to the way that class position continues to shape life chances. Studies of **social mobility** have shown that, although there is more mobility today than in the past, at the lower end of the class structure there is little evidence of routine intergenerational mobility. In short, class is a much more effective determinant of social position and status than vice versa. Social inequalities are also primarily generated and reproduced through structural economic changes and cannot be explained in terms of individual choices or esteem measures. As Crompton (2008) suggests, explaining material **poverty** and severe disadvantage demands an understanding of the socio-economic and occupational structures of society.

Continuing Relevance

Modern societies have become consumer societies, geared to the continual acquisition of material goods. Despite criticisms from class theorists, it may be that the status differences based on differing 'tastes' now tend to reinforce those of social class position (Bourdieu 1986). As modern societies have become consumer-oriented, social status has arguably become more rather than less significant. In a consumer society, people increasingly establish status distinctions through the purchase and consumption of goods as lifestyle choices. This leads to a heightened individualization as well as a de-identification with social class and other traditional identities. That does not mean social class is not significant, but it does mean that people are less likely to perceive it as the central feature of their personal identities. The shift towards **consumerism** allows for much more varied, complex and fine-grained status differences to be made, leading to a more comprehensive society-wide status competition.

In an interesting article, Mari Rege (2008) asks why people care about social status. She discusses the way that individuals are induced to care about their and other people's status positions during 'complementary interactions'. These are interactions – such as in business – in which a person can increase his or her own position by interacting with others with similar abilities. But, as 'ability' is not necessarily visible, status markers can be significant signs which connect people of similar talents. This thesis of complementary interactions may help to explain why certain status 'props' or material goods tend to be shared in certain contexts.

In business, for instance, the widespread adoption of Rolex watches and Armani suits may be because these items are widely acknowledged as visible signs of business ability, and, by investing in them, business people may increase their chances of making useful connections. Rege's argument implies that the old idea of 'keeping up with the Joneses' may not be as superficial as previously thought.

In Ridgeway et al.'s (2009) experimental study of the creation of status differences, gender is found to be a significant factor. This article explores the formation of strong status beliefs after just two social encounters with people with social differences. But Ridgeway's experiment found a significant gender divide. Although both men and women formed strong beliefs about a person's status, it was men who carried that belief into their next interaction, while women did not. In that sense, men seem to be 'first movers' in acting on their beliefs. However, once status distinctions were established, women were just as likely as men to treat people unequally. Although a small study, this piece suggests that social status distinctions are both readily drawn and powerful in the reproduction of inequalities.

References and Further Reading

Bourdieu, P. (1986) *Distinction: A Social Critique of the Judgement of Taste* (London: Routledge & Kegan Paul).

Chan, T. W. (ed.) (2010) *Social Status and Cultural Consumption* (Cambridge: Cambridge University Press).

Crompton, R. (2008) *Class and Stratification: An Introduction to Current Debates* (3rd edn, Cambridge: Polity).

Rege, M. (2008) 'Why Do People Care about Social Status?', *Journal of Economic Behavior and Organization*, 66(2): 233–42.

Ridgeway, C. L., Backor, K., Li, Y. E., Tinkler, J. E., and Erickson, K. G. (2009) 'How Easily Does a Social Difference Become a Status Distinction? Gender Matters', *American Sociological Review*, 74(1): 44–62.

6 Relationships and the Life Course

Community

Working Definition

A contested concept, but, simply, a group of people living in a particular locality, or who have a certain shared interest, who engage in systematic **interactions** with one another.

Origins of the Concept

The term 'community' has been used since the fourteenth century, when it denoted 'the common people' as distinct from those of rank. From the eighteenth century, community was used to describe the people in a particular district or those who had shared interests, as in 'a community of interest' (Williams 1987). By the nineteenth century it became increasingly common to see community used in contrast to **society**, with 'community' defined as smaller in scale than the more impersonal and large-scale 'society'. The German sociologist Ferdinand Tönnies ([1887] 2001) traced the decline of *Gemeinschaft* (or community bonds) as *Gesellschaft* (or 'associational' bonds) was rapidly expanding. This kind of contrast was repeated many times in sociological studies and social commentaries, and community acquired a normative element that became problematic when sociologists tried to use the concept for analysis.

Early community studies meant researchers becoming involved in specific localities in order to understand them better. However, too often these came to be seen as mere description and lacking theoretical rigour. By the 1970s, community studies looked rather quaint and fell quickly from favour among a new generation of sociologists. In the 1980s and 1990s, though, a renewed interest in the ideas of everyday life and lifestyles led to the reinvigoration of 'studies of communities', which allowed researchers to explore new interests in **gender**, **ethnicity** and other social inequalities at the local level. Over the last two decades, research has shifted again to study the relations between **globalization** and its local effects, online 'virtual' community-building and the impact of increasing geographical mobility on community relations.

Meaning and Interpretation

The concept of community is a difficult one to pin down, as it has taken on several meanings as well as carrying some damaging normative implications. Two basic meanings stand out, however. It has become commonplace to speak of an academic community, the gay community, the Muslim community, and many more. This definition is based on the notion of 'communities of interest', where the people and groups referred to may be geographically dispersed and never actually meet, yet still have some shared interest. What constitutes the 'communal' aspect of these varied groups is not entirely clear, though it could be a perception of a shared **identity** and common interests. On the other hand, some researchers continue to see communities as territorially based social groups of kinship networks, neighbours, businesses and friends, especially where these communities are small in scale. This spatial definition harks back to the early community studies tradition of the 1950s and 1960s. It is of course possible that the two definitions may overlap in some cases, such as the idea of a 'mining community', which may be localized and also involve shared interests and a shared sense of identity created in the workplace.

Lee and Newby's (1983) survey of community studies discerned three alternative definitions of community which were in play. First was community as a locality or bounded territory, within which people live. The problem with this is that it is more a geographical than a sociological definition. Lots of people may live in a particular area but have nothing to do with one another. The definition takes no account of social relations and whether people interact with one another or not. Second, some studies define community as 'a local social system', involving social relationships that operate within a locality. The problem here is that the social relations forming the social system may be rooted in antagonisms and hatred which serve to keep social groups apart. Is it legitimate to consider that situation as a single 'community'? Finally, community is defined as a type of relationship involving a shared sense of communal identity. Lee and Newby call this 'communion', as it may be that this shared identity continues to exist even after people move away from the locality.

Critical Points

One major problem with the concept of community is the constant danger that social analysis will shade into normative bias. Community has often been seen as both morally and socially superior to other, larger forms of human settlement. Tönnies's contrasting of *Gemeinschaft* and *Gesellschaft* is a clear example of this problem. Even though his study was in many ways an accurate depiction of some important social changes brought about by rapid urbanization and industrial development, there is a sense throughout that something more valuable and important was being lost in the process.

Community studies also tended, quite logically, to look inward, focusing on relations within a defined locale to produce rich accounts of community life. But the downside was an inability to connect the lives of people within the community to the world outside. As a result, many sociologists abandoned the concept altogether as a useful tool of analysis in favour of social **network** analysis, which offers a more objective approach to the study of social relations. One advantage of this approach is its ability to break through the boundaries of communities to link local social networks to those outside. This is a particularly important factor in the more mobile, globalizing world in which we now live. For example, patterns of global **migration** mean that networks exist across national boundaries, with migrant workers maintaining strong links with both their community of origin and the community of destination.

Continuing Relevance

There is reason to suspect that the idea of community will survive in sociology. In spite of the barrage of criticisms against the concept, it does draw our attention to something fundamental, namely the *quality* of people's lives as they are lived. Although the old community studies were probably too inward-looking, they did produce some very rich and informative accounts which are hard to reproduce using the more objective methods that came afterwards. What studies of community can provide is a better understanding of the meaningful relationships within which people live the bulk of their lives. Provided that such studies are inclusive enough to consider **conflict**, social inequalities and the wider social networks that have become more common today, the concept still has much to contribute to our understanding of global–local connections.

Clearly globalization is bringing about many changes in almost every aspect of social life and across the **life course**, and the effects of globalization on later life are discussed in Phillipson's (2007) study of old age and residency. Recent studies of older people's perceptions of community life suggest a widespread and strong nostalgia for previously existing 'imagined communities'. Not all of this is the result of global processes, however, as such attitudes pre-date the present period of rapid globalization. But this study argues that the economic, social and cultural aspects of globalization *are* transforming many residential environments and that new divides among older populations are emerging. This is especially so in relation to those who are able to move into retirement communities or second homes and others who view changing neighbourhoods as problematic for their sense of self and belonging. The detailed community study of 'lives in place' has much to offer the emerging research agenda as sociologists try to grasp global–local relations.

References and Further Reading

Blackshaw, T. (2010) *Key Concepts in Community Studies* (London: Sage).
Crow, G., and Allan, G. (1994) *Community Life: An Introduction to Local Social Relations* (Hemel Hempstead: Harvester Wheatsheaf).

Lee, D., and Newby, H. (1983) *The Problem of Sociology* (London: Routledge).

Phillipson, C. (2007) 'The "Elected" and the "Excluded": Sociological Perspectives on the Experience of Place and Community in Old Age', *Ageing and Society*, 27(3): 321–42.

Tönnies, F. ([1887] 2001) *Community and Society [Gemeinschaft und Gesellschaft]* (Cambridge and New York: Cambridge University Press).

Williams, R. (1987) *Keywords: A Vocabulary of Culture and Society* (London: Fontana).

Family

Working Definition

A social group consisting of individuals related by blood ties, marriage or adoption, who share a mutual commitment to the group.

Origins of the Concept

The concept of the family is as old as societies, and sociologists, from the classical founders to the present day, have had things to say about families. Many sociologists today believe that we cannot speak about 'the family' as if there is one universal model. There are many different family forms, such as step-families, lone-parent families, and so on, and sociologists speak of 'families' in the plural to reflect this diversity.

All ideas of a previous 'golden age' of family life in which children were reared in stable, harmonious families have been shown to be false. For instance, many politicians and commentators compare today's families with the apparent stability of the Victorians. But, in nineteenth-century England, death rates were high, the average length of marriages was less than twelve years, and more than 50 per cent of all children under the age of twenty-one had lost at least one of their parents. Similarly, the discipline of the Victorian family was based on very strict rules and physical punishments that would be unacceptable to most people today. Middle-class wives were more or less confined to the home, while many 'respectable' men frequented prostitutes and made regular visits to brothels. Child labour was also very common. Historical sociology has provided some timely reminders that our common-sense historical memories are very often nostalgic and unrealistic.

Meaning and Interpretation

Defining 'the family' today is fraught with difficulties, as sociologists now recognize that there exists a diversity of family forms both in any single national **society** and across the societies of the world. In some parts of the world, traditional family structures that have existed for more than a century continue today in relatively unchanged form. However, major changes have occurred in people's family arrangements in the developed societies that have necessitated new ways of studying family life.

In the developed countries, the presence of minority ethnic groups, for instance families of South Asian or West Indian origin, and the influence of movements such as feminism have produced considerable cultural variety in family forms. Persistent **class** divisions between the poor, the skilled working classes, and the various groupings within the middle and upper classes sustain major variations in family structure. Variations in family experience during the **life course** have also diversified. For instance, one individual might come into a family in which both parents had stayed together, and go on to marry and then divorce. Another person might be brought up in a single-parent family, be married several times and have children by each marriage.

Connections between parents, grandparents and wider family have also become weaker as family members move around the country and across the world with work, thus losing everyday contact with those left behind. On the other hand, more people now live into old age, and three 'ongoing' families might exist in close relation to one another: married grandchildren, their parents and the grandparents. There is also greater sexual diversity in family organizations than ever before. As homosexuality becomes increasingly accepted in many Western societies, partnerships and families are formed based on homosexual as well as heterosexual coupling and marriage.

The diversification of family types, structures and practices has outpaced wide-spread notions of an idealized family form based on the nuclear family. There have been numerous attempts to reinvigorate this now 'traditional' family type, which is seen by proponents as a more stable and reliable site for bringing up children. However, this idealization neglects the 'dark side' of family life such as intimate violence and the abuse of children, making it an inadequate and partial account of nuclear families. The relatively recent legalization of gay marriage in some developed countries and the normalization of step- or blended families in the wake of high divorce rates show that the gap between ideas of 'family' and the reality of 'families' may, slowly, be narrowing.

Critical Points

The mainstream idea that families are rooted in mutual help and support is open to question. Empirical studies have found that inequality is a common aspect of family life, with some members benefiting while others are disadvantaged (Pahl 1989). Capitalist production brought about a much sharper distinction between the domestic and work realms, resulting in male and female spheres or a public and private division. In contemporary developed societies, domestic tasks such as child care and housework continue to fall primarily on women, even those who work in the formal economy. Not only do women tend to shoulder concrete tasks such as cleaning and child care, but they also invest large amounts of emotional labour in maintaining personal relationships and looking after older relatives.

Feminists have drawn attention to the 'dark side' of family life, such as domestic violence, marital rape and the sexual abuse of children. This abusive side of family life had long been neglected, leaving the picture of families in sociology as unduly positive and optimistic – the haven in a heartless world. Feminist research shows that the intimate private setting of the family has been a key site for **gender** oppression and emotional or physical abuse. This body of work has served further to demystify the family.

Continuing Relevance

Although diversity has emerged as a central characteristic of family studies, there may also be some general patterns emerging as **globalization** brings cultures closer together. For example, Therborn (2004) argues that clans and other kin-based groups are declining in influence and that there is a widespread trend towards the free selection of a spouse. Women's rights are becoming more widely recognized in respect to both the initiation of marriage and decision-making within the family, while higher levels of sexual freedom, for both men and women, are developing in societies that were previously very restrictive. There is also a general trend towards the extension of children's rights and an increasing acceptance of same-sex partnerships.

In an analysis of official government statistics between 1981 and 2001, Ware et al. (2007) assessed the claim that the nuclear family is in long-term decline. Around one-third of residents lived in ostensibly 'nuclear' households in 2001, but family forms have diversified significantly, to include lone-parent, lone-person, multiple-person, couple-only, couple with extra adult, and extended nuclear types. However, the authors argue that the nuclear family remains important and, in particular, that those living in nuclear family forms in middle age are more likely to remain in that state. However, the routes into and out of the nuclear family have also changed significantly, given the relatively high rates of relationship breakdown and divorce which result in increased numbers of lone-parent and lone-person households.

As more step-families are created, an issue that arises is how such families are perceived. Are they seen in a negative light or have they become more widely accepted as normal types of family? In an Australian study, Planitz and Feeney (2009) found persistent negative stereotypes of the step-family which were actually shared by many members of step-families themselves. Some of these negative characteristics were 'unsupportive', 'broken ties' and 'a lack of affection'. Despite the apparent normalization of diverse family and household forms, this study illustrates the continuing **power** of stereotypes informed by ideals of the 'biological family'.

References and Further Reading

Chambers, D. (2012) *A Sociology of Family Life* (Cambridge: Polity).
Pahl, J. (1989) *Money and Marriage* (Basingstoke: Macmillan).

Planitz, J. M., and Feeney, J. A. (2009) 'Are Stepsiblings Bad, Stepmothers Wicked and Stepfathers Evil? An Assessment of Australian Stepfamily Stereotypes', *Journal of Family Studies*, 15(1): 82–97.

Therborn, G. (2004) *Between Sex and Power: Family in the World, 1900–2000* (London: Routledge).

Ware, L., Maconachie, M., Williams, M., Chandler, J., and Dodgeon, B. (2007) 'Gender Life Course Transitions from the Nuclear Family in England and Wales 1981–2001', *Sociological Research Online*, 12(4), www.socresonline.org.uk/12/4/6.html.

Life Course

Working Definition

The individual's movement through various socially created transitions during the course of their life.

Origins of the Concept

A longstanding view of human life is that there is a universal life cycle, through which we all pass, containing several fixed, biological stages. We are all infants, children, young people, adults and older people and, of course, eventually we all die. However, from the 1970s onwards, as childhood, youth subcultures and ageing became part of mainstream sociology, it became clearer that these apparently natural or biological stages are in fact part of the human life course, which must be understood as socially constructed.

Historical sociologists discovered that the experience of childhood was very different in feudal societies, with no distinct stage set apart from adulthood. Children looked and were treated very much as 'small adults' and were set to work as soon as possible. The creation of youth culture with its own characteristics emerged only in the post-1945 period and, as life expectancy has expanded, many more people can now expect to experience being 'old-old' (more than eighty) than ever before. For sociologists, the concept of the life course is preferable to that of the life cycle because it allows for the considerable variation in life stages that have been found in different societies and over time.

Meaning and Interpretation

The life course in a given **society** is the product of that society's social structure, **culture** and economic system. This means that the number and type of life course stages are likely to differ over time and across different societies. A simple example is dying and death. In most developed societies, where the average age of death is now over seventy-five, dying is considered to be intimately tied to ageing. However, in previous periods there was no functioning healthcare system or awareness of the causes of infection, the rates of infant mortality were very high, and consequently dying was not so strongly associated with later life. Other social factors, such as social **class**, **gender** and **ethnicity**, also influence the way that life-course stages are experienced. In the nineteenth century, upper-class children attended boarding schools and continued their **education** over an extended period of time, but for children from working-class families it was not unusual for boys of thirteen to work in coal mining and industry and girls of the same age to go into domestic service. Childhood was not a universal, age-related stage of the life course.

Similarly, birth cohorts (groups of people born in the same year) tend to be influenced by the same major events, which other cohorts are not. In this way whole generations have different life-course experiences too. Birth cohorts have common cultural and political reference points, particular governments, **conflicts**, musical trends, and so on. In more recent times, the 9/11 attacks and the invasions of Iraq and Afghanistan have all made their mark in generating a common currency of life-course experiences, though the way these events are interpreted will differ. 'Baby boomers', for example, had the first home televisions, new forms of spectacular youth culture, rising income levels, and more liberal attitudes to sex and morality. Their life course was, in many ways, very different to that of their parents and grandparents.

Sociologists have spent a good deal of time studying childhood, which seems an obvious and universal life stage. But childhood, as a distinct stage of life, is only around three hundred years old. Before this, it was usual for older infants to move directly into work without passing through a life-course stage called 'childhood'. By studying paintings and representations of the medieval period, the social historian Philippe Ariès (1965) noted that the concept and life stage we know as childhood was not present. Paintings show 'children' dressed in 'adult' clothing with faces that make them look much older than their years. The life-course stage we know as 'childhood' was socially created much later. Many children and young people today still work from a very young age and in a range of employment, from mining to agriculture, and the attempt by the United Nations to establish a universal definition of childhood and a universal set of children's rights is a tacit admission that childhood is not a universal life stage. And, of course, we could trace this **social constructionist** idea with all of the life stages with which we are familiar, including teenage, youth and middle age.

Sociologists have started to theorize a relatively new phase within the life course in the developed societies, which we can call young adulthood. Young adulthood is said to characterize those people in their twenties, and perhaps early thirties, who live relatively independent lives but have not yet married or had children; as a consequence, they are still experimenting with relationships and lifestyles. However, this stage is not seen as being experienced in the same way by all social classes and ethnic groups. It may be that it describes only small groups of wealthier individuals in their early twenties who have the time and are able to travel and explore alternative lifestyles. This stage of life is also likely to involve more young women who go on to university and forge careers instead of settling into traditional **family** life at an early age.

Critical Points

Clearly the social constructionist approach to the human life course has been productive, bringing a new dimension to studies of individual lives. Some post-modern thinkers argue it has not yet gone far enough. This is because life-course studies remain wedded to the idea of transitional stages that mark specific changes, perhaps suggesting a structure which no longer exists and harks back to the earlier biological model of the life cycle. The criticism here is that life-course studies have not yet broken decisively with the older studies of biological stages. For postmodernists, the human lifespan is a continuum rather than a set of distinct stages, and attempts to identify particular stages risk imposing an illegitimate ordering sequence. However, perhaps this criticism fails to take account of the full impact of the social markers associated with life-course stages such as compulsory schooling, entitlement to welfare benefits, and a forced retirement age and receipt of a pension. These are symbolic markers connected to shifts in people's perceptions of self.

Continuing Relevance

The concept of the life course is relatively underdeveloped in sociology. However, introducing the life course into studies of childhood, family life, youth cultures, the ageing process and personal relations has already shown that a new research agenda is possible which breaks with the older, biologically based life-cycle approach. The concept has also stimulated interest in new research methods such as biographical research and oral histories, which allow sociologists access to the ways in which differently situated individuals experience life-course stages. Studies in this vein may well offer new information on the **structure–agency** problem from the point of view of social actors at different stages of the life course.

Are events at different stages of the life course more significant than others for our perception of age in later life? Schafer (2008) suggests they may well be. His fascinating article looks at the phenomenon of 'subjective ageing' – people's perception of age. Schafer's statistical analysis finds that maternal death during childhood is associated with an older subjective age in adulthood, while paternal death at the same life stage does not have the same impact. He argues that there are important connections between the timing of key life-course transitions and the development of a person's social self, with implications for future subjective perceptions and health in adult life.

References and Further Reading

Ariès, P. (1965) *Centuries of Childhood* (New York: Random House).
Green, L. (2016) *Understanding the Life Course: Sociological and Psychological Perspectives* (2nd edn, Cambridge: Polity).
Priestley, M. (2003) *Disability: A Life Course Approach* (Cambridge: Polity).

Schafer, M. H. (2008) 'Parental Death and Subjective Age: Indelible Imprints from Early in the Life Course?', *Sociological Inquiry*, 79(1): 75–97.

Network

Working Definition

In sociology, a network is a group of people linked together by relatively loose social bonds or ties which may be informal (such as social media 'friends') or formal (such as work colleagues).

Origins of the Concept

Familial kinship and friendship networks have been studied by social scientists for many years, along with the social networks formed among groups of employees and business acquaintances. Arguably, Georg Simmel's theoretical ideas in the early twentieth century on the shifting dynamics of basic social forms such as dyads (two social units) and triads (three social units) was a precursor to the study of much wider social networks. Although networks are very old forms of human association, for some sociologists, as information technology creates many new opportunities for networking, they are becoming the defining organizational structure of contemporary societies. The inherent flexibility and adaptability of networks gives them enormous advantages over older types of **organization**, and some see businesses beginning to adopt networked structures to maximize their efficiency in a global economic environment.

Meaning and Interpretation

Sociologists refer to the connections between people and social groups as networks. Perhaps the best way to think about a network is to see it as a web-like structure, or maybe a matrix, in which the points where vertical and horizontal strands cross are 'nodes' – or, in sociology's case, individuals, groups or even organizations. Gaining access to the web potentially opens up a whole series of connections to other nodes (individuals, groups or organizations) which may then be used to gain advantages. Networks can be viewed as all of those direct or indirect links between people and groups, including friendship groups and those one step removed, such as friends of friends.

However, organizations can also be networked, and belonging to networked organizations can extend people's social reach and influence more widely. Similarly, many other social groups offer a range of networking opportunities for individuals that 'oil the wheels' of social life, from gaining access to a local councillor to finding a specific skilled tradesman. Some groups, such as political parties and charities, have an international reach which can provide valuable contacts for people travelling or moving to new countries.

Networks have many useful functions, even though their ties are relatively weak, but access to the more powerful networks tends to be strictly controlled. Women have long been excluded from key networks in business, politics and private schools, thereby limiting their opportunities in these and other areas of life. Some of the fee-paying schools in England, such as Eton and Harrow, admit only boys, thereby denying women access to such powerful connections. Sociologists have found that, in the labour market, women tend to have relatively weak networks compared to men, which, again, reduces their employment prospects. However, this may be changing slowly as more women move into higher **education** and are promoted to higher positions within workplaces.

For Castells (2009), the enormous advances in computing and technology have made networks more efficient than bureaucracies. Many administrative tasks, such as data processing, no longer require workers to be physically close in large office blocks but can be carried out by separate groups around the globe. Organizations and companies have taken advantage of this new flexibility to become more decentralized, reinforcing the tendency towards smaller, less rigid types of enterprises, including homeworking. Traditionally, organizations were located in defined physical spaces, such as an office building or university campus, where the bureaucratic model made sense. But today the physical boundaries of organizations are being eroded as new technology in an increasingly global environment allows the transcending of countries and time zones, increasing efficiency by working as part of wider networks involving other organizations. What we are witnessing, says Castells, is the slow disintegration of the dominance of **bureaucracy** as the most efficient and effective organizational form.

Critical Points

Is the combination of information technology with networks taking us away completely from Weber's pessimistic vision of the future of bureaucracy? We should probably be cautious about such a view. Bureaucratic systems are increasingly being challenged by other, less hierarchical forms of organization. But bureaucracies will probably not disappear altogether. It seems unlikely that the network **society** will ever reach the point at which no organizations at all will be housed within a physical space, and those that are may well continue to adopt a more bureaucratic structure. In the near future, there is likely to be a continuing push and pull between tendencies towards large size, impersonality and hierarchy in organizations, on the one hand, and opposing influences, on the other.

Continuing Relevance

Networks are undoubtedly more widespread, and the adoption of new digital technologies is likely to further this trend. Though social network analysis is not entirely novel, having been used to study kinship networks in anthropology and classical sociology, it does seem likely that the method will be employed to explore a much wider variety of social networks than sociologists have considered in previous times.

A good example of the utility of social network analysis is Nick Crossley's (2008) empirical study of networks within the early punk rock movement in London. Crossley argues that the structural properties of the network help to explain the emergence of the movement itself. For instance, he suggests that the punk movement originated in London rather than in other UK cities partly because key participants of what would become the 'inner circle' of the movement were already connected, which made collective action in London more likely. Similarly, early punk band members were connected to one another and moved between bands, sharing information. In short, a common dense network existed which legitimized the emerging punk dress styles and **culture** against attacks from those who saw them as deviant. Of course, the political and ideological elements of punk were also important, but they may not have found expression in a cultural movement without the favourable network structures that already existed.

Another innovative piece of research is Mayer and Puller's (2007) study of data on friendship networks gathered from the social networking website Facebook. The researchers analysed a large dataset from ten private and public universities to explore the key elements responsible for the formation of friendships among students. They found that campus networks exhibited similar characteristics to 'classic' social networks: they were 'cliquish', and those individuals with many ties were linked to others with a similarly large number of ties. However, two students were more likely to become friends if they shared the same political orientation, and among minority ethnic groups **'race'** was the strongest predictor of friendship formation. This pattern held regardless of university size or character and seemed to be based on student preferences, suggesting that policies aimed at encouraging a diversity of interactions may have a limited impact on the formation of student networks.

References and Further Reading

Castells, M. (2009) *The Rise of the Network Society* (2nd edn, Oxford: Wiley Blackwell).
Crossley, N. (2008) 'Pretty Connected', *Theory, Culture and Society*, 25(6): 89–116.
Mayer, A., and Puller, S. L. (2007) 'The Old Boy (and Girl) Network: Social Network Formation on University Campuses', *Journal of Public Economics*, 92(1/2): 329–47.

Sexuality

Working Definition

The sexual characteristics and sexual behaviour of human beings, involving social, biological, physical and emotional aspects.

Origins of the Concept

Until quite recently, much of what we have known about sexuality came from biologists, medical researchers and sexologists, whose studies can be traced back to the nineteenth century. However, these studies tended to focus on individual psychology rather than examining the kind of general patterns of sexuality and sexual behaviour that interest sociologists. Many early scholars also looked at animal behaviour to provide some clues about human sexuality, and some still do. Although there is a clear biological component to sexuality, such as the imperative to reproduce, sociologists view human sexuality as the complex intertwining of biological and social factors.

The first major sociological studies of sexuality came in the 1940s and 1950s, when Alfred Kinsey and his colleagues in the USA carried out their major surveys of sexual behaviour. Their findings shocked people, revealing a large difference between public norms and expectations and actual sexual conduct. Michel Foucault's studies of sexuality in the late 1970s also opened up a new interest in the history of sexuality and the ways in which sexualities are created, denied and suppressed. This was a major turning point which took sexuality studies out of biology and into the fields of history, politics and sociology.

Meaning and Interpretation

Sexual orientation refers to the direction of a person's sexual or romantic attraction, and this is the result of a complex interplay of biological and social factors. Most people, in all societies, are heterosexual, and heterosexuality has historically been the basis of marriage and **family**, though there are many other sexual tastes and inclinations. For example, Judith Lorber (1994) identified ten different sexual identities: straight (heterosexual) woman, straight man, lesbian woman, gay man, bisexual woman, bisexual man, transvestite woman (a woman who regularly dresses as a man), transvestite man (a man who regularly dresses as a woman), transsexual woman (a man who becomes a woman) and transsexual man (a woman who becomes a man). Sexual practices are even more diverse, and in all societies there are norms governing these, encouraging some and condemning others.

Michel Foucault (1978) showed that the concept of a homosexual person seems barely to have existed in Europe before the eighteenth century. The term 'homosexuality' was coined in the 1860s, and from then on the homosexual was increasingly regarded as a separate type of person with a particular sexual aberration. Homosexuality became part of a medical rather than a religious **discourse**, spoken of in clinical terms as a psychiatric disorder or a perversion rather than as a religious 'sin'. Homosexuals, along with other 'deviants' such as paedophiles and transvestites, were seen as suffering from a biological pathology that threatened the wholesomeness of mainstream **society**. Until just a few decades ago homosexuality remained a criminal activity in virtually all Western countries, and it remained a designated mental disorder in the USA until the American Psychiatric Association finally removed it in 1987. Its shift from the margins of society to the mainstream is not yet complete, but rapid progress has been seen over recent years.

Sexual attitudes have undoubtedly become more permissive over the past forty years in most Western countries. Important aspects of people's sexual lives have been altered in a fundamental way. In earlier societies, sexuality was tied tightly to the process of reproduction, but in our current age it has been separated from it. Sexuality has become a dimension of life for each individual to explore and shape. If sexuality once was 'defined' in terms of heterosexuality and monogamy in the context of marital relations, there is now a growing acceptance of diverse forms of sexual behaviour and orientations in a broad variety of contexts.

Sociologists steered clear of sexuality research for most of the discipline's history until the 1940s, when Kinsey's research team in the USA carried out a ground-breaking survey which helped to dispel the idea that homosexuality was a medical condition that needed a cure. Surveys of sexual behaviour are fraught with difficulties. Many people see their sexual behaviour, more than most other areas of their lives, as a purely personal matter and are not prepared to discuss such intimate aspects with strangers. This may mean that those who are prepared to come forward to be interviewed are essentially a self-selected sample, which is therefore unrepresentative of the general population.

Critical Points

Kinsey's research was attacked by conservative and religious organizations, partly for its inclusion of children under sixteen years of age. Academic critics took issue with Kinsey's broadly positivist approach, which involved the collection of large amounts of raw data but a failure to grasp the complexity of sexual desire that underpinned the diverse behaviour he uncovered. The research also failed to tackle the meanings people attach to their sexual relationships, and later research actually found lower levels of homosexual experience than Kinsey's team, so their sample may have been less representative than they had thought. Nevertheless, it would be uncharitable to expect a single study to have come to grips with all of these issues, especially in such a difficult area of research practice, and Kinsey deserves credit for effectively opening up sexuality to sociological research.

The validity and reliability of surveys of sexual behaviour have formed the subject of much debate. Many critics suggest that these surveys just do not generate reliable information about sexual practices. Publicly stated attitudes may simply reflect people's understanding of prevailing social norms rather than giving us accurate information about their private attitudes and sexual behaviour. However, this criticism could also be levelled at many other surveys of different aspects of people's lives, such as marriage, divorce, crime and **deviance**, yet sociologists manage to weigh the pros and cons of their data to bring us insights that have been helpful for policy-makers, and there is no conclusive reason why studies of sexuality should not do the same.

Continuing Relevance

One reason why sexuality has become part of sociological theorizing and research is that the 1960s movements for reform helped to change society, opening up a range of new subjects for sociologists. Since these movements integrated into mainstream society, there has been something of a restabilization of older norms relating to sexual behaviour. Recent surveys show large proportions of respondents in favour of discouraging sexual activity among young people and smaller numbers opposed to homosexual sex. In this context, sociological research needs to be sensitive to changing attitudes and public norms and may have to devise new methods that are better able to get to the truth of people's lives.

A little researched subject, the sexuality of disabled people, is discussed in an article by Kelly et al. (2009). This piece presents the findings from research which elicited the views of a group of people with intellectual disabilities in Ireland regarding their experiences of sexuality, relationships and what support structures they considered helpful. In Ireland, it is against the law for anyone to engage in sexual activity with a person who is unable to live without support or protect themselves from abuse unless those involved are married (a consultation on changing this law reported in 2011). Participants in this study said that they had not received enough sex education or information and that within their services relationships were not allowed, which led to the formation of 'secret' relationships. The authors argued that a change in the law is needed, as many people with intellectual disabilities are capable of having sexual relationships and protecting themselves from abuse.

Many countries have moved towards legislation allowing gay couples to seal their partnerships in a legal way, either through civil partnerships or in some form of marriage. Although such moves appear to be in line with wider acceptance of gay relationships, the question arises as to why marriage, a conventional heterosexual institution, would be attractive to homosexuals. Kelly (2006) suggests several possible reasons, including achieving formally equal legal status, working and welfare rights, healthcare rights (such as visitation) and tax benefits. However, debates continue within the LGBT movement on whether the apparently 'progressive' character of gay marriage is real or illusory.

References and Further Reading

Foucault, M. (1978) *The History of Sexuality* (London: Penguin).

Kelly, G., Crowley, H., and Hamilton, C. (2009) 'Rights, Sexuality and Relationships in Ireland: "It'd Be Nice to Be Kind of Trusted"', *British Journal of Learning Disabilities*, 37(4): 308–15.

Kelly, R. (2006) 'Gay Marriage. Why Now? Why at All', in S. Seidman, N. Fischer and C. Meeks (eds), *Handbook of the New Sexuality Studies* (London: Routledge), pp. 433–40.

Lorber, J. (1994) *Paradoxes of Gender* (New Haven, CT: Yale University Press).

Taylor, Y., and Hines, S. (2012) *Sexualities: Past Reflections, Future Directions* (Basingstoke: Palgrave Macmillan).

Weeks, J. (2016) *Sexuality* (4th edn, London: Routledge).

Socialization

Working Definition

The social processes through which new members of **society** develop awareness of social norms and values and help them achieve a distinct sense of self. Socialization processes continue throughout life.

Origins of the Concept

Socialization is a concept that is common to many sociological perspectives, though it was developed and fully explored within the functionalist tradition. Talcott Parsons in particular used the concept to resolve the 'problem of social order'. Interactionists, such as Mead and Cooley, also used socialization to study the creation of the **social self** during childhood. Socialization refers to the process which transforms a quite helpless human infant into a self-aware, knowledgeable person who is skilled in the ways of their society's **culture**. Socialization is essential for social reproduction, maintaining the continuity of society over time. Not only do children learn from adults during socialization, but adults learn how to deal with babies and children too. Parenting ties the activities of adults to children, usually for the remainder of their lives, and the same happens with grandparents. Socialization is normally discussed in terms of primary socialization, which is particularly intense and takes place in the early years of life, and secondary socialization, which continues across the life course.

Meaning and Interpretation

Socialization takes place through various agencies, such as the **family**, peer groups, schools and the media. The family is the main agent during primary socialization, though increasingly children attend some form of schooling or nursery care in this phase as well. In modern societies, social position is not inherited at birth, but the **ethnicity**, **gender** and social **class** of families, as well as region of birth, do influence patterns of socialization. Children learn gender in a largely unconscious way by observing and picking up ways of behaviour and language that are characteristic of their parents or others in their neighbourhood or **community**. Gender differences are also learned through the way infants and children are treated by adults. For example, young boys and girls are spoken to and handled differently by parents and other adults, and appropriate norms of behaviour are shaped by gendered expectations. Children are able to recognize their own and others' gender at a very early age, and this is reinforced throughout childhood through, for example, gender-specific toy choices and representations in books, films and television programmes. Yet gender socialization is not entirely unconsciously imbibed. Parents and peer groups actively enforce gender roles and expectations, and children who break gender norms face sanctions such as shaming, name-calling or chastisement. The combination of continuous unconscious learning, reinforced by sanctions and measures of enforcement, make gender socialization a very powerful process that continues into young adulthood and beyond.

This 'secondary socialization' begins in schools through both the formal and informal curriculum and continues into colleges and workplaces. Boys and girls begin to divide on subject lines as they pursue conventionally 'female' and 'male' subjects, a pattern that follows into college and university. Teachers' expectations play a part in this gendered pattern but so too do peer groups in schools and workplaces, and, as many families today are dual-earner families, peer groups have, arguably, increased in their impact.

In adulthood, socialization continues as people learn how to behave in relation to new areas of social life, such as work environments and political beliefs. **Mass media** – radio, television, CDs, DVDs and the Internet – are also seen as playing an increasing role in socialization, helping to shape opinions, attitudes and behaviour. This is especially the case with the advent of new media, which enable virtual interactions via chatrooms, blogs, and so on. Taken together, agencies of socialization form a complex range of contrary social influences and opportunities for **interaction**, which illustrates why socialization can never be an entirely directed or determinant process, particularly given that humans are self-aware creatures capable of forming their own interpretations of the messages with which they are presented.

Critical Points

The main criticism of theories of socialization is the temptation to exaggerate its influence. This was particularly the case with Parsons's structural functionalism, which some critics saw as treating people like 'cultural dopes', at the mercy of socializing agencies. It is certainly the case that some sociological theories have laid heavy emphasis on socialization to explain how social and cultural reproduction takes place. Dennis Wrong (1961) took issue with what he saw as an 'oversocialized conception of Man [*sic*]' in sociology, arguing that it treats people as mere role-players who follow social scripts according to mainstream social norms. If we look instead at Sigmund Freud's theory of self and **identity** formation, it is possible to build an alternative theory which sees individuals, even children, as active agents in the process rather than as passive vessels. Socialization is almost always a **conflict**-ridden, emotionally charged affair, unlike the smooth process depicted in some sociology textbooks. Today, theories of social and cultural reproduction are much more sensitive to the contradictions inherent in socializing processes, reflected in the work of Bourdieu, Willis or Mac an Ghaill.

Continuing Relevance

Socialization is a fundamental concept in sociology, helping to explain how societies transmit knowledge, social norms and values across generations. And though the critical points above can be conceded, socialization is a powerful social process, especially during the primary phase when children learn to control their impulses and develop a concept of self. It also allows us to assess the relative significance of socializing agents such as the mass media, peer groups and schooling across the **life course**. In addition, it enables comparative work covering socialization processes in different societies and in the same society over time. In short, socialization is a necessary, if not sufficient, concept in the explanation of social change as well as social reproduction.

A fascinating study of an unusual form of adult socialization effects can be found in Mennesson's (2009) account of men's participation in activities – such as ballet – that are widely seen as female. Mennesson interviewed fourteen male jazz and ballet dancers to gain an initial grasp of how men can develop a desire for female activities during socialization and how the gender identity of male dancers may then be influenced by being a male in a 'female' world. She found some evidence of similarities with women who play 'male' sports such as football or rugby. A 'reverse gender socialization' within certain family configurations seems to produce these kinds of preferences, while the socialization of the male dancers leads to specific outcomes, with some dancers keen to 'remain men' and others happier to describe themselves as both masculine and feminine.

References and Further Reading

Denzin, N. K. (2009) *Childhood Socialization* (New York: Transaction).

Maccoby, E. E. (2008) 'Historical Overview of Socialization Research and Theory', in J. E. Grusec and Paul D. Hastings (eds), *Handbook of Socialization: Theory and Research* (New York: Guilford Press), pp. 13–41.

Mennesson, C. (2009) 'Being a Man in Dance: Socialization Modes and Gender Identities', *Sport in Society*, 12(2): 174–95.

Wrong, D. (1961) 'The Over-Socialized Conception of Man in Modern Sociology', *American Sociological Review*, 26: 183–93.

Interaction and Communication

Culture

Working Definition

The way of life, including knowledge, customs, norms, laws and beliefs, which characterizes a particular **society** or social group.

Origins of the Concept

Because of its convoluted history, 'culture', like its presumed opposite, 'nature', is one of the most complex words in the English language, and one of the most difficult to pin down. From the fifteenth century one important meaning has been culture as in tending crops and animals. Once this meaning expanded to take in people, culture came to mean the 'culturing' of people's minds. In eighteenth-century Germany, culture came to be opposed to 'civilization', with the former seen as superior to the latter. By the nineteenth century a recognition of 'cultures' or cultural wholes developed, which is the start of modern social scientific usage. Culture in this sense refers to all of the elements of a society's way of life that are learned, among them language, values, social norms, beliefs, customs and laws. However, culture has not conventionally included material artefacts such as buildings or furniture, though this has changed as sociologists have become increasingly interested in 'material culture'. The comparative study of cultures in this sense is a very broad enterprise.

Meaning and Interpretation

For most of its history, sociology has studied culture as intimately bound up with social relations and the structure of society. Marxist studies, for example, tended to view the entire edifice of culture and cultural production as a superstructure standing on the foundations of the capitalist mode of production. Hence, religious beliefs, dominant ideas, central values and social norms were all seen as providing support for and legitimizing an exploitative economic system of social relations. Even before the age of television, the Frankfurt School of critical theory argued that the emerging mass culture was a form of **social control** that kept the masses inactive and uncritical, constructing them as passive consumers of undemanding entertainment. The irony of this Marxist critique is that it differentiated high culture from mass culture and saw more value in the former, even though this was the province of the educated upper classes.

Cultural reproduction involves not just the continuation and development of language, general values and norms but also the reproduction of social inequalities. For example, on the face of it, **education** should be a 'great leveller', enabling capable people from across **gender**, **class** and ethnic lines to achieve their ambitions. However, a large body of work over some forty years or so has shown that education systems work to reproduce existing cultural and social divisions.

The most systematic general theory of cultural reproduction to date is that of Pierre Bourdieu (1986). This connects economic position, social **status** and symbolic capital with cultural knowledge and skills. The central concept in Bourdieu's theory is *capital*, the various forms of which are used to gain resources and give people an advantage. Bourdieu identifies social capital, cultural capital, symbolic capital and economic capital as the key forms. Social capital refers to membership of and involvement in elite social **networks**; cultural capital is gained within the **family** environment and through education, usually leading to certificates such as degrees and other credentials; symbolic capital refers to the prestige, status and other forms of honour, which enable those with high status to dominate those with lower status; while economic capital refers to wealth, income and other economic resources. Bourdieu argues that these forms of capital can be exchanged.

Those with high *cultural capital* may be able to trade it for *economic capital*; during interviews for well-paid jobs, their superior knowledge and credentials give them an advantage over other applicants. Those with high *social capital* may 'know the right people' or 'move in the right social circles' and be able to exchange this for *symbolic capital* such as respect from others and increased social status, which increases their **power** chances. These exchanges always take place within fields or social arenas which organize social life, and each field has its own 'rules of the game' that are not transferable to others.

Cultural capital can exist in an *embodied state*, as we carry it around with us in our ways of thinking, speaking and moving. It can exist in an *objectified state* in the possession of works of art, books and clothes. And it can be found in *institutionalized forms* such as educational qualifications, which are easily translated into economic capital in the labour market. As many other sociologists have found, education is not a neutral field divorced from the wider society. The culture and standards within the education system already reflect that society, and schools systematically advantage those who have already acquired cultural capital in their family and through the social networks in which it is embedded. In this way, the education system plays a crucial part in the cultural reproduction of existing society with its embedded social inequalities.

Since the 1980s, an increasing interest in the contours of the 'consumer society' has brought the study of culture closer to the mainstream of sociology. Investigating the practices of buying and consuming products and services has meant revisiting the critique of mass culture, but this time round sociologists have approached this from the point of view of the consumer and the audience. As the previously uniform mass culture has diversified to target smaller and niche markets, the subject of taste and the existence of 'taste cultures' has arisen. Are people's cultural tastes directly related to class position, gender and **ethnicity** or do they vary independently of these structural positions?

Critical Points

In many critical studies of culture, there has been an assumption that popular culture is in some way inferior to high culture. Popular culture requires little effort, education or knowledge to enjoy, while high culture demands much knowledge and sensitivity to be properly appreciated. However, the legitimacy of high culture has rested on the underlying idea that making the effort is worthwhile as it cultivates 'better people' and a more civilized society. Steiner (1983) argued that this claim has been conclusively falsified. During the Second World War, at the same time as the German armed forces were carrying out mass murder in European concentration camps, classical concerts went on uninterrupted. The claim that high culture 'civilizes', says Steiner, is patently false.

Postmodern theorists also see that the distinction between high and popular culture cannot be sustained and have argued that these are just different preferences and taste choices unrelated to notions of superior and inferior forms. The flattening out of cultural differences is seen by some as liberating, allowing, for the first time, the serious study of popular cultural forms in sociology. More recent work has explored the cultural significance of Lady Gaga, David Beckham and representations of disability in TV soap operas. Others argue that the real test of cultural taste is how it impacts on life chances, as Bourdieu recognized.

Continuing Relevance

The 1980s 'cultural turn' in the social **sciences** brought the study of culture into mainstream sociology, and much of this work is insightful, exploring the roles of cultural production and consumption in shaping lifestyles and life chances. Studying culture also shows us that the world of symbolic representations, entertainment and media can tell us much about social relations. However, recent critique of cultural studies sees too much of this work as 'decorative sociology', privileging the study of texts, **discourses** and interpretation at the expense of real social relations and people's lives as lived (Rojek and Turner 2000). This is a legitimate concern, and studies of culture will need to ensure that structured power relations and the historical development of cultural institutions are not ignored.

Recent theories of the global mixing of cultures is given an interesting twist in Giulianotti and Robertson's (2006) analysis of the migrant experiences of Glasgow Celtic and Rangers supporters in the United States. Rather than assimilating into the more powerful sporting culture of the USA, the Scottish migrants in this study shifted their old identities, allegiances and antagonisms into the new context and made little attempt to develop an interest in the indigenous sporting culture. In addition, a majority of members of the North American Supporters' Clubs (NASCs) regard themselves as unambiguously 'Scottish' despite many having gained American or Canadian citizenship; the clubs hold traditional Scottish Burns suppers, and members have generally retained their dialects and accents. However, a key issue for the NASCs, given the different experience of their children in the North American cultural context, is 'the cross-generational transmission of cultural identities'.

References and Further Reading

Bourdieu, P. (1986) *Distinction: A Social Critique of the Judgement of Taste* (London: Routledge & Kegan Paul).

Featherstone, M. (2007) *Consumer Culture and Postmodernism* (2nd edn, London: Sage).

Giulianotti, R., and Robertson, R. (2006) 'Glocalization, Globalization and Migration: The Case of Scottish Football Supporters in North America', *International Sociology*, 21(2): 171–98.

Jenks, C. (1993) 'Introduction: The Analytic Bases of Cultural Reproduction Theory', in C. Jenks (ed.), *Cultural Reproduction* (London: Routledge), pp. 1–16.

Rojek, C., and Turner, B. S. (2000) 'Decorative Sociology: Towards a Critique of the Cultural Turn', *Sociological Review*, 48(4): 629–48.

Steiner, G. (1983) *In Bluebeard's Castle: Some Notes on the Redefinition of Culture* (New Haven, CT: Yale University Press).

Identity

Working Definition

The distinctive aspects of an individual's character or the character of a group, which relates to their sense of self.

Origins of the Concept

Identities are made, not given at birth. The work of both Cooley (1902) and Mead (1934) in the early twentieth century has been important for the development of theories of self and identity. Cooley's 'looking glass' theory argued that the evaluation that others have of a person affects and potentially alters that person's view of themselves. However, Mead's was the first systematic sociological theory of the formation and development of the self which insisted that the self is not an innate part of our biology, nor does it emerge simply with the developing human brain, but is formed in social **interactions** with others. What Mead demonstrated is that the study of the individual's self cannot be divorced from the study of **society** – and that requires a sociological perspective. The emergence of a sense of self is a necessary prelude to the formation of a personal identity. Studies of identity have multiplied over the last thirty years or so, as previously solid collective sources have become weakened in the face of **consumerism** and a heightened individualization which allows for more flexibility in the shaping of identities.

Meaning and Interpretation

A person's identity is, at root, their own understanding of who they are as an individual. But identities have clear social aspects because our identity is related to the identities of other people and their identities are related to ours. Human identities are both personal and social in another way, because they are formed in the continuing processes of interaction. Jenkins (2014) sees three central parts to an identity: an individual or personal element, a collective or social element and the embodiment of an identity. This last is important to include, as identity is always embedded within the physical body of a person. Identities are constructed from several sources and are multi-layered.

A basic distinction is made between primary and secondary identities that are linked to primary and secondary **socialization** processes. Primary identities are those formed in early life, such as **gender** identity or **ethnicity**, while secondary identities build on these and include social roles, occupations and **status** positions. Acknowledging this makes clear that identities are complex and fluid, changing as people gain new roles or leave behind old ones. It also means that identity is rarely fixed but is in a constant process of change. An important consequence is that identities mark out similarities and differences. Our individual identity often feels unique and different from others. Names, for example, are an illustration of individual differences. Today many parents actively seek out a unique name for their offspring that marks them out as special rather than choosing '**family**' names or ones in common usage. By contrast, collective identities display similarity with others. To identify yourself and be identified by others as, say, working **class**, an environmentalist or a professional sociologist can be a source of pride and group solidarity or even shame.

Whatever the perception we may have of our own identity, individual and social identities are tightly bound together within the embodied self. A good example of the close linkage between social identity and embodiment is in the study of '**stigma**' by Goffman ([1963] 1990). He shows how disabled people, for example, can be more readily stigmatized on the basis of readily observable physical impairments (discredit*ed* stigma), which make individual identities more difficult to 'manage', than with non-physical impairments, which can be more easily hidden (discredit*ing* stigma). Goffman adopts a theatrical analogy which suggests that interactions can be analysed as though people are actors playing roles on a stage or in a play. This is not meant to be taken literally but provides a way of seeing that social actors do, in fact, play numerous roles which carry expectations that partly shape how people act. The skill of impression management is that it helps individuals to manage how others see and behave towards them.

Social influences on gender identity flow through many diverse channels. Studies of parent–child interactions, for example, have shown distinct differences in the treatment of boys and girls even when the parents believe their reactions to both are the same. The toys, picture books and television programmes experienced by young children all tend to emphasize differences between male and female attributes; though the situation is changing, male characters tend to play more active, adventurous roles, while females are portrayed as passive, expectant and domestically oriented. Feminist researchers have demonstrated how cultural and media products marketed to young audiences embody traditional attitudes towards gender and towards the sorts of aims and ambitions girls and boys are expected to have.

Critical Points

Some recent theories challenge the very notion of 'identity' as something that is relatively fixed or assigned to people by socializing agents. Following Foucault, they argue that gender and **sexuality**, along with all of the other terms that come with these concepts, constitute a specific **discourse** of sexuality rather than referring to something that is objectively real. For example, Foucault argued that the male homosexual identity that today is associated with gay men was not part of the dominant discourse on sexuality in the nineteenth century and before. Therefore, this form of identification just did not exist for people until it became part of, or was created within, the discourses of medicine and psychiatry. Identities, then, can be seen as pluralistic, quite unstable and subject to radical change over a lifetime.

Continuing Relevance

Identity is a concept that has grown in significance and across numerous specialist fields. **Social movement** studies now explore how collective identity is built, studies of class look at shifting identification with social class groups, and sociologists of health have shown how personal identity can be disrupted at the onset and progression of chronic illness. The concept of identity is now very well established in sociology and is used to study many new subjects.

For most people there is a clear divide between the identity they perform while at work and that which pertains in their private, home environment. However, in some workplaces there has been an attempt to 'humanize' the working environment (especially offices, call centres and other service-oriented workplaces) by introducing opportunities and facilities for a range of 'fun' activities. In an analysis of the literature on this subject, Baldry and Hallier (2010) argue that, in spite of its appealing aspects, such attempts may backfire. Workers may resent management's perceived intrusion into their private identities and attempts to change their values. Rather than 'oiling the wheels' of productivity, workplace fun may lead to heightened levels of **alienation**.

Since the 1980s there has been a renewed interest in social movements as sources of identity, and Saunders (2008) explores the collective identities forged within environmental movement organizations. Movements are broadly based collectivities focused around some central ideas or ideological preferences. Yet the solidarity within movements tends to be created in some of the social movement organizations (such as Greenpeace or Earth First!) which constitute that broader movement. As activists tend to forge identities within organizations, their allegiance is strong and paradoxically can be one source of the internal divisions often found in social movement networks.

References and Further Reading

Baldry, C., and Hallier, J. (2010) 'Welcome to the House of Fun: Work Space and Social Identity', *Economic and Industrial Democracy*, 31(1): 150–72.

Cooley, C. H. (1902) *Human Nature and the Social Order* (New York: Scribner's).

Goffman, E. ([1963] 1990) *Stigma: Notes on the Management of Spoiled Identity* (London: Penguin).

Elias, N. (2000) 'Homo clausus and the Civilizing Process', in P. du Gay, J. Evans and P. Redman (eds), *Identity: A Reader* (London: Sage), pp. 284–96.

Jenkins, R. (2014) *Social Identity* (4th edn, London: Routledge).

Mead, G. H. (1934) *Mind, Self and Society*, ed. C. W. Morris (Chicago: University of Chicago Press).

Saunders, C. (2008) 'Double-Edged Swords? Collective Identity and Solidarity in the Environmental Movement', *British Journal of Sociology*, 59(2): 227–53.

Ideology

Working Definition

'Common-sense' ideas and widespread beliefs in a **society** that serve, often indirectly, the interests of dominant groups and legitimize their position.

Origins of the Concept

The concept of ideology was first used in France in the late eighteenth century to describe a putative **science** of ideas and knowledge – an idea-ology. In this sense, ideology was to be a discipline akin to psychology or ecology. This conception of ideology is now seen as 'neutral', which does not imply that ideas are biased or misleading, simply that there are a variety of ideas in society that can be studied and compared. In the 1930s and 1940s, Karl Mannheim attempted to revive this idea in his sociology of knowledge, which linked particular modes of thought to their social bases. Mannheim thought that, for example, the knowledge produced in different social **class** contexts could only be partial and that a sociology of knowledge should aim to bring the varied interpretations together to produce a better understanding of society as a whole. The neutral concept of ideology has not proved particularly popular.

A much more critical version of ideology has been the dominant conception in sociology. Karl Marx saw ideology as an important factor in the reproduction of capitalist class domination. He argued that powerful groups are able to control the dominant ideas circulating in society, legitimizing their own privileged position.

Thus, the dominant ideas of every age are those that support the ruling class. Ideology is a barrier to equality, and later Marxists spent a lot of time theorizing how ideologies could be combated to raise workers' awareness of their exploitation. Social analysts, they thought, should uncover the distortions of ideology so as to allow the powerless to gain a true perspective on their lives as a prelude to taking action to improve their life conditions. Today the concept of ideology is not as well used as it was in the 1970s and 1980s, and it is much more likely that sociological interest in the **power** of ideas will draw on the Foucauldian concept of discourses and their effects, which has shifted the focus away from ideas and beliefs towards language use, speech and documentary sources. However, the two concepts are not necessarily opposed.

Meaning and Interpretation

To describe an idea or statement as 'ideological' is to suggest that in some important respect it is false, misleading or a partial account of reality and one that can and should be corrected. The concept of ideology therefore implies that it is possible to get at the facts or the truth about society. Studies of ideology have been dominated by the Marxist tradition, which sees ideologies as intimately related to class domination. Religious beliefs of a natural order, as suggested in statements such as 'the rich man in his castle, the poor man at his gate, God made them high and lowly and ordered their estate', are one prominent source of ideology. Marxist theory sees such ideas as dripping with ideological intent, aiming to convince the dispossessed and exploited that inequality is natural and that their lowly position in society has been ordered by God.

In the twentieth century, members of the neo-Marxist Frankfurt School of critical theory studied what they called the '**culture** industry' of film, TV, popular music, radio, newspapers and magazines and argued that, in mass societies, cultural production had become just as profit-oriented as any other industry, churning out standardized products with little real value. Cultural differences have become levelled down and cultural products are targeted at the largest possible audience. For the Frankfurt School, this levelling down means mass culture is not challenging or educational but comforting and lifeless, discouraging criticism and encouraging passivity. One useful aspect of the critical concept of ideology is the way it links ideas and cultural products with power and power relations. Ideology is about the exercise of symbolic power – how ideas are used to hide, justify or legitimate the interests of dominant groups.

The Glasgow Media Group produced a body of work concentrating on factual news reporting which pointed out the ideological aspects of the ostensibly neutral process of news gathering and reporting. In a series of empirical studies using content analysis techniques, the group showed how TV news reporting systematically generates bias. For example, when dealing with industrial disputes, news reports tend to favour government and management views at the expense of those of striking workers. Management are said to make 'offers' while workers and trade unions make 'demands', and reports of industrial relations are presented in a selective and biased fashion. News journalists tend to be from middle-class backgrounds, and their views chime with those of dominant groups in society, who inevitably see strikers as dangerous and irresponsible. The main conclusion from this work is that news reporting must be selective and can never be neutral or 'objective'. News reporting is one more cultural product which reflects the unequal society within which it exists and, as such, is one more source of ideology.

Critical Points

As the **mass media** of communications have expanded both in the huge variety of their contemporary forms and in the proportion of the global population that is exposed to these, the scope for production of ideology has increased. Things may be changing, though, as more interactive forms such as websites, chatrooms and blogs rise to prominence, all of which enable a more direct relationship and **interaction** between content producers and their audiences. Blogging, tweeting, and so on, are becoming sources of information in their own right and have played a part in some recent conflicts, giving news as seen by people within **conflict** zones an alternative to mainstream news channels and reports.

Some news producers accused the Glasgow Media Group researchers of exercising their own biases, which lie with striking workers rather than with government and management. They pointed out that, while *Bad News*, for example, contained a chapter on 'The trade unions and the media', there was no chapter on 'Management and the media', indicating an 'ideological' bias on their part. Harrison (1985) gained access to transcripts of ITN news broadcasts in the UK for the period covered by the original 1976 study and argued that the five months analysed were not typical. An abnormal number of days were lost because of industrial action over the period, and it would have been impossible for the news to report all of these. He also thought the group was wrong to claim that news broadcasts concentrated too much on the effects of strikes, as many more people were affected by strikes than took part in them. In short, news reports were not ideologically biased.

Continuing Relevance

The concept of ideology has historically been associated with Marxism and its fate has been inextricably linked to it. With the collapse of Soviet communism and the apparent triumph of neo-liberal **capitalism** since the 1980s, we might assume that the concept of ideology would lose ground. Indeed, if we go by the number of articles mentioning '**discourse**' compared with those using 'ideology', then we can see that the influence of Foucault has shifted sociologists' interest towards social discourses and discursive practices. Since the 1970s there have been several attempts to write off the concept of ideology, but so far the various 'end of ideology' theses seem premature. As long as sociology studies class-divided societies there will be a place for studies of ideology, which form one important aspect of our understanding of cultural reproduction.

References and Further Reading

Freeden, M. (2003) *Ideology: A Very Short Introduction* (Oxford: Oxford University Press).

Glasgow University Media Group (1976) *Bad News* (London: Routledge & Kegan Paul).

Harrison, M. (1985) *TV News: Whose Bias?* (Hermitage, Berks: Policy Journals).

Heywood, A. (2012) *Political Ideologies: An Introduction* (5th edn, Basingstoke: Palgrave Macmillan).

Zeitlin, I. M. (1990) *Ideology and the Development of Sociological Theory* (4th edn, Englewood Cliffs, NJ: Prentice Hall).

Interaction

Working Definition

Any form of social encounter, in formal or informal situations, between two or more individuals.

Origins of the Concept

Routine daily encounters such as conversations, meetings and other seemingly trivial aspects of life may not appear to be 'proper' subjects for a scientific discipline. Yet the tradition of symbolic interactionism in sociology which developed rapidly from the 1920s has demonstrated that studying everyday occurrences such as these provides crucial insights into the character and structures of social life. Typically, social interactions involve both focused and unfocused exchanges. Focused interactions, usually called 'encounters', cover most of our meetings with friends and **family** members. Unfocused interactions are those that are common whenever we are co-present with others but not engaged in one-to-one encounters with them. Shopping, for instance, involves many unfocused interactions in the form of body language, facial expressions and gestures, all of which allow us to get around and perform our daily tasks while in the presence of large numbers of other people.

Other perspectives within the social action tradition, including phenomenology and ethnomethodology, have also concentrated on social interactions. Phenomenologists study how people manage to acquire their taken-for-granted assumptions about the world, while ethnomethodology explores the methods used by people in everyday life to make sense of and structure their worlds.

Meaning and Interpretation

Social interaction takes place partly through non-verbal communication such as bodily comportment and facial expressions. When we compare the human face with that of other species, it does seem remarkably flexible and capable of manipulation. Norbert Elias (1987) argued that studying the face shows how human beings, like all other species, have naturally evolved over a long period of time, but also that this biological basis has been overlaid with cultural features in the process of social development. The human face is naked and very flexible, able to contort into a wide variety of postures. Therefore, Elias sees its development as closely linked to the evolutionary 'survival value' of effective communication systems, and humans communicate a varied range of emotions on just the 'signalling board' of the face. Thus, we use facial expressions and bodily gestures of other people to add to what they communicate verbally and to check both how far they are sincere in what they say and whether we can trust them.

An enormous amount of sociological research in the interactionist tradition has focused on conversations or 'talk'. Language use has long been studied by linguistics, but sociologists are concerned with language primarily as 'talk in context' – that is, how people communicate in different social settings. A distinct perspective that concentrates on language use in context is ethnomethodology, so called because its focus is on the methods used in ordinary social contexts as people go about their everyday lives ('ethnomethods'). In particular, how do people *make sense* of the world in which they live and the behaviour of others? Often we can make sense of what is said in conversation only if we know the social context, which does not appear in the words themselves. The most inconsequential forms of daily talk presume complicated, shared knowledge brought into play by those speaking. The words used in ordinary talk do not always have precise meanings, and we 'fix' what we want to say through the unstated assumptions that underpin it.

Because interactions are shaped by the larger social context, both verbal and non-verbal communication may be perceived and expressed differently by men and women. In societies where men on the whole dominate women in both public and private life, men may feel freer than women to make eye contact with strangers. A man who stares at a woman can be seen as acting in a 'natural' or 'innocent' way, and if the woman is uncomfortable she can evade the gaze by looking away. But a woman who stares at a man is often regarded as behaving in a suggestive or sexually leading manner. In non-verbal communications, men tend to sit in more relaxed ways than women, leaning back with their legs open, while women tend to have a more closed body position, sitting upright with their hands in their lap and legs crossed. Some research has also shown that women seek and break eye contact more often than men. These seemingly small-scale, micro-level interactions provide subtle cues which demonstrate men's **power** over women in the wider **society**.

Critical Points

Sociologists study interactions of some kind in almost every research project, whether it be of micro-level exchanges or of interactions between states in the international arena of global politics. However, the interactionist perspective is often seen as ignoring issues of social structure, which shape the type and quality of interactions, concentrating on face-to-face interactions. Indeed, some micro-level theorists deny that there are such things as social structures at all and argue that the focus of sociologists should be social relationships and interactions which continually re-create social order; it is this routinized social order that some mistake for thing-like social structures. Other sociologists who do discuss social structure believe that, although we may not be able to see structures, their effects are real and observable. After all, we may not see gravity, but scientists seem to have no problem inferring its existence by measuring its effects on other observable phenomena.

Continuing Relevance

The concept of interaction is so fundamental it would be difficult to 'do sociology' without it. It has also proved to be a remarkably flexible and adaptive concept that has been applied in many different areas of human existence. Evidence of this can be seen in the latest round of studies that focus on making sense of social interactions in cyberspace, a technologically mediated environment that is, in many ways, very different from the everyday face-to-face world. Studying such very different interactions is likely to require new concepts to extend our understanding of social interaction.

Understanding communication and social interaction in virtual environments is a growing field of inquiry. Thomas Ploug (2009) argues that there are some key differences between people's interactions and ethical behaviour inside and outside cyberspace. For example, in cyberspace, people often perceive the online environment as in some way 'not real' – or not as real as the physical world they inhabit. Ploug suggests that this impacts on their approach to morality in the online world. Online environments also tend to exhibit a certain lack of persuasiveness compared to evidence in the 'real world'. There are reportedly many more episodes of arguing and expressions of displeasure online than in face-to-face interaction, and disagreements are expressed in much stronger and often aggressive or abusive ways. All this suggests that there is a need to understand exactly how and why online environments seem to produce different ethical standards and what consequences this may have for future online interactions.

References and Further Reading

Elias, N. (1987) 'On Human Beings and their Emotions: A Process-Sociological Essay', *Theory, Culture and Society*, 4(2–3): 339–61.

Garfinkel, H. (1984) *Studies in Ethnomethodology* (2nd rev. edn, Cambridge: Polity).

Goffman, E. (2005) *Interaction Ritual: Essays in Face-to-Face Behaviour* (2nd edn, New Brunswick, NJ: Aldine Transaction), esp. Joel Best's Introduction.

Ploug, T. (2009) *Ethics in Cyberspace: How Cyberspace May Influence Social Interpersonal Interaction* (New York: Springer).

Ten Have, P. (2004) *Understanding Qualitative Research and Ethnomethodology* (London: Sage), esp. chapters 2 and 3.

Mass Media

Working Definition

All communication forms which are capable of reaching a large audience, including radio, television, the worldwide web and much more.

Origins of the Concept

For most of human history the main means of communication was speech, with face-to-face communication being the norm. In oral **cultures**, information, ideas and knowledge were transmitted across generations by word of mouth. Once speech could be written down and stored, the first writing cultures began to emerge, initially in China around 3,000 years ago. An important precursor to modern mass media in the mid-fifteenth century was the Gutenberg movable type printing press, which enabled texts to be reproduced. More immediate transmission of messages became possible with the invention of radio and television, both of which proved enormously popular with audiences. Television in particular has attracted the interest of sociologists, as much for the quality of its content as its ability to reach a global population. In the late twentieth century, new digital technologies, such as the mobile phone, video games, digital television and the Internet, revolutionized the mass media yet again, introducing the possibility of interactive media, the impact of which sociology is yet fully to understand and evaluate.

Meaning and Interpretation

Early sociological work on the mass media tended to be broadly functionalist, looking at the integrative functions of the media. For example, media produce a continuous flow of information about **society** and the wider world, which creates a shared experience so that we all feel part of the same world. Mass media also explain world events and aid our understanding, which plays an important role in the **socialization** of children. And media content entertains, providing a welcome release from the mundane world of work. But the main problem with such accounts is that they seem only to describe certain positive aspects of the mass media and ignore the active interpretations of the audience itself. More seriously, functionalist accounts do not take into account major **conflicts** of interest and the production of **ideology** aimed at maintaining existing inequalities.

By contrast, political economy approaches show how the major means of communication have come to be owned by private interests. For example, in the twentieth century, a few 'press barons' owned a majority of the pre-war press and were able to set the agenda for news and its interpretation. In the global age, ownership of media crosses national borders, and media magnates now own transnational media corporations, giving them international recognition and influence. As in other industries, economic interests in media ownership work to exclude those voices that lack economic **power**, and those that *do* survive are those least likely to criticize the prevailing distribution of wealth and power.

Symbolic interactionist studies have become more popular since the late twentieth century. Thompson (1995) analysed the relationship between the media and the development of industrial societies, distinguishing between *face-to-face* **interaction**, *mediated interaction*, where a media technology is involved, and *mediated quasi-interaction*, where interaction is stretched across time and space but does not link individuals directly. The first two types are 'dialogical' – conversation or phone calls where individuals communicate in a direct way – but the third is 'monological' – a TV programme, for example, is a one-way form of communication. Mass media change the balance between the public and the private, bringing more information into the public domain than before and creating many avenues for debate.

Jean Baudrillard argued that the coming of the mass media, particularly electronic media such as television, has transformed the very nature of our lives. TV does not just 'represent' the world, it increasingly defines what the world in which we live actually is. Hence, the border between reality and representation has collapsed and we can no longer separate out media representations from reality. Baudrillard sees both as *part of* the hyperreal world. Hyperreality is a world in which the ultimate guarantor of authenticity and reality is to be seen on TV and in the media – to be 'more real than the real'. This may be one part of an explanation for the growth of our celebrity culture, where the only genuinely acceptable sign of success and significance is to appear on TV or in glossy magazines.

Critical Points

Research studies have repeatedly demonstrated that representations of girls and women in the mass media use traditional stereotypes of **gender** roles. Women are conventionally seen in domestic roles as housewives and homemakers, as objects of male sexual desire, or in working situations that extend the domestic role – such as nurses, carers or office workers. Such representations have been fairly consistent across news reports, drama and entertainment programming. Media representations of ethnic minorities and disabled people have also been seen as reinforcing rather than challenging stereotypes. Black and Asian people were noticeably absent from mainstream television until quite recently. Even when they were present – for example, in news reports and documentaries – this tended to be as problematic social groups. Disabled people have been all but invisible in TV drama and entertainment and, when they are included, are over-represented among criminals and mentally unstable characters or among 'the bad, mad and sad'. Sociologists argue that media representations are not the *cause* of discrimination, but stereotypical representations can *reinforce* existing negative ideas of social groups.

A fair amount of critical media theory treats the mass of people as passive recipients of media messages rather than as able to engage with and even to resist them. But many **social movement** organizations, such as Greenpeace, do try to compete with the mass media and create alternative versions of reality which motivate the uncommitted to environmental activism. More recent audience studies have also added balance, finding that people are active consumers who are quite able to interpret and critique media content.

Continuing Relevance

Sociological theories of the various forms of media show us that they can never be assumed to be politically neutral or socially beneficial. At the same time, though, the ills of the world cannot be placed at the door of mass media, and we should assume that people are not 'cultural dopes', incapable of perceiving bias. The next stage for sociologists of the media is studying the new digital media, which may well mean devising new theories that are able to understand them better. It seems unlikely that the theories developed to account for television and radio will also be able to deal with the Internet.

Media reports have often been blamed for creating health scares by exaggerating the **risks** associated with particular viruses or diseases. However, Clarke and Everest's (2006) content analysis of magazines in Canada investigated a more common issue, namely the reporting of cancer in the print media, which, they argue, is routinely linked to fear and fearfulness in the context of new medical breakthroughs as possible 'cures'. In particular, cancer was seen as almost inevitable, presented through sets of scary statistics, routinely conflated with fear and set within a medical **discourse**. In addition, the magazines focused predominantly on breast cancer as opposed to other types. One consequence of such representations is to reinforce public fears about cancer and the medical model as the dominant discursive frame for dealing with the issue.

Media reporting on contentious issues has been subject to much research, and, in the USA as elsewhere, there has been interest in the reporting of terrorism and government policy. Altheide (2007) conducted a qualitative analysis of American media sources after the 2001 terror attacks known as 9/11. He argues that previously significant changes in US foreign policy were not reported by major news organizations and therefore faced little or no challenge. Following 9/11, government media messages were reframed to fuse a new 'war on terror' agenda into the existing 'fear of crime' discourse. The result has been the presentation of everyday life as increasingly dangerous and risky.

References and Further Reading

Altheide, D. (2007) 'The Mass Media and Terrorism', *Discourse and Communication*, 1(3): 287–308.

Andreasson, K. (ed.) (2015) *Digital Divides: The New Challenges and Opportunities of e-Inclusion* (Boca Raton, FL: CRC Press).

Clarke, J. N., and Everest, M. M. (2006) 'Cancer in the Mass Print Media: Fear, Uncertainty and the Medical Model', *Social Science and Medicine*, 62(10): 2591–600.

Flew, T. (2014) *New Media: An Introduction* (Melbourne: Oxford University Press), esp. chapter 4.

Takahashi, T. (2010) *Audience Studies: A Japanese Perspective* (London: Routledge), esp. the Introduction.

Thompson, J. B. (1995) *The Media and Modernity: A Social Theory of the Media* (Cambridge: Polity).

Public Sphere

Working Definition

The arena of public debate and discussion in modern societies, consisting of many formal and informal spaces.

Origins of the Concept

Modern democracies developed along with the **mass media**, especially newspapers, pamphlets and other publications. In a very real sense, the mass media enabled and encouraged a democratic **culture**. A public sphere developed first in the salons and coffee houses of seventeenth- and eighteenth-century London and Paris, as well as in other European cities, where people would meet to discuss issues of the day. Although only small numbers of the population were involved in this culture, they were vital in the early development of **democracy** because the salons introduced the idea of resolving political problems through public discussion.

Today the mass media are seen negatively, as trivializing the democratic process and creating a climate of general hostility to the business of politics. How did such a radical shift happen and could it be reversed? The key figure in debates on the public sphere is the German philosopher and sociologist Jürgen Habermas, who, based on his studies of language and the process of democratization, developed themes from the Frankfurt School in different directions. He analysed the emergence and development of the mass media from the early eighteenth century to the present day, tracing the creation and subsequent decay of the 'public sphere'.

Meaning and Interpretation

For Habermas ([1962] 1989) the public sphere is an arena of public debate in which issues of general concern can be discussed and opinions formed, which is necessary for effective democratic participation and the democratic process. The public sphere – at least in principle – involves individuals coming together as equals in a forum for public debate. However, the promise offered by the early development of the public sphere has not been fully realized. Democratic debate in modern societies is now stifled by the development of the culture industry. The spread of mass media and mass entertainment causes the public sphere to wither away. Politics is stage-managed in Parliament and the mass media, while commercial interests seem to dominate. 'Public opinion' is formed not through open, rational discussion but through manipulation and control – as, for example, in advertising. On the other hand, the spread of global media can put pressure on authoritarian governments to loosen their hold over state-controlled broadcasting outlets, and many 'closed' societies such as China are discovering that the media can become a powerful force in support of democracy.

Yet, as they become increasingly commercialized, global media encroach on the public sphere in the way described by Habermas. Commercialized media are beholden to the **power** of advertising revenue and compelled to favour content that guarantees high ratings and sales. As a result, entertainment will necessarily triumph over controversy and debate, weakening citizen participation in public affairs and shrivelling the public sphere. The media, which promised so much, have now become part of the problem. But Habermas remains optimistic, arguing that it is still possible to envisage a political **community** beyond individual **nation states** in which issues can be openly debated and where public opinion will influence governments.

Richard Sennett ([1977] 2003) also argued that the private and public spheres have become separated, both physically – with the separate development of residential housing estates, workplaces and leisure developments (including shopping arcades) – and philosophically – in the way we think about our distinct private lives, for example. However, he sees the private sphere as tending to canalize – or take over – the public sphere, so that, for instance, politicians are now judged more on their personal characteristics, such as honesty and sincerity, rather than on their ability to perform a public role. The advent of modern visual media, especially television, has led to a highly developed presentation of self by political figures aimed at matching such expectations of their personalities. Sennett sees this as destructive of an effective political life and representative of the fall of the dedicated public official.

Critical Points

Habermas's ideas have been subject to an important critique. The salon culture that he holds up as an arena of civilized, rational debate was strictly limited to the higher social **classes** and was beyond the reach of the working class. It was an elitist pastime that bore little real resemblance to the needs of mass democratic participation. The public sphere was also constituted by excluding certain social groups, among them women, ethnic minorities and non-property owners. Even though it was essentially limited, the notion of a public sphere allowed middle-class men to perceive themselves and their role and to present it to others as universal.

Feminist scholars argue that Habermas does not pay enough attention to the gendered nature of the public sphere. In separating the public sphere from the domestic, private sphere, many issues that were important for women were simply excluded. Nancy Fraser (1992) argues that the 'public' sphere was never really 'public' if that means open to all. Some 'publics' – such as women – were quite deliberately blocked from participating, demonstrating that conflictual social relations underpinned the idealized conception of a common public sphere. The concept of a public sphere was an **ideology** that helped legitimize social inequalities. Habermas's view that the contemporary mass media are destructive of the public sphere has also been seen as misguided, as the media today may actually enable *more* public debate by airing a variety of public matters and encouraging a wider discussion in **society**. The Internet, with its innumerable forums, blogs and chatrooms, is just the latest example of this, which shows that the public sphere may in fact be expanding rather than contracting.

Continuing Relevance

Habermas's ideas have provoked a good deal of debate and much controversy. Currently, it appears that they have lost some ground in the wake of critique from those who defend the mass media as, on balance, a positive force in society but also from postmodern thinkers, who see fear and mistrust of the 'mass' public in his account. There is some truth in such critiques. And yet Habermas powerfully reminds us that the rational, modernist project still has much to offer social theory.

The mass media have often been singled out as playing a key role in trivializing politics and cultural life. This notion is explored in Graham Murdock's (2010) piece, which looks into the growth of celebrity culture, a more recent subject of interest to sociologists. Murdock analyses shifts in 'visible culture' since the advent of photojournalism in the early 1960s through a study of two British tabloid newspapers (*The Sun* and the *Daily Mirror*). Given the increasing volatility of voting behaviour, politicians have been forced to pay more attention to their own and their party's brand **identity**, which means an increasing concern with appearances and images as presented in the photo-led world of the mass-market press.

China is often seen as completely lacking a public sphere in which contentious issues are aired and decisions arrived at. Alternatively, a state corporatist perspective sees the Chinese authorities as willing to allow the creation of social groups and organizations provided they are licensed and accept state regulation. However, a public controversy in the media around the construction of a hydropower project on the Nu River led the Chinese government to halt the project. Yang and Calhoun (2007) discuss this event in terms of the emergence of a specifically 'green' public sphere in China. This developing public sphere consists of three main elements: 'greenspeak' or environmental **discourse**, groups which produce and consume greenspeak (primarily environmental NGOs), and the media forms which disseminate it. Rejecting the orthodox state corporatist position, the authors argue that it does not give enough weight in the current Chinese context to the creative actions of organizations within civil society.

References and Further Reading

Fraser, N. (1992) 'Rethinking the Public Sphere: A Contribution to the Critique of Actually Existing Democracy', in C. Calhoun (ed.), *Habermas and the Public Sphere* (Cambridge, MA: MIT Press), pp. 109–42.

Habermas, J. ([1962] 1989) *The Structural Transformation of the Public Sphere* (Cambridge, MA: MIT Press).

McKee, A. (2005) *The Public Sphere: An Introduction* (Cambridge: Cambridge University Press).

Murdock, G. F. (2010) 'Celebrity Culture and the Public Sphere: The Tabloidization of Power', in J. Gripsrud and Lennart Weibull (eds), *Media, Markets and Public Spheres: European Media at the Crossroads* (Bristol: Intellect Books), pp. 267–86.

Sennett, R. ([1977] 2003) *The Fall of Public Man* (Cambridge: Cambridge University Press).

Yang, G., and Calhoun, C. (2007) 'Media, Civil Society, and the Rise of a Green Public Sphere in China', *China Information*, 21(2): 211–36.

Health, Illness and the Body

Biomedicine

Working Definition

A Western model of medical practice in which disease is defined objectively, in accordance with the presence of recognized physical symptoms, and scientifically derived medical treatments are sought to restore the body to health.

Origins of the Concept

Before the industrial age and the advent of a scientific understanding of disease, people relied on the traditional remedies passed down through the **family** and a variety of healers who had a special status in the **community**. Some of these older forms of healing continue to exist today, though in the developed countries they come under the general umbrella of 'complementary therapies' or 'alternative medicine'. They are 'alternative' because, for more than two hundred years, Western ideas about medicine have been dominant, as expressed in the biomedical model of health. Biomedicine rose to dominance along with the modern scientific methods on which it is based, and both form the basis of most national healthcare systems across the world. As **science** was applied to illness, disease came to be defined objectively in terms of identifiable and objective 'signs' located in the body, as opposed to the symptoms being experienced by the patient. Formal medical care by trained 'experts' became the accepted way of treating both physical and mental illnesses. Medicine also became a tool of reform for behaviours or conditions perceived as 'deviant' – from crime to homosexuality and mental illness.

Meaning and Interpretation

The biomedical model of health has several central elements. Disease is viewed as a breakdown within the human body which diverts it from its 'normal' state of being or 'health'. To restore the body to health, the cause of the disease must be isolated, treated and eliminated. Biomedicine treats the mind and body separately, so, when patients attend for diagnosis, medical professionals view them as essentially 'sick bodies' rather than as rounded individuals. The focus is on curing their disease, which can be investigated and treated in isolation from all personal factors.

Medical specialists adopt a 'medical gaze', a detached approach to viewing and treating the sick patient. The treatment is to be carried out in a neutral, value-free manner, with information collected and compiled, in clinical terms, in a patient's official file. Properly trained medical specialists are considered the only experts in the treatment of disease and the medical profession adheres to a recognized code of ethics. There is no room for self-taught healers or 'non-scientific' medical practices. The hospital represents the most appropriate environment in which to treat serious illnesses, as these treatments often rely on some combination of technology, medication or surgery.

Critical Points

Over the past thirty years or so the biomedical model has been the object of growing criticism, and much of the sociological literature in this area has a critical tone. Some scholars claim that the effectiveness of scientific medicine is overrated. In particular, some historians of medicine argue that, in spite of the prestige that modern medicine has acquired, improvements in the overall health of populations have very little to do with the implementation of a bio-medical model of illness (McKeown 1976). Most of the dramatic public health improvements seen since the early nineteenth century can actually be attributed to social and environmental changes, such as public sanitation systems, more effective food production methods and better nutrition, alongside public health campaigns leading to effective hygiene practices. McKeown's argument is that these general social and environmental advances contributed more to lowering mortality and morbidity rates than the interventions of scientific medicine. The admittedly significant impact of pharmaceuticals, vaccinations and hospital treatment came to the fore only towards the middle of the twentieth century.

Ivan Illich (1975) even suggested that modern medicine has done more harm than good because of iatrogenesis, or 'physician-caused' disease. Illich argued that there are three types: clinical, social and cultural iatrogenesis. Clinical iatrogenesis is where medical treatment makes the patient worse or creates new conditions. Social iatrogenesis is where medicine expands into more and more areas, creating an artificial demand for its services. Social iatrogenesis, Illich maintained, leads to cultural iatrogenesis, where the ability to cope with the challenges of everyday life is progressively reduced by medical explanations and alternatives. To critics like Illich, the scope of modern medicine should be dramatically reduced.

A further line of criticism is that biomedicine discounts the opinions and experiences of the patients it seeks to treat. Because medicine is based on objective, scientific understanding, there is no need to listen to the individual interpretations that patients give. Critics argue that effective treatment can take place only when the patient is treated as a thinking, capable being with their own valid understanding. The division between medics and patients can often lead to misunderstandings and a lack of trust, social factors that can interfere with diagnosis and treatment.

Finally, scientific medicine presents itself as superior to any alternative form. However, alternative therapies, some old and some very recently devised, have risen to prominence over recent decades. Many people today are likely to make use of acupuncture, homeopathy, reflexology, chiropractic and many more. The reasons for this are complex, but sociologists suggest that people turn to alternative medicine when all biomedical treatments have failed, when they have lost faith in scientific medicine, or when their conditions are chronic and not easily 'cured'. The last point is highly significant.

Medical sociologists identified a shift over the twentieth century in the types of illnesses people face, away from acute and towards chronic, often lifelong ones such as diabetes, high blood pressure and arthritis. As chronic conditions become more common, medicine seems less powerful and the biomedical model seems less appropriate. As such conditions need to be managed rather than cured, patients themselves can become experts on how best to handle their own health, and this is tending to change the doctor–patient relationship as the patient's opinion and experience becomes crucial to treatment regimes. The patient has become an active, 'whole' being whose overall well-being – not just physical health – is important.

Continuing Relevance

Biomedicine has, over recent decades, faced an onslaught of criticism, which shows no sign of abating. However, we have to remember that it remains the dominant model for healthcare systems around the world, and the preventative vaccinations against life-threatening conditions such as polio and tuberculosis have transformed infant mortality rates and saved many lives. In times of health crisis, such as the swine flu outbreak of 2009 or the emergence and spread of HIV/AIDS in the 1980s, people still look to medical science to provide effective treatments, which probably indicates an underlying assumption that biomedicine is a superior form.

However, it is now generally accepted that chronic and disabling conditions have become much more salient and politically significant, and the sociology of health and illness needs to embrace disability studies if the field is to remain vibrant. Scambler and Scambler's (2010) edited collection brings together some of the innovative scholarship in this area, uniting around the contention that chronic illness and disabilities amount to 'assaults on the lifeworld' which demand that we grasp the interrelation of the psychological, biological and sociological if we are to understand them properly.

The rise of alternative medicine presents a constant challenge for mainstream healthcare – should alternative therapies be kept out or allowed in? The relationship between these two systems is explored in a study by Mizrachi et al. (2005) which looks at collaborations in an Israeli hospital setting between biomedical practitioners and alternative therapists, mainly acupuncturists. Alternative therapists had managed to 'invade the fortress', but they had signally failed to shift the boundaries between the two systems. Biomedical professionals adopted a strategy of 'boundary at work' or 'on the job' rather than a formal top-down policy, in order to contain the potential competitor while also avoiding increasing tensions. Using a variety of subtle methods, biomedical professionals are able to control the alternative practitioners but also have to afford them a measure of legitimacy.

References and Further Reading

Illich, I. (1975) *Medical Nemesis: The Expropriation of Health* (London: Calder & Boyars).

McKeown, T. (1976) *The Role of Medicine: Dream, Mirage or Nemesis?* (Oxford: Blackwell).

Mizrachi, N., Shuval, J. T., and Gross, S. (2005) 'Boundary at Work: Alternative Medicine in Biomedical Settings', *Sociology of Health and Illness*, 27(1): 20–43.

Nettleton, S. (2013) *The Sociology of Health and Illness* (3rd edn, Cambridge: Polity), esp. chapter 1.

Scambler, G., and Scambler, S. (eds) (2010) *New Directions in the Sociology of Chronic and Disabling Conditions: Assaults on the Lifeworld* (Basingstoke: Palgrave Macmillan).

Medicalization

Working Definition

The process through which lifestyle matters, such as weight, smoking or sexual practices, become transformed into medical issues to be treated by medical professionals.

Origins of the Concept

The concept of medicalization was devised in the 1960s and 1970s as part of a critical attack on the perceived dangers of an expanding medical profession, which some saw as becoming too powerful. Critics such as Ivan Illich, Irving Zola, R. D. Laing, Thomas Szasz and Michel Foucault saw medicine as a form of **social control**, with patients falling under the supervision of medical professionals. Szasz, for example, criticized the growing expertise of psychiatry and described many conditions that were labelled 'mental illness' as simply 'problems with living'. Some behaviours which were best characterized as adaptations to difficult circumstances were being medicalized and people brought under the control and supervision of experts with the **power** to detain them. Since the 1970s, the concept of medicalization has moved into the mainstream of sociological studies of health and illness.

Meaning and Interpretation

For sociologists who are critical of the biomedical model, the medical profession as a whole holds a position of power that they perceive as unwarranted and even dangerous. One aspect of this social power comes from the ability of the medical profession to define exactly what does and what does not constitute illness and health. By doing so, medics are arbiters of 'medical truth', and their views have to be taken seriously by governments and the general public. However, a more stringent criticism of modern medicine concerns the way that, over time, it has continually expanded into more and more realms of life that were previously considered private or just part of everyday lifestyles. This long-term process is described as medicalization.

Feminist sociologists have shown how many aspects of women's lives, such as pregnancy and childbirth, have been medicalized and appropriated by modern medicine. In the developed world, childbirth routinely takes place in hospitals under the direction of predominantly male specialists. Pregnancy, a common and natural phenomenon, has come to be treated as something akin to an 'illness' that is laden with **risks** and dangers and thus has to be constantly monitored using the latest technologies, such as ultrasound scans and other examinations. Although this may seem a 'good thing', as medicine has helped to lower the child mortality rate, ensuring that a majority of babies and mothers survive child-birth, feminists see that as a partial story. Women have also lost control over this process, a key part of their lives, and their opinions and knowledge are deemed irrelevant by the new experts.

Similar concerns about the medicalization of apparently 'normal' conditions have been raised in relation to hyperactivity in young children, unhappiness or mild depression – commonly regulated with the help of medications such as Prozac – and persistent tiredness, which has been redefined as chronic fatigue syndrome. An issue with such episodes of medicalization is that, once diagnosed in medical terms, the 'cure' tends to be found in medicines and drugs which bring with them side effects.

Ivan Illich argued forcefully that the expansion of modern medicine has done more harm than good because of iatrogenesis, or 'physician-caused' illness. According to Illich, one type of iatrogenesis is social iatrogenesis, or medicaliza-tion, which creates an artificial demand for medical services. As medicalization progresses, people become less able to deal with their own health and more dependent on healthcare professionals. This dependency leads to a greater demand for health services and the expansion of medical services in a vicious upward cycle that pushes health budgets higher at the expense of other services. For Illich, the key to changing this is to challenge the power of medics in society.

Critical Points

Critics of medicalization see the thesis as somewhat overplayed. There are some problems with the expansion of medicine into new areas, but medicalization also brings many benefits. Moving childbirth into hospitals may have sidelined some local 'experts', but the major benefit is that the overwhelming majority of babies are born safely and even very premature babies are likely to survive. Historical accounts of childbirth before modern medicine now read like horror stories, and it was common for babies and/or mothers to die in the process. Surely no one would want to deny that hospital childbirth, for all its faults, is genuinely an improvement? Similarly, medicalization can allow people with some conditions to have them taken seriously and to find help. Those suffering with chronic fatigue syndrome were often seen as malingerers, people with ME struggled to convince others of the reality of their symptoms, and children with ADHD were seen as just plain naughty before the condition was identified as a genuine medical problem. Medicalization may not be as damaging or dangerous as some social theorists believe.

Continuing Relevance

The medicalization thesis has been an important strand of criticism in many sociological studies, and the recent challenges to biomedical dominance seem to suggest that the thesis has found a receptive audience. But we do need to temper our criticisms with the recognition that modern healthcare systems are capable of change, such as the introduction of some less invasive complementary therapies into the mainstream. What was once a radical and, in truth, rather eccentric and marginal approach to **biomedicine** and health has in the twenty-first century quite rapidly become part of many accounts of health and illness.

The issue of obesity is now seen as a global medical problem which threatens to overwhelm national health systems. Wray and Deery (2008) look at the way that body size has been brought under the gendered medical gaze, with particular implications for women's body image and self-esteem. In particular, large body size has come to be seen as symbolic of broader moral failures and unnecessary over-indulgence. The authors argue that this illegitimate connection threatens to undermine women's perceptions of an equal right to healthcare as well as leading them to question their sense of self.

What has sleep to do with medicalization? One study of newspaper representations of the health problems of insomnia and snoring suggests that sleep may be yet another part of life to be medicalized (Williams et al. 2008). The authors show that two quite similar and related issues – insomnia and snoring – are treated differently in media reports of sleep problems. In the case of insomnia, the condition is reported as a symptom rather than an illness, and one that is related to the individual's habits. In this way, although quite sympathetic, newspapers suggest behavioural changes, with pills and treatments viewed as a 'last resort'. By contrast, snoring is seen as akin to passive smoking – affecting others – and a clear health problem in its own right, leading potentially to serious conditions such as sleep apnoea. Not just medical professionals, then, but journalists too play a key role in the social processes leading to medicalization.

References and Further Reading

Nye, R. A. (1995) 'The Evolution of the Concept of Medicalization in the Late Twentieth Century', *Journal of the History of the Behavioral Sciences*, 39(2): 115–29.

Williams, S. J., Seale, C., Boden, S., Lowe, P. K., and Steinberg, D. L. (2008) 'Medicalization and Beyond: The Social Construction of Insomnia and Snoring in the News', *Health*, 12(2): 251–68.
Wray, S., and Deery, R. (2008) 'The Medicalization of Body Size and Women's Healthcare', *Health Care for Women International*, 29(3): 227–43.

Sick Role

Working Definition

A concept devised by Talcott Parsons to explain the social expectations attached to illness and the behaviour of sick people, deviation from which leads to sanctions and social **stigma**.

Origins of the Concept

When people fall ill they seek advice from medical professionals, who examine them, provide a diagnosis, and suggest a course of treatment aimed at restoring them back to health. This is an apparently simple and self-explanatory process – but not according to the American sociologist Talcott Parsons. Parsons (1952) observed that, although health and illness appear to be simple matters that lie outside the remit of sociology, in fact there is good reason to believe that we should approach them as social phenomena, using standard sociological concepts. Parsons argued that when people are ill they behave in certain socially approved ways, and if they deviate from these they may not be accepted as 'ill' at all. He also saw that there exist some key gatekeepers who sanction our illness as well as our return to health. The concept of a 'sick role' fell out of favour along with general functionalism in sociology during the 1970s and 1980s, but there has been some interest in reviving it for use in the comparative study of sickness across societies.

Meaning and Interpretation

For sociologists, people are not only individually sick, they also have to learn what **society** expects of them when they are sick. Parsons argued that there exists a sick role, a way of 'being ill', which societies impose on individuals. This is necessary in order that the disruptive impact of illness on the smooth operation of social institutions can be minimized. When we are ill it often becomes impossible to continue to attend work, perform routine household tasks or play our usual part in **family** life. As a result, our illness has an impact on work colleagues, family members and friends, and the ripples of our inability to participate fully in society effectively spread the burden of illness to others. The sick role is therefore a way of establishing what we should expect of ill people and how they should behave. For Parsons, people have to learn *how* to be ill. That is, they have to understand what is expected of them when they are sick and to put that knowledge into action should they fall ill.

People are not personally responsible for being sick and therefore they cannot be blamed. Scientific medicine understands most illnesses are not the fault of the individual sick person and that the onset of illness is unrelated to the individual's behaviour or actions. Second, the sick role entitles people to some rights and privileges, including the withdrawal from work and family duties, while behaviour that would normally be unacceptable will be tolerated. Third, the sick person must work to regain their health by consulting a medical expert and agreeing to become a 'patient'. This is crucial. The sick role is strictly temporary and 'conditional', contingent on the sick person actively trying to get well. In order to occupy the sick role, an individual must receive the sanction of a medical professional who legitimates their claim of illness. The patient is expected to cooperate in his or her own recovery by following 'doctor's orders', but should they not comply their special **status** may be revoked.

A useful threefold distinction was provided by Freidson (1970), who identified conditional, unconditional and illegitimate sick roles. The conditional legitimate sick role is generally a short-term role performed by those who are ill but are expected to get well again quite soon. By contrast, the unconditional legitimate role applies when individuals have chronic conditions that require management but are unlikely ever to be cured completely. Consequently, this sick role is expected to be a permanent one, and no stigma or sanctions will be enforced if the person does not get well. The illegitimate sick role occurs when people suffer from conditions for which they are widely perceived to be, at least partly, responsible. Illnesses related to alcoholism, obesity or smoking are current examples for which people may well be treated with suspicion or be stigmatized. Freidson's typology helps us to make sense of the reasons for the different ways that groups of people are treated when they are ill.

Critical Points

Parsons's thesis of the sick role has been very influential, linking individual illness to the institutional structure of society. But as Parsonian functionalism lost ground, so too did his thesis of the sick role. One missing element is the actual experience of 'being ill'. How do people experience acute or chronic illness and what impact does it have on their self-identity? This simple question led to a raft of new empirical studies in medical sociology which paid little heed to the ideas of Parsons. The consensual character of his ideas has also been seen as failing accurately to describe many encounters between patients and medical professionals. Empirical work since Parsons has detailed numerous cases of **conflict** as patients challenge the competence and diagnoses of medics. Such challenges have arguably become more widespread given the less deferential attitude towards 'experts' since the late twentieth century. The increased take-up of alternative and complementary therapies shows that many people are prepared to look beyond the dominant biomedical model.

The sick role itself is also far more complex and unclear than Parsons's model suggests. People who develop symptoms may avoid visiting the doctor, sometimes for years, and live without a diagnosis or playing a sick role, but they are clearly still ill. Additionally, the sick role model does not take account of misdiagnoses and medical errors and negligence. Perhaps more seriously, as the disease burden has swung away from acute illness towards chronic conditions such as diabetes and arthritis, there is no universal set of role expectations for people living with such conditions, the impacts of which are many and varied. Hence the concept of a sick role may be less helpful today than was once the case.

Continuing Relevance

Parsons's concept of the sick role is often thought to be less useful in today's age of healthcare consumers, who are more knowledgeable and reflexive than the more deferential recipients of the 1950s. However, Turner (2009) argues that most societies *do* develop sick roles, but these differ. In many Western societies, for example, there exists an individualized sick role, which means that hospital stays for non-life-threatening conditions are generally quite short, visiting hours are limited and the number of visitors is strictly controlled. However, in Japan, a more communal sick role is the norm. Patients tend to stay in hospital longer after their medical treatment is completed and the average hospital stay is much longer than in Western societies. Hospital visits are also more informal, with family and friends often eating together and staying for longer periods. Turner suggests that we can still learn much about the social bases of health from such a comparative sociology of sick roles.

The sick role may appear simple and obvious, but, as Glenton (2003) argues, some people struggle to achieve it and, by not being able to do so, become more rather than less dependent on doctors. In her study of back pain sufferers, many express the fear that they are not believed, that they are seen as malingerers or hypochondriacs, or that they have a form of mental illness. Essentially their status as 'patient' is undermined by the problems of presenting their illness adequately for medical diagnosis, which can lead to delegitimation. Glenton interprets this problem as a failure to achieve the sick role. As such, this shows that Parsons's description still pertains for medics and patients and provides useful evidence that, in spite of the common assumption to the contrary, chronic conditions are not beyond the reach of his original thesis.

References and Further Reading

Freidson, E. (1970) *Profession of Medicine: A Study of the Sociology of Applied Knowledge* (New York: Dodd, Mead).

Glenton, C. (2003) 'Chronic Back Pain Sufferers: Striving for the Sick Role', *Social Science and Medicine*, 57(11): 2243–52.

Parsons, T. (1952) *The Social System* (London: Tavistock).

Shilling, C. (2002) 'Culture, the "Sick Role" and the Consumption of Health', *British Journal of Sociology*, 53(4): 621–38.

Turner, B. S. (2009) *Medical Power and Social Knowledge* (2nd edn, Thousand Oaks, CA: Sage), esp. chapter 3.

White, K. (2009) *An Introduction to the Sociology of Health and Illness* (London: Sage), esp. chapter 6.

Social Model of Disability

Working Definition

An approach which locates the 'cause' of the disadvantages associated with disability within **society** and its organization rather than within the individual person.

Origins of the Concept

Until very recently, Western societies contained a dominant individualistic model of disability. This model suggested that individual limitations or 'disabilities' are the main cause of the problems experienced by disabled people in finding work, moving around, and becoming full citizens in society. In the individual model of disability, bodily 'abnormality' is seen as causing some degree of 'disability' or functional limitation. Medical specialists played a central role in the individual model because it is their job to offer curative and rehabilitative diagnosis to disabled people. For this reason the individual model is often described as a 'medical model'. This model of disability was challenged by activists from within an emergent disabled people's movement from the 1970s onwards.

In late 1960s America and Britain, an alternative perspective was developed which rejected the dominant model and saw disability as a political rather than a medical issue. A new 'social model' of disability emerged which separated impairments (individual problems such as loss of a limb) from disability (disadvantages caused by **organizations** not making provision for people with such impairments). The social model has been the subject of much research and development since then and has strongly influenced equal rights legislation aimed at forcing organizations to make 'reasonable provision' for disabled people. However, in more recent years there has been criticism that the social model needs to be amended to take account of the actual experience of disability.

Meaning and Interpretation

In the UK, the Union of Physically Impaired against Segregation (UPIAS) adopted, in its 1976 manifesto, a radical definition of disability based on the separation of impairment and disability. UPIAS accepted the definition of physical 'impairment' as a biomedical property of individuals, extending it to include non-physical, sensory and intellectual forms of impairment. Disability, though, was understood no longer as the problem of individuals but in terms of the social barriers that people with impairments face in order to participate fully in society. Disability was therefore a denial of full **citizenship** and a form of discrimination.

Mike Oliver (1983) was the first theorist to make explicit the differences between the individual and the social models of disability, and the social model soon became the focus of disability activism and academic studies. The social model provided a coherent explanation of why the social, cultural or historical barriers against disabled people have come about. Historically, many barriers were erected against disabled people's full participation in society, especially during the Industrial Revolution, when they were effectively excluded from the labour market as capitalist factories began to base employment on individual waged labour. Many disabled people were unable to keep or retain jobs, and the state's response was harsh deterrence and institutionalization. Indeed, even today, disabled people's presence in the workforce remains very small.

The social model has been enormously influential in shaping the way that we think about disability today. Although it originated in the UK, the social model has gained global influence. In focusing on the removal of social barriers to full participation, it allows disabled people to concentrate on political strategy. This has led some to argue that, in accepting the social model, disabled people have formed 'a new **social movement**'. In replacing the individual model, which identifies the 'invalidity' of the individual as the cause of disability, with a model in which disability is the result of oppression, the social model has been seen by many disabled people as 'liberating'.

Critical Points

Since the late 1980s, several lines of criticism have been developed against the social model. Some see that it pays no attention to the often painful or uncomfortable experiences of impairment, which are central to many disabled people's lives. Shakespeare and Watson (2002) state: 'We are not just disabled people, we are also people with impairments, and to pretend otherwise is to ignore a major part of our biographies.' Against this, advocates of the social model maintain that, rather than denying everyday experiences of impairment, the social model merely seeks to focus attention on the social barriers to full participation in society.

Medical sociologists often reject the social model, arguing that the division between impairment and disability, on which it rests, is false. These critics claim that the social model separates impairment, which is defined biomedically, from disability, which is defined socially. Medical sociologists see both disability and impairment as socially structured and closely interrelated. For instance, it is not easy to define where one ends and the other begins. Failure to design suitable wheelchair access to a building clearly creates a socially constructed disabling barrier to wheelchair users, but there are many more cases where it is impossible to remove all the sources of disability. Some argue that to be impaired by constant pain or significant intellectual limitation, for example, disables the individual from full participation in society in a way that cannot be removed by social changes. Hence, any full account of disability must also take into account disability caused by impairments, not just those caused by society.

Continuing Relevance

The social model was a radical move in both the academic study of disability and the political engagement of disabled people with the rest of society. And, despite the criticisms noted above, there do not seem to be any alternatives forthcoming to challenge it. The concept of disability itself has been transformed by the social model, and the sociology of disability was only possible after its introduction. The social model has shown, above all else, that disability is not something that can be left to the medical profession; it needs to be studied across all of the social **sciences** too.

The social model approach was adopted by Guo and her colleagues (2005) to examine some of the social barriers to Internet use in China. Using a survey method, the study sampled 122 people across twenty-five provinces. The survey found that only a minority of disabled people were Internet users, but for these individuals the Internet did increase the frequency and quality of their social interactions and helped to reduce social barriers. They were also able to interact with a much larger group of people than would be possible in the 'real world'. However, the findings suggest that a clear digital divide is emerging among disabled people in China, with the majority currently unable to access the Internet. The social model suggests that solutions to this problem are to be found in the reorganization of existing social life and the reshaping of social policies.

References and Further Reading

Barnes, C., and Mercer, G. (2008) *Disability* (Cambridge: Polity), esp. chapters 1 and 2.

Gabel, S., and Peters, S. (2004) 'Presage of a Paradigm Shift? Beyond the Social Model of Disability toward Resistance Theories of Disability', *Disability and Society*, 19(6): 585–600.

Guo, B., Bricout, J., and Huang, J. (2005) 'A Common Open Space or a Digital Divide? A Social Model Perspective on the Online Disability Community in China', *Disability and Society*, 20(1): 49–66.

Oliver, M. (1983) *Social Work with Disabled People* (Basingstoke: Macmillan).

Sapey, B. (2004) 'Disability and Social Exclusion in the Information Society', in J. Swain et al. (eds), *Disabling Barriers – Enabling Environments* (London: Sage), pp. 273–9.

Shakespeare, T., and Watson, N. (2002) 'The Social Model of Disability: An Outdated Ideology?', *Research in Social Science and Disability*, 2: 9–28.

Social Self

Working Definition

The formation of self-awareness that is created as the individual human organism reacts to the varied reactions of others towards it.

Origins of the Concept

It has often been said that human beings are the only creatures who know that they exist and that they will die. Sociologically, this means that human individuals have an awareness of self. George Herbert Mead's (1934) ideas on how the self is created constitute one of the most influential and genuinely sociological theories of self-formation. Mead insisted that a sociological perspective is necessary if we are to understand how the self emerges and develops, and his ideas formed the main basis for the symbolic interactionist tradition in sociology. He argued that, although the self, once created, amounts to the ability to 'think things through', it is an embodied self which resides within a real human individual and, unlike similar concepts such as the 'soul' or 'spirit', cannot be conceived without this.

Meaning and Interpretation

Mead's theory aims to understand how infants begin to develop a sense of themselves as social beings through imitation and play. Young children can be observed mimicking the actions of parents and other children – holding pretend tea parties, digging in plant pots or vacuuming carpets with toy cleaners – having seen adults do similar things. This is the start of the self-formation process. When they move on to playing games, around the age of four or five, the next stage begins. Engaging in play means children have to start to take on aspects of social roles rather than simply mimicking what they see. Mead calls this 'taking the role of the other', which demands that children see their play from the standpoint of other people; it is at this point that a social self starts to emerge. In taking the role of others and effectively seeing themselves 'from the outside', as it were, they also begin to grasp that they are separate people from those others.

Mead's theory is based on the idea of a two-part self: an 'I' and a 'me'. The 'I' represents the human organism, the unsocialized element of the self. The 'me' develops through social interactions, beginning with imitation and play, as discussed above. The social 'me' starts to form at the age of around eight or nine, when play moves on into more organized games with numerous players. To learn organized games, children must understand not just the rules of the game but their place within it, along with the other roles that exist in the game. Children start to see themselves as if from the outside and, rather than adopting a single role, take on the role of a 'generalized other'. It therefore becomes possible for individuals to develop self-consciousness through an 'internal conversation' between the individual, organismic 'I' and the socially generated 'me'. And it is this internal conversation that we ordinarily refer to as 'thinking', a way of 'talking to ourselves', as it were. Developing a sense of self is the bedrock on which quite complex personal and social identities are constructed.

Critical Points

One criticism of Mead's thesis is that the process of self-formation appears relatively unproblematic. But others have suggested that the process is full of **conflict** and emotional turmoil and can leave scars which last a lifetime. This is particularly the case in early **socialization**, when children acquire their sense of **gender** identity. Sigmund Freud and later Freudians argue that unconscious thoughts and feelings play a much more important role in self-formation and gender **identity** than Mead's theory allows for. The process through which boys and girls break their intimate ties with parents can be traumatic for many. Even where the process is relatively smooth, it can lead to boys growing up with difficulty in forming personal relationships. Self-formation is difficult and involves the repression of unconscious desires, an aspect that is absent from Mead's thesis. Others argue that Mead has little to say about the effects of unbalanced parental **power** relationships on the socialization of children, which can lead to selves that do not function well and are riven with internal tension and contradictions.

Continuing Relevance

Mead's theory was very important for the development of sociology. It was the first genuinely sociological theory of self-formation, which insisted that, if we are properly to understand ourselves, we must start with the social process of human **interaction**. In this way he showed that the self is not an innate part of our biology, nor does it emerge simply with the developing human brain. What Mead demonstrated is that the study of the individual self cannot be divorced from the study of **society**, and that requires a sociological perspective.

We may perceive ourselves as individuals, but what happens to our individual selves within intimate relationships and how does their breakdown affect the self? This is explored in an article that looks at the breakdown of romantic relationships and its impact on people's self-concept or sense of 'me' (Slotter et al. 2009). In strongly committed romantic relationships, people's selves become intertwined and less clearly defined, evidenced in the routine use of terms such as 'we', 'our' and 'us'. The ending of such relationships often results in distress and sadness, but it can also lead to changes in the content and structure of the self as individuals reorganize and reshape their lives. This study shows that many people subjectively perceive post-breakup confusion about their self and feel the self to be smaller. As both Mead and Elias argue, our experience of individuality actually belies the fact that the self is inevitably a social self that is shaped in interactions and relationships.

Sociologists have discussed the radical social changes of recent decades, including **globalization**, the spread of information technology, mass **migration**, travel and the compression of time and space, and restructured gender relations, to name a few. We would expect such changes to have an impact on people's sense of self, and Adams (2007) brings together accounts of macro-social change and theories of shifting forms of self-identity. For instance, some theorists suggest that, as **class** identification diminishes, people's individual selves are effectively cut adrift and become more vulnerable to uncertainty and **anomie**. Yet others see this shift as offering the possibility for a more reflexive form of social self that is capable of taking advantage of newly available freedoms. Adams helps us to understand recent theories of large-scale social change and their impact on self-formation.

References and Further Reading

Adams, M. (2007) *Self and Social Change* (London: Sage).
Burkitt, I. (2008) *Social Selves: Theories of Self and Society* (2nd edn, London: Sage).
Mead, G. H. (1934) *Mind, Self and Society*, ed. C. W. Morris (Chicago: University of Chicago Press).
Slotter, E. B., Gardner, W. L., and Finkel, E. J. (2009) 'Who am I without You? The Influence of Romantic Break-Up on the Self Concept', *Personality and Social Psychology Bulletin*, 36(2): 147–60.

Stigma

Working Definition

Physical or social characteristics that are identified as demeaning or are socially disapproved of, bringing opprobrium, social distance or discrimination.

Origins of the Concept

Sociological studies of stigma and processes of stigmatization have been conducted largely within the symbolic interactionist tradition from the 1960s onwards. Some early work, such as that of Goffman ([1963] 1990), theorized how stigmatizing processes work to produce discrimination and also investigated how the stigmatized person responds. For Goffman, there are some important differences depending on the type of stigma, which governs the extent to which people can manage their self-**identity** and protect their sense of self. Another source of ideas on stigma came from the disabled people's movement. An important early challenge to the individual model of disability was Paul Hunt's *Stigma: The Experience of Disability* (1966). Hunt argued that, rather than disabled people's problems being seen as arising from their impairments, it was **interactions** between disabled people and able-bodied people that led to the stigmatizing of disability. In more recent times the concept has been successfully used to explore the situation of people with HIV/AIDS and other health-related conditions.

Meaning and Interpretation

The most successful and systematic account of the production of stigma is that of Erving Goffman. Goffman's work is an excellent example of the close linkage between social identity and embodiment, as he shows how some physical aspects of a person's body can present problems once these have been categorized by others as sources of stigma. He shows, for example, how disabled people can be stigmatized on the basis of readily observable physical impairments. Nonetheless, not all sources of stigma are physical, as stigma can reside in biographical features, character 'flaws' or personal relationships.

Stigma can take many forms. Physical stigma, such as a visible impairment, can often be hard or impossible to hide from others, and Goffman argues this can make the management of identities more difficult. Where this is the case, we can refer to a '*discredited*' stigma – one that has to be acknowledged in interactions. Biographical stigma, such as a previous criminal conviction, can be easier to hide from others, and in this case we can speak of a '*discrediting*' stigma – one that may lead to stigmatizing should it become more widely known. Managing this type may be somewhat easier, but it does still have to be continually controlled. A character stigma, such as associating with drug users, may also be a discrediting stigma, but it may turn into a discredited stigma if the person is observed with the wrong crowd. Note that Goffman is not suggesting people *should* hide stigma; he is just trying to make sense of how the process of stigmatization works in the real world and how people use strategies to avoid becoming stigmatized.

Goffman argued that stigma is a social relationship of devaluation in which one individual is disqualified from full social acceptance by others. Stigmatization often appears in a medical context as people become ill and their identity is changed – sometimes temporarily, but at other times, such as with chronic illnesses, permanently. Goffman argued that inherent in the process of stigmatization is **social control**. Stigmatizing groups is one way in which **society** at large controls their behaviour. In some cases, the stigma is never removed and the person is never fully accepted into society. This was true of many early AIDS patients and it continues in some countries.

Homosexuality has long been stigmatized in many countries around the world, and since the 1960s the hatred of gay men and lesbians has been described as *homophobia*. This may take the form of derogatory language and name-calling but also outright violence. In 2016, a gunman targeted gay men in a nightclub in Orlando, Florida, killing forty-nine people and injuring fifty-three others – the worst mass shooting in US history. One of the key settings for homophobic abuse has long been schools in which terms such as 'poof', 'sissy', 'queer' and many more have been and continue to be common currency in the playground. Given that childhood is crucial in the formation of the **social self**, homophobic abuse in schools has been seen as a key aspect in the reproduction of 'heterosexism' in society. Sarah Nettleton (2013) notes that, because AIDS was first found among gay men in the USA, it was originally called GRID – Gay Related Immune Deficiency – and it was suggested that a 'fast-lane' gay lifestyle actually *caused* the disease, which was often referred to in the media as a 'gay plague'. Although this was false, epidemiological interpretations of gay men as part of 'high-risk groups' tended to reinforce the division between such groups and the 'heterosexual general public'.

Critical Points

One of the deficiencies with studies of stigma is the relative lack of interest in resistance to stigmatizing processes. At the individual level, people may simply refuse to accept the stigmatizing label, though in isolation they are not very likely to be successful. However, collective forms of resistance can be very significant in challenging stigma. Disabled people's movements and gay and lesbian movements challenged mainstream interpretations of their discredited and discrediting stigmas, often by protests and direct action campaigns. Highly visible symbolic protests and the head-on tackling of discriminatory language and **labelling** generated pressure for change and new equal rights legislation and helped to shift attitudes in society. Stigmatizing processes are perhaps more open to change than the earlier theories allowed for.

Continuing Relevance

The concept of stigma continues to be useful. Research into self-injurious behaviour, for example, shows how those who engage in practices of self-harm are keenly aware of the possible stigmatizing of their behaviour, choosing the body sites that are most easily hidden from view in public situations in order to avoid their discrediting stigma becoming discredited. Similarly, studies of eating disorders such as anorexia nervosa show that people go to great lengths to try and keep their behaviour hidden in order to manage their presentation of self, and thus their identity, rather than losing control over it to others and in the process facing the imposition of social stigma.

The continuing relevance of the concept of stigma is clear in the study of sexual promiscuity labels and AIDS in Thailand by Kit Yee Chan (2009) and her colleagues. This research used a mixed-methods approach to explore the perceptions of nurses in Bangkok towards the risk of being accidentally exposed to HIV in their work roles. The authors found that nurses' fear of HIV was rooted mainly in the social ostracism they associated with being HIV-positive rather than in the medical consequences of infection. Although the nurses were well aware that the probability of actual infection at work was very low, they still had a fear which was sustained by what they perceived to be the social consequences of HIV. This social fear was reinforced by their observation at close hand of the stigma attached to their patients.

Goffman argued that stigma can accrue from almost any aspect of people's lives. Caroline Howarth (2006) looked at how conceptualizing **'race'** as a social stigma may help us to understand the process of stigmatizing 'race' but also how communities can contest and change the processes that lead to discrimination. Drawing on material from three qualitative studies, Howarth argues that, as the stigma attached to 'race' cannot be hidden or disguised, resistance and attempts to overthrow the stigmatizing regime have to be collaborative. Her article describes various examples of this in schools and church groups which aim to provide 'social psychological spaces' in which the operation of stigma can be challenged.

References and Further Reading

Chan, K. Y., Rungpueng, A., and Reidpath, D. (2009) 'AIDS and the Stigma of Sexual Promiscuity: Thai Nurses' Risk Perceptions of Occupational Exposure to HIV', *Culture, Health and Sexuality*, 11(4): 353–68.

Goffman, E. ([1963] 1990) *Stigma: Notes on the Management of Spoiled Identity* (London: Penguin), esp. chapters 1 and 2.

Green, G. (2009) *The End of Stigma: Changes in the Experience of Long-Term Illness* (London: Routledge), esp. chapters 1 and 2.

Howarth, C. (2006) 'Race as Stigma: Positioning the Stigmatized as Agents, Not Objects', *Journal of Community and Applied Social Psychology*, 16(6): 442–51.

Hunt, P. (1966) *Stigma: The Experience of Disability* (London: Chapman).

Nettleton, S. (2013) *The Sociology of Health and Illness* (3rd edn, Cambridge: Polity).

9 Crime and Social Control

Anomie

Working Definition

A feeling of severe anxiety and dread resulting from the experience of a lack of effective social norms, often produced during periods of rapid social change.

Origins of the Concept

Social change in the era of **modernity** is so rapid that it often gives rise to major social problems, as traditional lifestyles, morals, religious beliefs and everyday routines are disrupted, sometimes without being replaced. Durkheim linked these unsettling conditions to anomie – feelings of aimlessness, dread and despair when people no longer know 'how to go on'. For example, the traditional moral rules and standards provided by organized **religion** were undermined by early industrial capitalist development. Without such moral rules and behavioural norms to guide them in their everyday lives and routines, many people felt a deep sense of anxiety, disorientation and uncertainty. This is precisely the condition Durkheim described as anomie.

This general concept was later used by Robert Merton in the USA, but he changed its meaning for use in empirical research on crime and **deviance**. For Merton, anomie exists where people experience a social strain between **society**'s cultural goals and the individual's ability to meet them. In this century, Messner and Rosenfeld (2001) produced a modified version of anomie theory – institutional anomie – referring to a situation where there is too much emphasis on a market ethic which tends to override and undermine social norms that regulate behaviour.

Meaning and Interpretation

When individuals commit crimes and acts of deviance, it seems reasonable to assume they are rational beings who know exactly what they are doing. But sociologists have found that there are patterns of crime and deviance that vary according to **gender**, **class** and ethnic group, and this raises some new questions about causation. Why should certain social class groups commit more crimes than others, for instance? In the relatively rich societies, where even poorer groups have many material possessions and better lifestyles than their parents and grandparents, crime rates are still relatively high. Robert Merton used Durkheim's concept of anomie to provide an explanation and, in doing so, argued that the very structure of American society was part of the answer.

Merton (1938) started from a well-established observation from official statistics across many developed societies: that a high proportion of 'acquisitive' crimes – those committed for immediate financial gain – are committed by the 'lower working class' – a common phrase at the time describing those from unskilled, manual backgrounds. Merton noted that American society contains generally held cultural values that promote the pursuit of material success as a legitimate goal, encouraging self-discipline and hard work as the means of achieving it. The idea that people from any background can succeed if they just work hard enough, no matter what their starting point in life, came to be known as the 'American dream'. This has clearly proved attractive to many groups of immigrants who have settled in the USA. Merton explained that, for lower-working-class groups, this 'dream' has become an **ideology**, masking the fact that the legitimate opportunities for success are not open to all. Those who do not achieve high materialistic lifestyles, in spite of working hard, find themselves condemned for their apparent inability. Worse, they are told they are to blame for not working hard enough. This puts great pressure on them to try and get ahead by other, illegitimate means, and the result is higher levels of acquisitive crime among these groups as they experience the social strain between deeply held cultural values and their own social position.

In short, Merton argued that America was a highly unequal and divided society which promoted goals that only some of its population could realistically hope to achieve. Many working-class people, especially young men, have imbibed the cultural goal and seek all the symbols of material success, such as technological gadgets, cars and clothes, but turn to acquisitive crimes such as burglary, shoplifting, stealing, and handling stolen goods to get them. Merton says they 'innovate' around the means available to them to achieve their goals, and this helps to explain why young, working-class men are over-represented in the official criminal and prison statistics. It is not individual character flaws but deep and longstanding social inequalities which create the strain that pushes some people towards a certain type of crime.

Critical Points

Critics point out that, in focusing on individual responses, Merton failed to appreciate the significance of subcultures in sustaining deviant behaviour. If all lower-working-class people are in a position to experience social strain or anomie, why don't they all turn to acquisitive crime? The formation of gangs and deviant subcultures helps to explain this, as most people within this class fraction do not commit crimes, but those who do will often band together to legitimize their actions. Merton's reliance on official statistics is also problematic, because these have since been shown to be flawed and unreliable, with some sociologists arguing that they should not be used as sources of information at all. If Merton's thesis overestimates the amount of lower-working-class crime, then conversely it under-predicts middle-class crime. Later studies of white-collar and corporate crime showed a surprising amount of criminality – fraud, embezzlement, the breaking of health and safety rules, and so on. This acquisitive crime by social groups that have already achieved material success is not accounted for in Merton's scheme.

Continuing Relevance

Merton's creative adaptation of Durkheim's concept of anomie was significant as it reinvented the concept for use in empirical research in other fields of inquiry. His research question – 'What causes crime rates to rise during periods of economic growth and increasing wealth?' – tackled an important social problem in American society. His answer was both a heightened sense of *relative deprivation* among those who feel left behind and severe social strain. This conclusion drew attention to the enduring significance of social class divisions in the USA, despite the country's self-image as a relatively 'classless', open society.

Merton's original argument was relevant for the 1940s and 1950s, but how does it hold up in the twenty-first century? Baumer and Gustafson (2007) analysed official datasets in the USA, including Uniform Crime Reports and the General Social Survey, and found that instrumental crime rates remain higher in areas where there is 'a strong commitment to money success' alongside 'a weak commitment to legitimate means'. This is the central proposition of modern anomie theory, and this study provides some statistical evidence in favour of a version of Mertonian strain theory.

Waring, Weisburd and Chayet (2000) deal with the issue of whether anomie theory has anything to offer the study of white-collar crime. Though it has often been assumed that it does not, this study suggests ways in which Merton's typology can be extended to take middle-class crime into account. The authors remind us that Merton did not suggest a direct link between poverty and crime and, in fact, saw white-collar criminals as 'innovators' who accept the cultural goal of material success but innovate around the means to achieve it. In many 'lesser white-collar jobs', fraud, embezzlement, and so on, may not involve huge sums of money, but there exists a similar strain between goals and means, often created by blocked opportunities for advancement due to bias on class, gender, **ethnicity** or educational grounds. In principle, some types of white-collar crime are explicable using Merton's concepts.

In another interesting piece, Teh (2009) also draws on Merton's theory, as well as Messner and Rosenfeld's arguments, in a study of rising crime rates in Malaysia during a period of strong economic development. Again, Merton's thesis seems to have maintained its relevance, in this case even outside of the developed countries for which it was devised, suggesting that a general sociological theory of crime is possible.

References and Further Reading

Baumer, E. P., and Gustafson, R. (2007) 'Social Organization and Instrumental Crime: Assessing the Empirical Validity of Classic and Contemporary Anomie Theories', *Criminology*, 45(3): 617–63.

Merton, R. H. (1938) 'Social Structure and Anomie', *American Sociological Review*, 3(5): 672–82.

Messner, S. F., and Rosenfeld, R. (2001) *Crime and the American Dream* (Belmont, CA: Wadsworth).

Teh, Yik Koon (2009) 'The Best Police Force in the World Will Not Bring Down a High Crime Rate in a Materialistic Society', *International Journal of Police Science and Management*, 11(1): 1–7.

Waring, E., Wesiburd, D., and Chayet, E. (2000) 'White Collar Crime and Anomie', in W. S. Laufer (ed.), *The Legacy of Anomie Theory* (New Brunswick, NJ: Transaction), pp. 207–77.

Deviance

Working Definition

The undertaking of actions which do not conform to the norms or values that are widely accepted in **society**.

Origins of the Concept

Nineteenth-century biological and psychological studies of criminality assumed that deviance was a sign of something 'wrong' with the individual. They saw that, if a scientific criminology could identify the causes of deviant and criminal behaviour, it would be possible to intervene and prevent such behaviour. In this respect, both biological and psychological theories of crime were positivist in nature, looking to apply natural scientific methods to the study of the social world.

Sociological approaches to the study of deviance began with Durkheim in the late nineteenth century. He viewed deviance as in many ways 'normal' and as performing some useful functions for the maintenance of social order, though he also recognized that too much deviance could become dysfunctional. From the 1950s, the concept was used to study youth subcultures and their relationship to mainstream society, and by the 1960s a radical interactionist theory of deviance was developed. This defined deviance simply as any form of behaviour that has come to be labelled as such by powerful gatekeepers in society. **Labelling** perspectives took the sociology of deviance about as far from the early positivist conception as possible, suggesting that it results from the social process of labelling through which some actions come to be defined as such.

Meaning and Interpretation

Deviance is behaviour that 'deviates', or departs, from the rules or norms considered acceptable or 'normal' within a given society. Most of us transgress generally accepted rules of behaviour at some point, though generally we follow social norms as a result of childhood **socialization**. Deviance and crime are not synonymous, even though in many cases they do overlap. Deviance is much broader than crime, which refers only to non-conformist conduct that breaks a law. The concept of deviance can be applied both to individual behaviour and to the activity of groups. The study of deviance also directs our attention to the issue of **power**, and when we look at deviance we have to bear in mind the question as to *whose* rules are being broken. In the sociology of deviance, no single theory has emerged as dominant, and several theoretical perspectives remain relevant and useful.

Durkheim saw crime and deviance as social facts and argued that both were inevitable and, in some ways, 'normal' features of all societies. In the developed world there are relatively high levels of individualism and personal choice, fewer strictly observed, rigid rules and constraints on behaviour, and more tolerance of low-level deviant acts. Durkheim also considered deviance to fulfil two important functions. First, it can be innovative, bringing new values and ideas into society and challenging time-honoured traditions. In doing so, it can help to bring about significant social change. Second, when deviant acts provoke a negative reaction, they actually perform a useful function, which is to remind everyone what the current rules and norms are. In sociological terms, the response to deviance helps to shore up society's boundary maintenance of acceptable and unacceptable behaviour. On the other hand, if levels of deviance become too high, they can interfere with the smooth operation of society, and in that instance the forces of law and order would need to intervene.

Probably the most widely used theory of deviance is the labelling perspective, which interprets deviance not as a set of characteristics of individuals or groups but as a process of **interaction** between deviants and non-deviants. We must therefore discover why some people come to be tagged with a 'deviant' label. Labelling not only affects how others see a person but also influences the individual's own sense of self. Edwin Lemert (1972) advanced a model for understanding how deviance can either coexist with or become central to one's **identity**. He asserted that, contrary to what some might think, deviant behaviour is actually quite commonplace and people usually get away with it. For example, many traffic violations rarely come to light and small-scale theft from the workplace is often 'overlooked'. Lemert called these initial acts of transgression *primary deviance*. In most cases, they remain marginal to the person's self-identity and the act becomes 'normalized'. In some cases, though, normalization does not occur and the person is labelled a criminal or delinquent. Lemert argued that people may take on board the label they are given so that it becomes part of their self-identity and they act in accordance with it. When their adopted label leads to more criminal and deviant acts, we may call this a type of *secondary deviance*. Labelling can be a very powerful process, and for some individuals the label of 'criminal' may override all the other aspects of their identity, effectively becoming a 'master **status**' which leads to a criminal career.

Critical Points

Functionalist theories of deviance have the clear advantage of linking deviance and crime with everyday conforming behaviour, showing that a lack of opportunity can be the differentiating factor between those who engage in criminality and those who do not. Nonetheless, we must remember that the vast majority of people in all social **class** groups never become career criminals and most do not routinely commit crimes. Labelling theory has sometimes been criticized for its focus on the minority, the exotic and the extreme aspects of society, as well as for 'humanizing the deviant', rather than trying to understand why most people do *not* break the rules or the law. Some have also suggested that, rather than governments intervening to bring unacceptable levels of deviance down when they become too high, it is more usual to redefine what counts as deviance and crime in order to bring previously unacceptable behaviour into the mainstream. In redefining what counts as deviance in the first place, Durkheim's optimistic idea that we could know what constituted acceptable and unacceptable levels becomes impossible.

The constructionist stance of the labelling perspective has also been criticized. Outside wartime, some deviant acts are not just defined as such by powerful gatekeepers but are universally and consistently prohibited across societies. Murder, rape and robbery, for example, are usually seen as unacceptable regardless of the views of the authorities. Labelling is also seen as having little to offer policymakers. If all deviance is relative, how then are we to decide which actions should be controlled and prohibited and which should be allowed? If such decisions have to be based on the harm caused, it would seem that, contrary to labelling theory, deviance really is a quality of the act and does not lie merely in its social definition and labelling.

Continuing Relevance

The concept of deviance has had a long career in sociology that continues to produce interesting and insightful studies of rule-breaking and its control. Indeed, it is hard to see how the sociology of crime and criminology can do without it. Because deviance forces us to consider the roles of many social actors, including deviants and criminals, opinion-formers and moral entrepreneurs, police forces, courts and politicians, it is an important concept which links 'bad' behaviour to the social context in which it takes place. Studying deviance forces us to think differently about society's current standards of 'normality'.

Deviance studies have often delved into hidden worlds, and Goldschmidt (2008) carries on this tradition. His small-scale study looked at the way ten police officers engaged in deviant behaviour during the course of their job, such as unlawful instances of stop and search, planting evidence, writing false reports and committing perjury. The study examines the rationales given. Primarily the officers saw their deviance as being 'in a noble cause', namely catching criminals and protecting the **community**, though they also believed that victims approved of their methods. However, they also benefited professionally from their actions and had developed effective techniques for neutralizing moral guilt.

The concept of deviance is applied to a much wider range of behaviour than crime, and Adler and Adler's (2007) qualitative research with eighty people who self-injure shows how useful it can be in understanding the practice. Their paper explores the way that self-injurious behaviour (or 'self-harm') was formerly classified by the psychological and medical professions as an illness to be treated. However, drawing on interview data and Internet sources, the authors find that, in the late 1990s and early 2000s, self-harm was in the process of being redefined and reclassified by those who engage in it as 'a voluntarily chosen deviant behavior' and not a medical problem. This reflects the interactionist maxim that deviant behaviour is that which is so labelled.

References and Further Reading

Adler, P. A., and Adler, P. (2007) 'The Demedicalization of Self-Injury', *Journal of Contemporary Ethnography*, 36(5): 537–70.

Goldschmidt, J. (2008) 'The Necessity of Dishonesty: Police Deviance, "Making the Case" and the Public Good', *Policing and Society*, 18(2): 113–35.

Henry, S. (2009) *Social Deviance* (Cambridge: Polity).

Lemert, E. (1972) *Human Deviance, Social Problems and Social Control* (Englewood Cliffs, NJ: Prentice Hall).

Labelling

Working Definition

The process through which some individuals and social groups are identified as having certain characteristics by others who have the **power** and influence to make such labels stick.

Origins of the Concept

The concept of labelling was developed in the 1950s and 1960s by sociologists working in the symbolic interactionist tradition. Labelling perspectives were particularly influential in the study of crime and **deviance**, where they drew attention to the way that deviance is defined and created in processes of social **interaction**. Edwin Lemert distinguished between primary and secondary deviance, and labelling tended to concentrate on secondary deviance. Howard Becker (1963) argued, for example, that deviance was best seen as a process during which some actions were defined and categorized as deviant and treated accordingly. Becker's central focus was on the impact of that process on the **identity** of 'deviants' themselves, who had effectively been made into 'outsiders', stigmatized and marginalized from mainstream **society**.

Meaning and Interpretation

The study of crime and deviance owes much to interactionism and, in particular, to the sociological perspective known as labelling theory. The starting point for labelling theories is that deviant behaviour is a social process involving interactions between those who are able to impose labels and those who are labelled. For example, police officers, judges, courts and the **mass media** have the power to define what constitutes deviance, while others are subject to such definitions. For some, the labelling process reflects the distribution of power in a society because those groups which make the rules tend to be white, older, middle class and male. However, we must be careful not to trivialize labelling, as it is not a sociological version of simply 'giving a dog a bad name' but the end product of a long social process involving many actors.

Howard Becker's work showed how deviant identities are produced through labelling processes rather than through deviant motivations or behaviour. Becker argued that 'deviance is not a quality of the act the person commits, but rather, a consequence of the application by others of rules and sanctions to an "offender". The deviant is one to whom that label has been successfully applied ... deviant behaviour is behaviour that people so label.' This definition has stimulated much research, though it has been criticized too. Becker was highly critical of criminological approaches which saw a clear distinction between the 'normal' and the 'deviant'. For Becker, their behaviour is not the determining factor in why people become 'deviants'. Rather there are processes, unrelated to the behaviour itself, which are more influential in determining whether or not someone is so labelled. A person's dress, manner of speaking or country of origin could be the key factors that determine whether or not this label is applied.

One particular irony of the criminal justice system pointed out by labelling theory is that those institutions charged with reducing criminality, such as the police, courts and prisons, very often play a crucial part in the creation and maintenance of deviant and criminal identities. For labelling theorists, this is a clear demonstration of the 'paradox of **social control**' resulting in deviancy amplification. Wilkins (1964) was interested in how deviant identities are 'managed' and integrated into daily life. Deviancy amplification refers to the unintended consequence of labelling behaviour as deviant, when an agency of control actually provokes more of that same deviant behaviour. The labelled person incorporates the label into his or her identity through secondary deviance in a cycle of escalating amplification. Labelling perspectives are important because they teach us that we cannot assume that any act or individual is criminal or deviant by nature. To do so would be illegitimately essentialist. Instead, we need to examine deviance and crime as social constructions that are always subject to change.

Critical Points

Labelling views primary deviance as relatively unimportant because it is so widespread. However, in focusing so heavily on secondary deviance, labelling theorists neglect the processes that lead people to commit acts of primary deviance, leaving these unexplained. But any rounded theory would surely need to deal with both primary and secondary deviance. It is also not clear whether labelling really does have the effect of increasing deviance. Youth offending tends to escalate following conviction, but other factors, such as greater interaction with other offenders or learning about new criminal opportunities, may be involved as well. Labelling also raises issues of structural power relations but fails to address them. How did some powerful groups come to acquire their positions? Answering this question needs sociological theories of society, such as Marxism or other **conflict** theories, and labelling has no general theory of society to offer.

Continuing Relevance

Deviance tends to be thought of as negative, but all societies have to allow space for individuals and groups whose actions do not conform to mainstream norms. Those who follow orthodox ways often initially regard people who develop new ideas, in politics, **science**, art or other fields, with suspicion or hostility. In this sense, both labelling theory and the sociology of deviance more generally have proved a useful counterweight to criminology, which concentrates only on crime and crime reduction. And, though labelling does not address all of the questions its studies raise, it has opened up the issue of deviance and the creation of deviant identities to wider scrutiny, which has enabled later sociologists to follow new lines of interest.

Labelling perspectives continue to be useful in the study of groups that experience discrimination. Joy Moncrieffe (2009) uses labelling to explore the position of 'street children' and 'restavecs' in Haiti. 'Restavec' is a label given to children sent from rural households to live and work in urban homes, and Moncrieffe argues that the majority are badly treated, as there is strong evidence of beatings, long working hours and rape. However, government officials have varying views on restavecs, with some believing the system is a 'sore' on Haiti's reputation and others viewing it as performing a useful economic function. The label 'street children', on the other hand, brings a much more negative response, as the 'most reviled of the groups within Haiti'. These labels tend to be reproduced among all groups and **organizations**, even those aiming to alleviate **poverty**, such as missionaries. Moncrieffe shows how the classic labelling process is closely tied to stigmatization.

The concept of deviance stands in opposition to conformity to social rules. But can deviance be applied in a context where the normalization of rules has not yet been established? Given the relatively 'lawless' world of cyberspace, it may be thought that definitions of deviance and normality would be fairly random, but people still tend to bring 'offline' conventions and norms to bear in the 'online' environment. In an interesting discussion of this issue, Denegri-Knott and Taylor

(2005) investigate the online sharing of MP3 music files and 'flaming' (the use of inflammatory language) in virtual environments, in which social norms are still evolving, to explore whether 'deviance' is an appropriate concept for some of the behaviours they observed.

References and Further Reading

Becker, H. S. (1963) *Outsiders: Studies in the Sociology of Deviance* (New York: Free Press).
Denegri-Knott, J., and Taylor, J. (2005) 'The Labeling Game: A Conceptual Exploration of Deviance on the Internet', *Social Science Computer Review*, 23(1): 93–107.
Hopkins Burke, R. (2013) *An Introduction to Criminological Theory* (4th edn, Abingdon and New York: Routledge), esp. chapter 9.
Moncrieffe, J. (2009) 'When Labels Stigmatize: Encounters with "Street Children" and "Restavecs" in Haiti', in R. Eyben and J. Moncrieffe (eds), *The Power of Labelling: How We Categorize and Why it Matters* (London: Earthscan), pp. 80–96.
Wilkins, L. T. (1964) *Social Deviance: Social Policy Action and Research* (London: Tavistock).

Moral Panic

Working Definition

The societal overreaction to a certain group or type of behaviour that is taken as symptomatic of a more general social and moral malaise.

Origins of the Concept

The process of deviancy amplification was examined in a highly influential study conducted by Stanley Cohen, published in 1972 as *Folk Devils and Moral Panics*. In this classic work, Cohen examined **labelling** processes in relation to the emergence and control of youth **cultures** in the UK. He observed some of the minor clashes in 1964 between so-called Mods and Rockers in the seaside town of Clacton but could not reconcile what he had witnessed with newspaper reports the following day. The exaggeration of this event and the subsequent labelling of others he saw as an instance of a moral panic in which 'youth' became a scapegoat for wider social problems and, as in other labelling studies, media attention led to a cycle of deviancy amplification. Later studies have used the concept of the moral panic to investigate the rising social concern with dangerous dogs, drug-taking, rowdy 'ladettes', immigration and lots more. Some theorists argue that the moral panic has become so widespread and diffused as a **social control** mechanism that it is today one aspect in the social reproduction of **society**. Perhaps the era of the discrete moral panic is over.

Meaning and Interpretation

Following gatherings at a British seaside resort in 1964, newspapers carried lurid headlines declaring 'Day of Terror by Scooter Groups', 'Wild Ones Invade the

Seaside' and 'Youngsters Beat up the Town'. Intrigued by this reaction, Cohen set about reconstructing the actual events of the day from eyewitness accounts, court records and other documentary sources. What he found was that newspaper reports were very wide of the mark. No serious violence had in fact occurred, no one had been hospitalized, and vandalism was no worse than on previous holiday weekends. However, this response set the tone for future reporting. Cohen argued that, in presenting young people's activities in such a sensationalized way, the press contributed to a climate of fear and a panic that society's moral rules were under threat. In doing so, they inadvertently helped to construct new forms of youth identities rather than just reporting on them. Before 1964, 'Mods' and 'Rockers' did not exist as discrete youth cultures, and their supposed mutual antipathy was fuelled by media presentations. In subsequent years, all such gatherings came to be described within this master frame of oppositional youth cultures and their propensity for violence against both each other and mainstream society.

For Cohen, this social process of labelling a group as outsiders – or 'folk devils' – helped to focus many people's concerns about the direction of society as a whole. Fears of growing permissive attitudes, indiscipline as National Service ended in 1958, **family** breakdown, and a materialistic generation with more money in their pockets than ever before – all came to be loaded onto the scapegoat of youth subcultures. Many moral panics are brought to an end with the passing of legislation, and new laws on criminal damage helped to assuage concerns about out-of-control youth in the 1960s. However, there have been similar panics around almost every youth culture since, from punk to rave culture.

Moral panics follow a typical pattern. They start when something or some group is identified as a threat to common moral values. The threat is then exaggerated and simplified in the **mass media**, sensitizing the public to the issue and heightening concern. In turn, this leads to calls for 'something to be done', and there is increasing pressure on the authorities to act, usually by introducing new legislation. In some cases, the panic persists until the media attention cycle ends. Since Cohen's work there have been many more studies of moral panics, and historians have found episodes back in the nineteenth century and perhaps even earlier.

Geoffrey Pearson found a specific example in the 1860s, when a type of robbery with violence appeared to be out of control in London. Press reports of 'garrotting' focused on the use of knives and teamwork in the robbery of wealthy citizens, remarking that this was a very 'un-British' crime which might be linked to the then recent Italian immigration. Pearson argued that the panic was the result of social fears that government was getting 'soft on crime' as transportation, flogging and other physical punishments were abolished. In the wake of the panic, flogging was reintroduced, which brought the panic to a close. Moral panic theory is a good example of interactionist sociology, linking moral entrepreneurs, opinion-formers, police, judiciary, legislators, the general public and, of course, 'deviants' within a process of **interaction**.

Critical Points

Critics argued that the main problem with the theory was how to differentiate between an exaggerated moral panic and a serious social problem. For example, would the societal response to the terrorist acts in the name of Islam in the twenty-first century be part of a moral panic, or is this such a serious matter that extensive media coverage and new laws are appropriate? Where does the boundary lie between an unnecessary panic and a legitimate response, and who decides? A further criticism is that, in recent years, moral panics have arisen over matters such as youth crime and drug use and 'bogus' asylum-seekers. This has led some sociologists to argue that moral panics are no longer discrete or confined to short bursts of intense activity but have become chronic features of everyday life in modern societies and, as such, been normalized. If so, then it becomes much harder to separate the concept of **deviance** from normality.

Continuing Relevance

We know a lot about moral panics and how they progress, but the other side of this coin is less well understood: why do some social issues just not become moral panics at all? This issue is taken up by Jenkins (2009) in a fascinating discussion of the social response to Internet child pornography. Although there has been much comment and discussion of people's fears of child pornography online and some well-publicized convictions, the issue of child pornography on the Internet has not generated a classic process of moral panic. This is strange as, on the face of it, all the necessary facets are in place for it to do so. Jenkins suggests that one reason for this lies in the lack of a proper understanding of the phenomenon among law-enforcement agencies, mainly on account of a lack of knowledge regarding the technology involved and its use.

Cohen's early study is particularly important because it successfully combined theories of deviant labelling with ideas of social control and the creation of deviant identities. In doing so, it created the framework for a very productive research agenda in the sociology of deviance which continues today. For example, Lumsden (2009) investigated the subculture of car enthusiasts known as 'Bouley Bashers', or boy racers, in Aberdeen, Scotland, which was the focus of a localized moral panic. It has been suggested that contemporary 'folk devils' are better able to resist being labelled, as they now produce their own blogs and other media as a counter to mainstream labelling. However, this case followed the process of a classic moral panic. The boy racers were marginalized, labelled and stigmatized by the media, other groups and government (via antisocial behaviour legislation). Despite their attempts to redefine the situation, ultimately the label was made to stick.

References and Further Reading

Cohen, S. (1972) *Folk Devils and Moral Panics: The Creation of the Mods and Rockers* (Oxford: Martin Robertson).

Goode, E., and Ben-Yehuda, N. (2009) *Moral Panics: The Social Construction of Deviance* (Oxford Wiley-Blackwell), esp. chapter 10, on the 'witch craze'.

Jenkins, P. (2009) 'Why do Some Social Issues Fail to Detonate Moral Panics?', *British Journal of Criminology*, 49: 35–47.

Lumsden, K. (2009) '"Do We Look Like Boy Racers?" The Role of the Folk Devil in Contemporary Moral Panics', *Sociological Research Online*, 14(1), www.socresonline.org.uk/14/1/2.html.

Thompson, K. (1998) *Moral Panics* (London: Routledge).

Restorative Justice

Working Definition

A theory and process of criminal justice focusing on repairing the harm caused to victims by crime and which requires the involvement of all stakeholders.

Origins of the Concept

Restorative justice is a form of **community**-based justice and represents a departure from the retributive (punishment-oriented) justice systems of the developed countries. However, community justice systems have a very long history, especially among most small, non-state societies in the past. In these societies, justice involved dispute resolution, with offenders and their families making reparations to their victims and to the community at large (Strickland 2004: 2–3). The retributive justice systems that are widespread today can be seen as relatively novel, with a history that dates back only to the eighteenth century. The invention and increasingly widespread use of incarceration as the punishment for crimes of all kinds marked a distinct shift away from community justice. The contemporary restorative justice movement, which drew inspiration from the restorative models of Maori communities in New Zealand and Aboriginal groups in Australia (McLaughlin et al. 2003), emerged at the end of the 1970s. However, among criminologists, the impetus for this movement was a growing disillusionment with conventional retributive policies, stubbornly high recidivism rates and a feeling that 'nothing works'.

Meaning and Interpretation

Restorative justice is a form of criminal and community justice which forces offenders to acknowledge the impact of their behaviour on victims, families and the community more generally. In this sense it begins from the premise that offenders are part of and not separate from their communities. Retributive justice systems work by removing offenders from the community into prisons, often far away from the site of the offence, and therefore they shield the offender from the aftermath of their actions. Advocates of restorative justice argue that offenders should be exposed to the impact of their offences in a meaningful way that helps reintegrate them back into the mainstream of social relationships (Graef 2001). Restorative processes therefore aim to find creative new ways of reducing reoffending by giving victims and communities a central role in the justice system.

A key founder of restorative justice studies is John Braithwaite ([1989] 1999), who argues that restorative justice is most effective if it is based on 'reintegrative shaming'. That is, offenders are made keenly aware of both the victim and **society**'s disapproval in ways which shame them into 'freely chosen compliance'. The process through which this is achieved should adopt three basic principles: mutual respect for each other, mutual commitment to each other and intolerance towards offending behaviour (Van Ness and Strong 2014). For Braithwaite, shaming is the best way to convey to offenders the justifiable resentment of their victims and make them take responsibility as citizens. But shaming can easily turn into stigmatization, which may turn offenders into 'outsiders' and push them into criminal careers in deviant subcultures. Hence, it is crucial that the justice process is 'reintegrative' and faithful to the basic principles noted above (Strang and Braithwaite 2001).

In restorative justice approaches, offenders may be required to meet or communicate with their victims, usually through some form of mediation. This allows victims to ask questions, express their feelings directly, receive a formal apology and make clear the consequences of the offender's actions. It may also help victims to move on with their lives. But it also forces offenders to take responsibility for their actions, to understand how their offending affects others and to reassess their future behaviour (Liebmann 2007: 29). However, the second part of restorative justice is reparation – repairing the harm that has been caused. Although a prison sentence may still be appropriate for serious crimes of violence, it is much more likely that a 'community sentence' will be more fitting in most cases. This could be providing services to the community, performing unpaid work or assisting with projects in the community.

Critical Points

The use of shame in the criminal justice system may appear more suitable for some kinds of offender than others. Much of the literature and examples of restorative justice seem to concentrate on a similar set of offences – opportunist burglary, theft, domestic violence, motoring offences and vandalism, for example. There have been some instances of successful reintegration in these areas, though there is a real lack of robust empirical data which supports the notion that restorative justice reduces reoffending. Is it really likely that organized gangsters, rapists, murderers or those involved in paedophile rings could be pushed towards responsible **citizenship** through reintegrative shaming? Similarly, it may not be accidental that the model of restorative justice is taken from small-scale, relatively homogeneous communities in which community reparations have the best chance of success. In large, multicultural cities and urban areas, impersonality and segregation are the norm. In this context, it is very difficult to discern what 'community' might mean. And, in the absence of community identification, shaming and restorative measures are unlikely to carry any force.

Some scholars also take issue with the underlying principles of restorative justice. Acorn (2004) argues that, of course, the best way to deal with offences and disputes is to try and resolve them through dialogue and agreement. However, the idea that restorative justice could form the basis of the whole justice system is misguided and possibly dangerous. Acorn maintains that all justice systems are ways of dealing with relationships between people precisely when mutual respect, sympathy and compassion do not exist. Therefore, restorative justice reflects a failure or an unwillingness to face up to the reality of modern life in which these qualities may be in short supply. Restorative justice does not really contain a genuine conception of justice at all but is simply 'tied to the age-old human hope for the convergence of love and justice' (Acorn 2004: 22). Suggestions that the existing system should be dismantled in favour of such unworldly sentimentality are positively dangerous.

Continuing Relevance

As a relatively recent innovation, the restorative justice approach is still being tried in many countries and for a range of diverse acts of crime and deviance. As a result, finding out whether it actually reduces recidivism rates still lags behind. One of the growing areas of research in this field is systematic evaluations of restorative approaches, and we can expect these to continue. Even so, some scholars suggest that a simple focus on recidivism rates may not demonstrate all of the benefits of restorative justice, which include victim satisfaction with the process and increased community involvement in the justice system.

This latter point is made by Young and Goold ([1999] 2003) in their comparison of 'old-style' police cautions and 'new-style' restorative cautioning in one town in the UK. Police cautions are usually, though not always, delivered in police stations, the intention being to avoid minor offences going to court, where a 'degrading' form of shaming might be perceived as unfair and lead to the adoption of a deviant **identity**. However, the authors argue that the mode of delivery of conventional police cautions constitutes a form of 'dressing down' and therefore of degrading shaming. Restorative cautions take much longer – typically 30 to 40 minutes – allowing offenders to describe their offence and victims to ask questions and explain their feelings. Young and Goold argue that this new model, compared with the older type, should be valued for its involvement of victims and relative openness and not assessed solely on preventing reoffending.

References and Further Reading

Acorn, A. (2004) *Compulsory Compassion: A Critique of Restorative Justice* (Vancouver: UBC Press).

Braithwaite, J. ([1989] 1999) *Crime, Shame and Reintegration* (Cambridge: Cambridge University Press).

Graef, R. (2001) *Why Restorative Justice? Repairing the Harm Caused by Crime* (London: Calouste Gulbenkian Foundation).

Liebmann, M. (2007) *Restorative Justice: How it Works* (London: Jessica Kingsley).

McLaughlin, E., Fergusson, R., Hughes, G., and Westmarland, L. (eds) (2003) *Restorative Justice: Critical Issues* (London: Sage).

Strang, H., and Braithwaite, J. (eds) (2001) *Restorative Justice and Civil Society* (Cambridge: Cambridge University Press).

Strickland, R. A. (2004) *Restorative Justice* (New York: Peter Lang).

Van Ness, D. W., and Strong, K. H. (2014) *Restoring Justice: An Introduction to Restorative Justice* (5th edn, Abingdon and New York: Routledge).

Young, R., and Goold, B. ([1999] 2003) 'Restorative Police Cautioning in Aylesbury: From Degrading to Restorative Shaming Ceremonies?', in E. McLaughlin, R. Fergusson, G. Hughes and L. Westmarland (eds), *Restorative Justice: Critical Issues* (Buckingham: Open University Press), pp. 94–104.

Social Control

Working Definition

All of the formal and informal mechanisms and internal and external controls that operate to produce conformity.

Origins of the Concept

Control theories are often traced back to the seventeenth-century philosopher Thomas Hobbes, who argued that, in a **society** of self-interested individuals, a great **power** – the state – was necessary to prevent a 'war of all against all'. A contract between state and the individual existed which exchanged citizens' loyalty to the state for the state's protection of individuals. As the study of social control entered social **science**, more complex, sociological perspectives were developed.

In the late nineteenth century, Edward Ross suggested that social control involves all of the pressures on people to conform to social rules, though this was a very general approach. Talcott Parsons (1937) offered an alternative based on **socialization**. He argued that conformity was not just produced through fear and external agencies but was also internalized in the norms and values that people imbibed during the socialization process. A more specific answer was provided by Travis Hirschi (1969), who considered that juvenile delinquency occurred when the individual's bonds to society were weakened or broken. This theory focused attention on the attachments people have to **family**, peers and social institutions. For Marxist theorists, though, the state is a key actor in the production of social control, which in capitalist societies is really the control of the working class.

Meaning and Interpretation

Social control is the flipside of **deviance**. While sociologists of deviance and crime look at why people break social norms and laws, social control theorists ask the opposite question: why do people conform? One way to think about the various theories of social control is to divide them into 'conformity-producing' and 'deviance repressing' approaches (Hudson 1997). Conformity-producing theories tend to concentrate on the learning of social roles and the internalizing of social norms, while deviance-repressing theories look at the links between deviant behaviour and the measures introduced to reduce it. Arguably, better theories are those that are able to combine these two approaches.

Parsons tried to address what he called 'the problem of social order' – that is, how societies manage to produce enough conformity from generation to generation. He argued that people's conformity does not appear to be forced or reticently given and that most people conform actively. This is because social norms exist not just 'out there' in legal manuals and manners books but also within our own selves. Socialization ensures that our sense of self is bound up with conformity to rules, which helps to shape our self-image as 'good people'. In a real sense, we are our own censors and do much of the 'policing' of our own behaviour. For example, David Matza's (1964) study of youth delinquency found that even those who break the law share the general values of mainstream society and have to devise what he called 'techniques of neutralization' – self-narratives of why they broke the laws – in order to commit offences while, at the same time, maintaining their self-image.

Hirschi's theory of social control saw conformity as based on attachments and social bonds. These are created through attachment to friends, family and peers, commitment to conventional lifestyles, involvement in normal, legal activity, and beliefs such as respecting the law and **authority** figures. These attachments and bonds act on the individual to keep them involved in mainstream activity and away from the opportunities for deviant behaviour. Hence the causes of deviance lie not simply in individual pathology or selfish individualism but also in a lack of attachment to society and its central agencies and institutions, which leaves them cut adrift and vulnerable to deviant temptations. Deviance does not need explanation, as it occurs wherever opportunities exist.

One example of this is the gendered pattern of crime, which is perhaps the most striking aspect within the official crime statistics. Why do women commit far fewer crimes and why do men commit so many? On Hirschi's theory, the answer lies in the differential control of girls and boys by parents and social **organizations**. Boys are encouraged to go out into the public world from an early age and to take **risks** which help them to grow up in ways that enable them to adapt to the adult masculine roles they will be expected to fill. The more time boys spend outside the home, the more opportunities exist for them to become involved in deviant activity. Young girls, on the other hand, are kept closer to the parental home for much longer and discouraged or even prevented from engaging with the outside world, especially after dark, and this reduces their opportunities for breaking with social norms.

Critical Points

Parsons's sociological approach to social control shifted attention from external controls to internal self-controls, which added a new dimension to our understanding. However, critics argue that it is heavily reliant on socialization in the production of conformity – a burden socialization may not be able to carry. This is because many see socialization and self-formation processes as inherently conflictual rather than smooth, with many emotionally charged tensions involved. This means there can be no guarantee that the same set of social norms and values will be internalized by all. There must be more to the production of conformity than Parsons allows for.

Later theories of social control include the **labelling** perspective, which views social control and deviance as intimately tied together. The relationship between them is deeply ironic, though, as the more agencies of social control try to prevent deviance, the more likely it becomes that more will be created. A series of interactionist studies of deviance since the 1960s has shown how social control has a tendency to lead to more behaviours being labelled as deviant and a subsequent expansion of 'deviant activity'.

Continuing Relevance

The concept of social control and problems of social order have long been the subject of sociological theory. Tackling the latter has led sociologists to consider problems of structure and agency, micro- and macro-level phenomena, and related issues of socialization and conformity. But all of these cannot be divorced from studies of crime and deviance, as they are essentially two sides of the same coin. This being so, then, as long as there are studies of crime and deviance, there will also be interest in the implications of these for our understanding of social control.

Dealing with antisocial behaviour has led to some innovative schemes, one of which is the combination of social housing management with policing. Brown (2004) argues that the concept of 'antisocial behaviour' in the UK is a recent creation which enables the state to address specific types of activity previously considered outside the remit of the criminal justice system. She argues that, in one way, this move indicates that a new model of social control is emerging which involves both the caring and the control professions. Yet it also suggests that the previous model has failed.

Hirschi's control theory argued that strong attachments immunize people against deviancy, but this thesis is revisited with an eye on **gender** differences in Booth et al.'s (2008) school-based survey of social control, gender and delinquency. In contrast to earlier research suggesting that parental attachment had a greater impact on girls, this study found that parental attachment had little impact on risky behaviour or serious delinquency in either boys or girls. By contrast, involvement in pro-social activities such as sports, church and school activities had multiple effects. Church and non-sport school activities reduced serious delinquency in boys but not in girls, while involvement in sports reduced delinquency in girls but not in boys. This suggests that some of the conventional ideas about sport keeping boys away from crime and church or non-sports doing the same for girls may be ineffective. The authors conclude that there are crucial differences in social bonding which necessitate gender-specific rather than general analyses of deviance.

References and Further Reading

Booth, J. A., Farrell, A., and Varano, S. P. (2008) 'Social Control, Serious Delinquency, and Risky Behavior', *Crime and Delinquency*, 54(3): 423–56.

Brown, A. P. (2004) 'Anti-Social Behaviour, Crime Control and Social Control', *Howard Journal of Criminal Justice*, 43(2): 203–11.

Hirschi, T. (1969) *Causes of Delinquency* (Berkeley: University of California Press).

Hudson, B. (1997) 'Social Control', in M. Maguire, R. Morgan and R. Reiner (eds), *The Oxford Handbook of Criminology* (2nd edn, Oxford: Oxford University Press), pp. 451–72.

Innes, M. (2003) *Understanding Social Control: Crime and Social Order in Late Modernity* (Buckingham: Open University Press), esp. chapters 1 and 2.

Matza, D. (1964) *Delinquency and Drift* (New York: John Wiley).

Parsons, T. (1937) *The Structure of Social Action* (New York: McGraw-Hill).

Political Sociology

Authority

Working Definition

The legitimate **power** which one person or group holds over another.

Origins of the Concept

Max Weber's ([1925] 1979) political sociology is the starting point for most studies of power, politics and authority. Weber saw power as the ability of people or groups to get their own way, even against opposition, but people can be said to be in positions of authority only when they are able to issue commands and have a reasonable expectation that those commands will be carried out. Authority therefore rests on the belief among those receiving commands that the person giving them is doing so legitimately. That is, their position is accepted as authoritative. Authority can be seen in operation in adult–child relations; within families, where the head of household makes decisions; within **organizations**, where managers are seen as having the right to give orders; in the armed forces, where a strict system of rank and authority is in place; and in politics, where governments introduce laws which they expect to be obeyed.

Meaning and Interpretation

Weber argued that systems of authority differ across societies and also over time. He distinguished three types of authority in history: traditional, charismatic and rational-legal. However, all three are **ideal types** – heuristic tools devised to assist researchers as they approach real-world phenomena. And though Weber's scheme may appear chronological – from traditional to charismatic to rational-legal – any of the three types could become dominant, and it is more usual for two or three to exist at the same time.

Traditional authority is power that is legitimized through respect for long-established cultural patterns transmitted over generations. In this system, people obey commands on the basis of the traditional **status** of rulers. The legitimacy of traditional authorities comes from the knowledge and acceptance that this is the way things have been organized in the past. Weber gives the example of hereditary **family** rule of nobles in medieval Europe, echoes of which continue in aristocratic and royal families. In traditional authority, people's allegiance is to particular individuals and not to the rules they put in place. In practice, this means that people obey rulers, not rules, and feel they owe them personal fidelity.

Charismatic authority tends to disrupt traditional forms and has been the source of innovation and change in history. Charismatic authority is based on the devotion felt by subordinates towards a leader by virtue of her or his exceptional qualities which inspire devotion. The concept of charisma has proved difficult to pin down, though, as it is unclear whether its special qualities actually inhere in the personality of the leader or whether it is the perception by others that the leader has such qualities. Historical examples include Jesus Christ, Adolf Hitler and Mahatma Ghandi, though heroic soldiers, 'saintly' individuals and political leaders have all been described as 'charismatic'. One thing all charismatic leaders must do is to provide occasional 'proof' of their special qualities, and if such proof is not forthcoming the charismatic person may come under challenge. Weber saw that this made charismatic authority essentially unstable, reinforced by the fact that, when the leader dies, a crisis of belief and legitimacy is likely to follow. When charismatic systems begin to take on more routinized form, they tend to be transformed into traditional or legal-rational systems.

With the emergence of **capitalism**, Weber saw traditional authority giving way to a new form of *legal-rational authority*. This is power that is legitimized through legally enacted rules and regulations and combines a belief in the law with formal rationality in decision-making. It is found in modern organizations and bureaucracies and in democratic systems of government that direct the political life of a **society**. Rational-legal authority can only be exercised when decisions and commands have been arrived at through 'due' process, not according to tradition or individual whim. **Bureaucracy** is the typical form of legal-rational authority.

Critical Points

One longstanding criticism of Weber's typology is that, although he identified four types of social action, there are only three systems of authority. The 'missing' category appears to be *value-rational authority*, where legitimacy rests on the absolute value attached to a set of norms. Essentially this is an ideological form of authority in which legitimacy is given to leaders on the basis of their pursuit of a goal or end. This fourth logical type rests on obedience to the ideological goal rather than on individuals, and commands issued are legitimized to the extent that they relate to the ultimate goal. Examples would include strongly 'ideological' systems such as religious organizations or early Soviet communism.

In recent years sociologists have discussed the emergence of a celebrity culture which glorifies individuals on the basis of their media presence rather than their achievements. This **culture** has also impacted on political life, and leading politicians now tend to be evaluated on their personalities as presented in the **mass**

media. Some sociologists have suggested that this undermines or short-circuits legal-rational democratic processes and presents a threat to democratic values. Neil Postman (1986), for example, warned that politics was in danger of becoming a mere adjunct of show business.

Continuing Relevance

Weber's classification allows for mixtures of the three types to coexist, even though one may be dominant. For example, modern Britain has a system of legal-rational authority, but in political life the House of Lords plays a part in government and the monarch still has a constitutional place. This mixing of ideal types gives Weber's scheme flexibility and continues to be useful for political sociologists. However, the spread of celebrity culture into the world of politics has raised some questions about the basis of a political leader's authority. It is commonplace today for politicians to manage their public image and for political parties to court popular celebrities such as pop stars, actors and sportspeople. Similarly, in the USA, two former actors, Ronald Reagan and Arnold Schwarzenegger, became president and a state governor respectively. This encroaching of celebrity into political life has often been seen as obviously pernicious.

However, Street (2004) argues not only that celebrity politics can be traced back to at least the eighteenth century but that the advent of the celebrity politician is not incompatible with the authority of representative democracy. Indeed, rather than being at odds with the principles of democratic representation, celebrity politics can be seen as an extension of them. 'Representativeness' is not a concept that is restricted to party manifestos and policy proposals; it also includes the style, aesthetics and attractiveness of politicians. All of these elements help to forge identification between politicians and those they claim to represent. And it is through political style and appearance that politicians communicate their relationship to voters and their future plans, reducing complex political arguments into a form with which citizens can identify.

Political scientists have often seen small political parties as relying more on a charismatic leader to help bridge the resource gap with the major parties. But do charismatic leaders really carry the authority to help small parties win votes? Van der Brug and Mughan (2007) bring empirical evidence from Dutch elections to bear on this issue. They analysed three elections, looking at the performance of right-wing populist parties, and concluded that the influence of their leaders was essentially no greater than that of the leaders of the larger established parties. The study also rejects the notion that those who vote for right-wing parties are motivated primarily by a vague sense of dissatisfaction rather than actually supporting the policies promoted by party leaders. Right-wing voters, they suggest, make the same kinds of considerations as all other voters, and their choices are no less 'rational' or swayed by charismatic forms of authority.

References and Further Reading

Morrison, K. (2006) *Marx, Durkheim, Weber: Formations of Modern Social Thought* (2nd edn, London: Sage), esp. pp. 361–73.

Postman, N. (1986) *Amusing Ourselves to Death: Public Discourse in the Age of Show Business* (London: Heinemann).

Street, J. (2004) 'In Defence of Celebrity Politics: Popular Culture and Political Representation', *British Journal of Politics and International Relations*, 6: 435–52.

Van der Brug, W., and Mughan, A. (2007) 'Charisma, Leader Effects and Support for Right-Wing Populist Parties', *Party Politics*, 13(1): 29–51.

Weber, M. ([1925] 1979) *Economy and Society: An Outline of Interpretive Sociology* (Berkeley: University of California Press).

Citizenship

Working Definition

A **status** accorded to individuals within a specific nation or political **community** which carries with it certain rights and responsibilities.

Origins of the Concept

The concept of citizenship originated in the city states of ancient Greece, where the status of 'citizen' was afforded to some of those living within the city boundary. In that sense, citizenship was a symbol of social status. In many societies before the modern period, the monarch or emperor ruled over a mass of people who had no proper means of being part of a system of governing. Indeed, in many societies with low levels of literacy, the bulk of the population had very little knowledge of government and politics at all. The idea that ordinary people could have individual rights or take part in political decision-making was quite alien, as such privileges were restricted to high-status members of the **society**. Today, people are considered to be and see themselves as citizens, usually part of a national community, with the rights and responsibilities that go with that status. Marshall ([1950]1973) saw citizenship as emerging alongside **industrialization** and traced the evolution of citizenship in Britain (specifically England) from eighteenth-century civil rights, through nineteenth-century political rights, to twentieth-century social rights.

Meaning and Interpretation

In the modern world, citizenship is a social status granted to members of **nation states** on the basis of residence. Citizenship therefore grants certain privileges, though these are balanced by duties which citizens are expected to accept. For example, citizens have the right to expect the state to protect them, but the state also expects citizens to act reasonably and not to take up arms against other citizens or government. The concept of citizenship has been divided into different types, with each new form building on the previous type.

Civil citizenship emerged with modern property ownership, as this imposed certain mutual obligations on people to respect one another's right to property, leading to a mutual responsibility for the maintenance of social order. Political rights were restricted to property owners, and large numbers of people were left outside formal politics. In a second stage, *political citizenship* involved the gradual extension of voting rights to working-class groups and women, and certain rights of free association were introduced, such as those allowing the formation of trade unions, while ideas of free speech also emerged. The third stage, *social citizenship*, saw citizenship rights extended to social welfare and a shared responsibility for collective provision of welfare and other benefits. People were expected to contribute to the social fund used for supporting the vulnerable and, as a result, enjoyed the right to a share of the welfare safety net when they needed it.

In recent years, some have argued that we are moving into a fourth stage, described as *environmental citizenship*. In this stage, citizens have new rights to expect a clean, safe **environment** but also a new duty not to pollute the human or natural environment. A more radical version of 'ecological citizenship' envisages the protections embedded within human rights of citizenship being extended to some animals. Ecological citizenship would involve new obligations to non-human animals, to future generations of human beings, and to maintaining the integrity of the natural environment. New obligations to future generations of human beings also mean working towards sustainability over a long time period. In essence, ecological or environmental citizenship introduces a new demand for people to take account of the human 'ecological footprint' – the impact of human activity on the natural environment and natural processes.

Critical Points

Marshall's conception of citizenship is problematic as it is based on the experience of one nation state, Britain. In France, Germany and other countries, citizenship did not 'evolve' in the way he describes. Some have also seen his approach as simply a *post hoc* description – this is what happened – rather than being genuinely explanatory. Why were political rights granted to the working classes and women at a specific historical moment, for instance? Was this really just part of a natural 'evolution'? Trade unions, for example, had to fight hard for an extension of the franchise, which other groups fought equally hard against. Similarly, even in Britain, the voting age for men and women did not reach parity until 1928, well into the twentieth century, which is much later than Marshall's scheme allows for. In short, it is not clear exactly why civil rights had to lead to political rights, which then had to lead to social rights, and this process requires proper explanation.

The attempt by administrations in both the USA and the UK in the 1980s to cut government spending and 'roll back the state' shows that citizenship is never so firmly established that it cannot be reversed. The politics of austerity that followed the 2008 financial crisis also led many governments to cut back on public spending and to extend the principle of conditionality to more welfare benefits, thus changing the content of social citizenship rights. Recent **globalization** theories have challenged the basis of the nation-state-based model of citizenship. For instance, the European Union offers a regional form of citizenship which grants some rights, such as the right to travel and to work, which nation states have to respect. European citizens can also challenge legal decisions made at nation-state level at the regional European level. Cosmopolitan thinkers see the possible extension of citizenship to the global level, with individuals having the status of global citizen, though we are a very long way from this vision at present.

Continuing Relevance

Though there are some issues and challenges to the nation-state model of citizenship, the basic concept of citizenship as involving rights and duties remains sound. Indeed, some of the more recent political debate has involved a rethinking of how to enable citizens to become more active as a means of reinvigorating politics and community life. The continual pressure for the expansion of rights and responsibilities continues to inform our understanding of what citizenship is and should be.

Redley and Weinberg (2007) tackle the question of whether the liberal democratic model of citizenship is capable of integrating people with learning disabilities. Can this democratic model, which demands intellectual ability and independence as prerequisites, politically empower those with intellectual impairments? This ethnographic study explored what can be learned from a UK initiative, the Parliament for People with Learning Disabilities (PPLD). The PPLD embraced a clear liberal democratic preference for 'self-advocacy' by people with learning disabilities. However, the study found several practical interactional obstacles to the liberal democratic preference for self-advocacy. Some participants were just not audible, some spoke 'inappropriately' (that is, did not move the discussion forward) and others did not take the floor when invited to do so. While the authors support the basic principle of self-advocacy, they argue that this principle needs to be bolstered by a concern with care, security and well-being if full citizenship is to be realized for people with learning disabilities.

The citizenship experience of two generations of British-Pakistani Muslims is explored in Hussain and Bagguley's (2005) **qualitative** research in the aftermath of the 2001 'riots' in some northern English towns and cities. In particular, the authors maintain that citizenship is a form of **identity** as well as a set of entitlements and that the identity of being a citizen is not necessarily shared by all. First-generation migrants from Pakistan did not generally consider themselves to be British citizens but reported that they lived in Britain, which remained an essentially foreign country to them. However, second-generation British Pakistanis had a strong sense of themselves as British-born citizens with all the rights that identity confers. For this second generation, the electoral success and overt racist language of the far-right British National Party posed a direct threat to their status as British citizens as well as to their ethnic identity.

References and Further Reading

Bellamy, R. (2008) *Citizenship: A Very Short Introduction* (Oxford: Oxford University Press).

Dobson, A., and Bell, D. (eds) (2006) *Environmental Citizenship* (Cambridge, MA: MIT Press).

Hussain, Y., and Bagguley, P. (2005) 'Citizenship, Ethnicity and Identity: British Pakistanis after the 2001 "Riots"', *Sociology*, 39(3): 407–25.

Marshall, T. H. ([1950] 1973) *Class, Citizenship and Social Development* (Westport, CT: Greenwood Press).

Redley, M., and Weinberg, D. (2007) 'Learning Disability and the Limits of Liberal Citizenship: Interactional Impediments to Political Empowerment', *Sociology of Health and Illness*, 29(5): 767–86.

Civil Society

Working Definition

The sphere of **society** made up of all those **networks**, voluntary associations, businesses, clubs, **organizations** and families formed by citizens independently of government.

Origins of the Concept

The concept of civil society can be traced right back to ancient times, when it was tied to notions of civility and people treating one another with respect. However, modern conceptions of civil society draw from Alexis de Tocqueville's nineteenth-century idea of 'civic associations', such as lodges, charities and religious groups, which he found in abundance in the USA. Tocqueville saw the existence of thousands of such associations not just as performing useful functions but as fundamental to sustaining the country's democratic culture (Eberly 2000). For much of the twentieth century, sociologists and political theorists had little to say about civil society, but there has been a resurgence of interest since the 1980s. Of late, interest has shifted to cosmopolitan theories of a global civil society which, for the first time, offer the promise of an effective global form of **citizenship**.

Meaning and Interpretation

The concept of civil society is close to that of the **public sphere**. However, the latter is generally taken as all of those public spaces in which discussion and debate about society and its political decisions take place. In contrast, civil society consists of voluntary groups, clubs and other organized forms of civic association. However, there are many disagreements about what civil society entails. For some it does not include businesses, for others families are excluded, and yet others see three distinct realms: state, market and civil society.

There are also fundamental disagreements about the nature of civil society. For some, it represents a space for the expression of active citizenship and a democratic bulwark against authoritarianism. This view glosses over the distinct possibility that organizations and voluntary groups are, to some extent, in competition with one another (for resources and members) and the relations between them may be much less cooperative than the more positive assessments suggest. In the Marxist tradition, civil society is even less of a progressive arena of voluntarism and creativity. Marx saw civil society, along with the rest of the cultural superstructure, as implicated in transmitting the ideological and cultural dominance of **capitalism** and its values. However, later neo-Marxists, especially Gramsci, acknowledged that such ideological domination was never complete and that civil society at least offered opportunities to build a counter-cultural challenge (Edwards 2014).

Reinvigoration of the concept of civil society in the late 1980s seems to have been stimulated by events in Eastern Europe and the collapse of Soviet-style communism. Strengthening civil society seemed a useful way of counterbalancing the power of states, and in recent years it has also been invoked as an effective means of peacemaking in places such as Northern Ireland, Kosovo and Afghanistan (Harris 2003: 2). Establishing inclusive voluntary associations and networks could help to build strong social foundations beyond the actions of governments.

The concept has been extended more recently by cosmopolitan thinkers whose research agenda has become established in the social **sciences**. Beck (2006) argues that the ideas of a universal citizenship and global civil society were historically the preserve of well-travelled and well-connected social elites who *voluntarily* chose to see themselves as 'Europeans' or 'citizens of the world'. But, due to processes of **globalization**, this outlook now has much stronger roots in reality and is potentially more effective. As global communications and interactions become more common, a global civil society may be evolving. For example, campaigners against landmines, tax avoidance by multinational companies, and fundamentalist terrorists are able to link up with sympathizers around the world in global networks that help to constitute a global civil society (Kaldor 2003).

Critical Points

Some studies assume that a strong civil society inevitably strengthens **democracy** and that the development of the two runs in tandem. However, this is not necessarily the case. Many voluntary organizations and clubs are far from democratic, and there is no reason to suppose that they should be. Promoting civil society as a panacea for democratic deficits in formal politics or as balancing authoritarian leadership may therefore be misguided. Some voluntary groups may enjoy high levels of social capital – such as the National Rifle Association in the USA – and have access to government, which gives them much more **power** than other groups to influence policy without having to run for election.

Not everyone agrees that civil society is in a state of rude health. Robert Putnam's (2000) study of civic associations in America found much evidence that civic ties and membership of voluntary bodies was actually declining. He argued that parent–teacher associations, the National Federation of Women's Clubs, the League of Women Voters and the Red Cross had all experienced membership declines of roughly 50 per cent since the 1960s. Fewer people reported that they socialized with neighbours or even trusted them. Similar, if less dramatic results were also found in the UK and Australia, though Sweden, the Netherlands and Japan had stable or rising levels of social capital (social networks) (Halpern 2005). The picture is therefore mixed, but it does not augur well for ideas of a global civil society.

Cosmopolitan theories which perceive a global form of civil society emerging seem poorly supported by the evidence. So far, cosmopolitan mentality and practice seem to be restricted to Western activists and academics who hold a normative commitment to the project or to wealthy global tourists who are able to take full advantage of opportunities for international mobility. For most people, a commitment to the nation or the local community remains the dominant source of identification.

Continuing Relevance

In contrast to some of the more optimistic perspectives on the possibility of a future global civil society, the 2008 global financial crisis has led to some much less sanguine analyses. One example is Pianta's (2013) paper on the prospects for a concerted response from within civil society. Noting the 'democratic deficit' in the EU, Pianta argues that the eurozone crisis has heightened awareness of this, as decisions are made and imposed on citizens without their proper involvement. On the other hand, there have been strong reactions across Europe from civil society actors, illustrating the potential strength of citizens' groups. However, so far, these groups are not united in their approach and remain divided on how best to increase democratic participation.

It is often remarked that the spread of the Internet is a key factor in the constitution of an emerging global civil society, enabling global communications, debate and **interaction**. However, Naughton (2001) argues that the Internet may not be as unproblematic as it appears. Most studies assume that it is simply a resource to be used. But this is rather naïve. While the open source nature of the Internet is in line with the values of a global civil society, this radical openness is not inevitable, and there are governments and corporate interests that are pressing for change. The increasing web presence of corporate advertising in many subtle and not-so-subtle forms shows how the character of the Internet may be changing. The huge digital divide between the information-rich and information-poor countries is also a barrier to global communications. Naughton claims that, for too long, cyberspace has been seen as very different from the 'real world', but in fact the two are converging around essentially similar power struggles between civil society and corporate and government interests.

References and Further Reading

Beck, U. (2006) *Cosmopolitan Vision* (Cambridge: Polity).
Eberly, D. E. (ed.) (2000) *The Essential Civil Society Reader* (Lanham, MD: Rowman & Littlefield).
Edwards, M. (2014) *Civil Society* (3rd edn, Cambridge: Polity).
Halpern, D. (2005) *Social Capital* (Cambridge: Polity).
Harris, J. (ed.) (2003) *Civil Society in British History: Ideas, Identities, Institutions* (Oxford: Oxford University Press).
Kaldor, M. (2003) *Global Civil Society: An Answer to War* (Cambridge: Polity).
Naughton, J. (2001) 'Contested Space: The Internet and Global Civil Society', in H. A. M. Glasius and M. Kaldor (eds), *Global Civil Society* (London: Sage).
Pianta, M. (2013) 'Democracy Lost: The Financial Crisis in Europe and the Role of Civil Society', *Journal of Civil Society*, 9(2): 148–61.
Putnam, R. (2000) *Bowling Alone: The Collapse and Revival of American Community* (New York: Simon & Schuster).

Conflict

Working Definition

The struggle for supremacy between social groups, which involves tensions, divisions and competing interests.

Origins of the Concept

Conflict is as old as human **society** and, though today we may see it as unacceptable and something to be prevented, in broad historical terms, conflict and conquest have shaped the human world and led to the spread of humanity across the globe. Western colonial expansion was based on the naked exploitation of subject populations and natural resources, but, by creating new conflict relationships over a larger geographical spread, colonialism also promoted more global interconnectedness. For Georg Simmel, conflict is a form of human association in which people are brought into contact with one another and through which unity can be achieved. This is an important starting point because it helps us avoid the idea that conflict is the ending of relationships and **interactions**. Simmel's point is that conflict forces parties to acknowledge each other even though the relationship may be antagonistic.

Sociological studies of conflict are often seen as forming a 'conflict tradition', though there appears to be little common theoretical ground apart from a general focus on clashes of interest between large social groups. Most studies have adopted either a Marxist or a Weberian approach to conflict, and a majority explore intra-society conflicts such as those centring on major inequalities, among them social **class**, **gender** and **ethnicity**. Conflict sociologies were popularized in the 1960s, partly as a reaction to the dominant structural functionalist paradigm and partly in response to increasing conflicts within and between societies at that time. Functionalism seemed better able to explain consensus and conformity than conflict, and many sociologists turned away from Parsons and Durkheim and moved towards Marx and Weber for inspiration. Today conflict theories are well established, and sociology is better equipped to understand and explain phenomena such as **social movements**, terrorism and war.

Meaning and Interpretation

Conflict is a very general term that takes in both disputes between two individuals and international war between many states and encompasses everything in between these two extremes. In practice, sociology has concentrated on the structured social conflicts which are embedded within society rather than, say, wars between **nation states**, which have been relatively neglected until quite recently. The quest for **power** and wealth, attempts to gain **status**, and social inequalities lead to the formation of distinct social groups with shared interests and identities that pursue those interests against others. Conflict theory therefore sees the potential for strife as always present.

The conflict perspective is one of the main traditions of inquiry in sociology, which includes numerous theoretical approaches. Marxism, feminism, many Weberian perspectives and more – all use some version of conflict theory. Conflict theories investigate the importance of those social structures within society which produce chronic tensions and opposition that occasionally flares into violence. Some theories, such as Marxism, put structured class conflicts at the centre of society as the dynamic that drives forward social change. Simmel's point is worth restating here, namely that, although they are in conflict, social classes are also embedded within relationships of mutual dependence. Under **capitalism**, workers depend on capitalists to provide them with the jobs and income they need to survive, but capitalists need workers to deliver the products and services that make profits.

Conflict theories are by no means all Marxist. Many conflict studies have been influenced more by the ideas of Max Weber, who saw much broader conflicts arising on more than a class basis. Conflicts can be based on political differences, status competition, gender divisions or ethnic hatred, all of which may be relatively unrelated to or independent of class. Patriarchal power works to the advantage of men and the disadvantage of women wherever they are situated in the class structure, though class position may well exacerbate the multiple problems faced by working-class women. Similarly, the episodes of genocidal violence by Hutus against Tutsis in Rwanda (1994) and by Serb armed forces against Bosniaks in Srebrenica (1995), as well as the mass murder committed by the German Nazi state against Jewish populations in Europe during the Second World War (1939–45), have been viewed primarily as arising from traditional ethnic rivalries and racist hatred rather than class conflict. None of this suggests that class is not important, of course – merely that the true importance of class, gender, **'race'**, ethnicity, and so on, can only be assessed in real-world research studies.

Critical Points

The difference between conflict and competition are sometimes elided in conflict theory. Social groups may be in competitive relationships over access to resources, but competition does not always lead to conflict actions. Unless competitive relations lead to actions aimed at achieving supremacy over an identified enemy, then the competition may not develop any further. Similarly, is it correct to describe, say, class relations as class conflict? It may be possible to demonstrate that social class groups have some differing interests, but, unless these lead to attempts to establish supremacy over the class 'enemy', is there any real basis for theorizing class in conflict terms?

Over recent decades, there has also been a move towards analysing peace processes rather than simply conflict situations. Sociologists have started to apply themselves to the study of dispute resolution, reconciliation processes and peacekeeping efforts, and this growing body of work may well take conflict theories in different directions.

Continuing Relevance

Conflict theory and studies of conflict in sociology have never been so numerous. Research into 'civilizational' clashes, anti-capitalist protests, the 'new terrorism', 'new wars', genocide, hate crimes and lots more has expanded over the last thirty years, and sociologists have had to use their conceptual and theoretical tools to analyse these new episodes of serious conflict. As **globalization** processes have gathered pace, and following the end of the Cold War, there has been an emergence of new conflicts.

An up-to-date account of the scholarship in the field of conflict and its resolution can be found in Bercovitch, Kremenyuk and Zartman's (2009) edited collection. The authors remind us that the historical evidence shows conflict to be 'normal, ubiquitous and inevitable ... an inherent feature of human existence' (2009: 3). It is important to be realistic about this fact. However, what should be possible is the management and/or control of the violent expression of conflict, and this has become the focus of recent academic research. Given the multiple dimensions of human conflict, including political issues, personal motivations and shifting international context, it is not surprising that the analysis of conflict resolution is a multidisciplinary endeavour, and there are numerous examples in this book.

Nonetheless, a thoroughly sociological perspective is John Brewer's (2010) theoretical perspective on peace processes and their likelihood of success – a previously neglected issue. Brewer identifies three basic types of peace process after a violent conflict has subsided: conquest, cartography and compromise. Broadly, the *conquest* situation exists after wars between nation states or in civil and colonial wars; the *cartography* situation is when peace is achieved mainly by geographical separation; and *compromise* covers situations in which previous combatants have to negotiate to end violence and agree a reasonable settlement. However, which of these processes is possible does depend both on the extent of shared nationality, values and norms, and on the degree to which participants retain or lose their historical and cultural capital. Brewer's scheme aims to bring a better sense of what is realistic and achievable in specific post-conflict situations.

References and Further Reading

Bercovitch, J., Kremenyuk, V., and Zartman, I. W. (2009) 'Introduction: The Nature of Conflict and Conflict Resolution', in J. Bercovitch, V. Kremenyuk and I. W. Zartman (eds), *The Sage Handbook of Conflict Resolution* (London: Sage).

Brewer, J. (2010) *Peace Processes: A Sociological Approach* (Cambridge: Polity).

Joseph, J. (2003) *Social Theory: Conflict, Cohesion and Consent* (Edinburgh: Edinburgh University Press).

Democracy

Working Definition

A political system providing for the participation of citizens in political decision-making, either directly or through the election of political representatives.

Origins of the Concept

The concept of democracy comes from the Greek *demokratia*, bringing together *demos* ('the people') and *kratos* ('rule' or 'power'). The radical nature of this concept is clear; it suggests that societies should be ruled by 'the people' themselves, rather than by emperors, monarchs or unelected dictators. However, although a direct type of mass democratic participation was practised in ancient Greece, important decisions of governance were taken by a much smaller group of 'citizens' with special rights not afforded to the rest of the population. Democratic rule has also taken differing forms at varying times and in different societies, not least because what is meant by 'the people' has changed over time and location. At various times, the concept of 'the people' has been restricted to adult men, just to those who owned property, and to male and female adults – but only those beyond a certain age. Representative democracy – in which people elect representatives to act on their behalf – has become the normal method of achieving 'rule by the people'. With the ending of Eastern European communism in the 1990s, representative forms of 'liberal' democracy have been seen as the dominant model around the world.

Meaning and Interpretation

Democracy is generally seen as the political system most able to ensure political equality, protect liberty and freedom, defend the common interest, meet citizens' needs, promote moral self-development, and enable effective decision-making which takes everyone's interests into account (Held 2006). Representative democracy is a political system in which decisions affecting a **community** are taken not by its members directly, but by those they have elected. In national governments, representative democracy takes the form of elections to congresses, parliaments or similar national bodies. Representative democracy also exists at other levels, such as in provinces or states within an overall national community, cities, counties, boroughs and other regions. Countries in which voters can choose between two or more parties and in which the mass of the adult population has the right to vote are usually called 'liberal' democracies and include Britain, the USA, Japan and Australia.

Since the early 1980s, a number of countries in Latin America, such as Chile, Bolivia and Argentina, have undergone the transition from authoritarian military rule to democracy. Similarly, following the collapse of the communist bloc in 1989, many Eastern European states – Russia, Poland and Czechoslovakia, for example – have become democratic. And, in Africa, a number of previously undemocratic nations – among them Benin, Ghana, Mozambique and South Africa – have come to embrace democratic ideals. Democracy is no longer concentrated primarily in Western countries but is now endorsed, at least in principle, as the desired form of government in many areas of the world.

One reason for this may be that other political systems have simply failed. In that respect, perhaps democracy has shown it meets the needs of the mass of people better than other systems. However, although some have made this argument, it seems likely that globalizing processes have played an important role in spreading democracy around the world. Increasing cross-national contacts have invigorated democratic movements in many countries, while a global media and advances in information and communications technology have exposed people in non-democratic states to democratic ideals, increasing internal pressure on political elites.

More importantly, global media and instant communications spread news of democratic revolutions and mobilizations. News of the revolution in Poland in 1989 travelled rapidly to Hungary, providing pro-democracy activists there with a useful, regionally appropriate model for their own protests, while the so-called Arab Spring in 2011 saw a wave of demonstrations and protests that forced out leaders in Tunisia, Egypt, Libya and Yemen, as well as leading to a destructive civil war in Syria. International **organizations** such as the United Nations and the European Union play an increasingly important role in global politics and have put external pressure on non-democratic states to change.

Critical Points

The dominance of representative democracy is not absolute. Aspects of participatory democracy play a part in democracies even today. Small communities in New England, USA, still hold annual 'town meetings', for example, while referenda in many countries may be gaining in popularity. This is possible where direct consultation can be made on specific issues with just one or two questions to be answered. Referenda are regularly used at the national level in some European countries to inform important policy decisions, such as whether national governments should sign up to a new European Constitution. They have also been used to decide contentious issues of secession in ethnic nationalist regions such as Quebec, the predominantly French-speaking province of Canada, and, as in the UK's referendum in 2016, to give the public a say on remaining in or leaving the EU.

The general trend towards democracy should not be seen as inevitable. In Poland, the Czech Republic and Hungary, liberal democracy seems to be taking a firm hold. But in other countries, such as the former Central Asian Republics of the Soviet Union, Yugoslavia and even in Russia itself, democracy is still fragile. Another reason not to assume democracy has 'won' is that, almost everywhere, established democracies are facing internal problems. In Britain, for instance, the numbers who vote in European, general and local elections have declined considerably since the early 1990s. A perception that political elites do not properly represent the people's interests – particularly evident during the expenses scandal of 2009 – has led to a loss of trust in politicians and formal democratic politics. There is also evidence that people may be turning to less formal ways of 'doing politics', such as forming **social movements** or voluntary groups to campaign on specific issues.

Continuing Relevance

Francis Fukuyama ([1992] 2006) once argued that the ideological battles of earlier eras are over and we stand at 'the end of history'. No one defends monarchism, fascism and communism any more; **capitalism** has won the struggle with socialism, and liberal democracy is the unchallenged victor. Certainly recent evidence supports this contention. However, cosmopolitan thinkers now argue that national democracies are no longer able to handle the demands of global processes.

Cosmopolitan democracy is seen by many advocates as an ambitious project of post-national politics. However, Calhoun (2007) argues that not only is this project rather premature but it may also be positively dangerous. It is premature because, since the early 1990s, a series of violent **conflicts**, episodes of genocide (including within Europe), terrorism and responses to it, and international economic recession have shown that cosmopolitanism remains an illusory dream. It is also a dream that has accompanied **modernity** from its inception, and it may well be bound up with nationalism rather than being its direct opposite. More than this, nationalism is a key source of identification for large numbers of people and many liberation movements and is by no means inherently dangerous. Indeed, national identification remains a vital force in the struggle for democracy, social integration and **citizenship** and is easily underestimated by cosmopolitan thinkers. Calhoun's is one of the more spirited and constructive critiques of cosmopolitan democracy currently available.

Democracies take time to become established, and some scholars suggest that newer democratic regimes tend to be less stable on account of the failure by political parties to instil loyalty among supporters. However, in an historical analysis of democratic development and political affiliations in Argentina over an entire century, Lupu and Stokes (2010) found that electoral stability grew in periods of democracy but declined again during dictatorships. Their study suggests that new and putative democracies can be severely disrupted by military coups, which prevent a democratic **culture** from taking root. One aspect of this is that the constant disruption of democracy by military coups effectively interrupts elections, erodes grassroots party activity, and thus presents an obstacle to the cumulative partisan loyalty needed to stabilize democratic systems.

References and Further Reading

Calhoun, C. (2007) *Nations Matter: Culture, History and the Cosmopolitan Dream* (London: Routledge).

Fukuyama, F. ([1992] 2006) *The End of History and the Last Man* (London: Hamish Hamilton).

Held, D. (2006) *Models of Democracy* (3rd edn, Cambridge: Polity).

Lupu, N., and Stokes, S. (2010) 'Democracy, Interrupted: Regime Change and Partisanship in Twentieth-Century Argentina', *Electoral Studies*, 29(1) March: 91–104.

Nation State

Working Definition

The combination of a large **community** (nation) and a territorial, political form (state), creating a cultural-political entity, now the most widespread 'survival unit' across the world.

Origins of the Concept

The nation state appears to be the normal, even natural, political-cultural entity in the modern world. But, like all social phenomena, nation states have a history that can be traced. Most scholars agree that the modern nation state is relatively recent, dating from the late seventeenth and the eighteenth century. Between the fifteenth and eighteenth centuries, Europe was ruled by absolutist and constitutional monarchies that had absorbed many smaller political units to produce fewer but much stronger states which coexisted in a competitive struggle for power. This system of sovereign states produced the Westphalian conception of international law (1648), based on the right of states to self-government and with interstate disputes being legitimately settled by force.

The Westphalian system laid the foundations for the transition to the modern nation state, which was ushered in by the English Revolution of 1640–88 and the French Revolution of 1789, symbolically marking the end of feudal social relations. However, it was the demands of **industrialization** that created the need for a more effective system of government and administration, and, since the basis of **society** was no longer the local village or town but a much larger unit, mass **education** and a planned education system based on an 'official language' became the main means whereby a large-scale society could be organized and kept unified. Nation states are thought to have become dominant due to their gaining a monopoly of the legitimate means of taxation and violence, which gave them both enormous military **power** and the loyalty of large populations.

Meaning and Interpretation

The cluster of concepts including the nation, the nation state, nationalism and national **identity** are some of the most contested and difficult to pin down in the whole of sociology. Yet they may appear quite simple. For instance, a nation is a large community, while a state is the political form which guarantees that community its security. However, nations are not necessarily homogeneous cultures with a shared language, history and traditions. The United Kingdom, for example, is a nation state consisting of England, Scotland, Wales and Northern Ireland and has several languages and different historical traditions. It is also a multicultural society with many more cultures and traditions – hence British citizens are an extremely diverse group with many languages and numerous **religions**.

Benedict Anderson (2006) argues that nations are 'imagined communities' rather than concrete 'things', with diverse groups bound together by a perception or imagination of what constitutes the cultural entity to which they feel they belong. Just because they are 'imagined', though, does not mean they have no reality. When many people act on the basis of a perceived national community, they bring about a shared national identity that binds them together.

Nationalism is in some ways quite modern, but it also draws on sentiments and forms of symbolism that go back much further into the past. Smith (1986) has argued that there is often a line of descent between a nation and historical ethnic communities – what he calls 'ethnies'. Over time, Western European countries and regions saw one ethnie gradually becoming dominant over others. For instance, in France, several language communities vied with each other until the nineteenth century. However, once the state made French the official and only language that was taught and used in schools, competing ethnies rapidly lost ground. A similar process occurred in the UK, where English became the dominant language across the constituent nations of the union. Other languages did not completely disappear in this process. For example, Welsh, Scottish Gaelic and Irish Gaelic are still spoken in parts of the UK, while Basque continues to be used in parts of Spain and France (in the Basque Country). Survival of these languages is an important aspect of keeping alive the continuity of past and present for the ethnies which use them.

Critical Points

Sociologists are happier to discuss states than nations, simply because the concept of the nation is so hard to pin down. But the concept of the nation state can also be seen as rather woolly at the edges, as there exist several types of 'nations without states'. A nation state may accept cultural differences within its minorities and grant them a certain amount of active development, as with Scotland, Wales and Northern Ireland within the UK as a whole. In 1999, Wales and Scotland achieved more autonomy with the introduction of a Scottish Parliament and a Welsh Assembly respectively. However, Scotland and Wales are not independent nation states. The Scottish independence referendum of September 2014 delivered a majority against independence and in favour of remaining within the United Kingdom state. The National Assembly of Quebec (a French-speaking province of Canada) and the Flemish Parliament (a Dutch-speaking area of northern Belgium) are other examples of devolved political bodies in nations that are not fully independent states. Many other nations within states still have no legal status or recognition, including Tibetans in China and Kurds in the region that takes in parts of Armenia, Turkey, Syria, Iran and Iraq.

Nation-building and nation states in the developing world have generally not followed the same path as the developed countries. In large measure this is because many developing countries were colonized by Western states and achieved independence only in the latter part of the twentieth century. The creation of many nation states in the developing world was the subject of quite arbitrary boundary decisions that failed properly to consider historically developed ethnic and cultural divisions. Post-independence, the mix of ethnies and other groups made the promotion of a distinct national identity much more difficult and politically contentious in these countries. The same issues and problems did not arise to the same extent in regions that did not suffer colonization, such as Japan, China and Korea, which were already more culturally unified.

Continuing Relevance

Arguably, one of the main factors in changing national identity today is **globalization**, which creates conflicting pressures between centralization and decentralization. On the one hand the powers of business **organizations** and political units (such as transnational corporations and organizations) become more concentrated, but on the other there is pressure for decentralization. As a result, globalization creates a dual threat to national identity: centralization creates pressures from above and decentralization creates pressures from below. Some scholars have forecast the end of the nation state as the key actor in international politics as the forces of globalization create a 'borderless world', in which state power is reduced in comparison to market forces. Ohmae (2007) explores the rise of regional economies such as the EU and the way states behave in relation to them. Although regionalization is short of a fully globalized system, it does suggest that nation states have lost control of key economic functions to emerging 'region states'.

On the other hand, the collapse of Soviet communism led to the creation of many more independent nations. Hence, there are actually far more sovereign nations in the world today than there were even thirty years ago. It is still too early to say with any certainty how the nation state will fare in the twenty-first century, but the impact of globalization on states and national identities is a growing area of interest in sociology. The Internet has been seen as promoting a global **culture** and, in principle, should also contribute to breaking down national identities. Yet, in a fascinating piece, Eriksen (2007) argues that 'nations thrive in cyberspace'. This is precisely because nations are 'imagined communities' whose members are able to maintain a web presence, promoting a sense of national identity much more effectively across large distances. Paradoxically, therefore, in an age of global communications and mass migration, the Internet facilitates the strengthening rather than the destruction of national identities.

References and Further Reading

Anderson, B. (2006) *Imagined Communities* (London: Verso).
Eriksen, T. H. (2007) 'Nationalism and the Internet', *Nations and Nationalism*, 13(1): 1–17.
Held, D. (1989) *Political Theory and the Modern State* (Cambridge: Polity), esp. chapter 1.
Ohmae, K. (2007) *The End of the Nation State: The Rise of Regional Economies* (London: HarperCollins).
Smith, A. D. (1986) *The Ethnic Origins of Nations* (Oxford: Blackwell).

Power

Working Definition

The ability of some individuals, groups and communities to get their own way, or to achieve their goals, against challenges and resistance from those who are opposed to them.

Origins of the Concept

Power is probably the central concept in political sociology, and yet its precise meaning and nature are disputed and there is still no agreement on exactly what it is. In sociology, the study of power has to take account of the ideas of Max Weber. For Weber, power can be defined as 'the chance of a man or a number of men to realize their own will in a command action even against the resistance of others who are participating in the action'. Many sociologists have followed

Weber in making a distinction between forms of power that are coercive and those that have **authority** and are rooted in legitimacy. For example, on Weber's view, the invasion of Iraq in 2003 would be a type of coercive power, as it did not have explicit authority from the United Nations and could thus be construed as lacking international legitimacy.

The most systematic treatment of the concept since Weber is that of Steven Lukes ([1974] 2004), who started with Weber's definition and extended it to take in more instances. Lukes saw Weber's concept as one-dimensional and argued that it was possible to develop two- and three-dimensional concepts of power. The work of Michel Foucault has also been very influential. Rather than seeing power as something people can hold, give away or take from others, Foucault conceives it as productive of social relations, running through **society** and having intimate connections with knowledge. Power works through **discourses** which provide frameworks through which we understand the world.

Meaning and Interpretation

Weber's perspective remains a valuable starting point for political sociologists and appears to be self-evidently correct. In **conflict** situations it seems a simple matter to decide who holds power, as the person, group or army with most power will win out over the other side. The ability to get your own way determines how much power you have. Power can also be exercised in decision-making processes, as some groups are able to ensure that decisions are made that are in the interests of particular people and to the disadvantage of others. However, this is quite a limited view.

Lukes (2004) argued that a two-dimensional perspective on power goes further. Some groups exercise power by controlling the agenda by which decisions are brought to public attention. Power is exercised by keeping some issues out of politics altogether, which effectively prevents some social groups from pursuing their interests. One way that governments have exerted their power, for example, is by placing restrictions on what the media can report. In doing so, they are able to prevent grievances and contentious matters from being aired and gaining wider support. To understand the operation of power we need to look not just at the observable decisions but also at how the decision-making process itself is created.

Lukes also proposed another, three-dimensional or 'radical' concept of power, which can be summarized as the manipulation of people's wants and desires. The shaping of desires can occur in subtle ways. The Frankfurt School argued that capitalists exercise power over workers by shaping their desires through the media, advertising and other means of **socialization**, so that they adopt the **status** of 'consumer'. This kind of seductive and ideological exercise of power is not visible or even measurable, but it can still be inferred when people act in ways that are against their own interests. In recent years there has been much concern about personal debt levels in the developed economies, and yet individuals may still be unable to resist the desire to spend even more on consumer goods. The manipulation of desire which pushes people to act against their own interests demonstrates the power of consumer **capitalism**. In this way, Lukes's three-dimensional concept of power takes in a wider range of situations than allowed for by Weber's version.

Sociology has also been influenced by Michel Foucault's ideas. Foucault argued that power was not concentrated in an institution such as the state, nor was it held by a social group or an individual. Older models of power, including that of Lukes, all relied on the notion of intentional action. Foucault maintained instead that power operates at all levels of social **interaction** and in all social institutions, and that it involves everyone. Power runs through society, oiling the wheels of our interactions, a sort of 'micro-physics' of power that has to be analysed at that level. Foucault also argued that power and knowledge are closely tied together, reinforcing each other. Scientific knowledge claims, for example, are also claims to power, as they are put into practice in various social contexts.

Critical Points

Lukes's and Foucault's concepts of power appear to have moved decisively beyond Weber's original concept, but there are some events which seem to fit better into Weber's model. Foucault's ideas have gained popularity, and his version of power breaks down the simple division between authoritative and coercive forms, replacing these with a single concept of power as something that is found in all social relations rather than being exercised only by dominant groups. Critics argue that, while he has provided a more subtle account of the way it works in everyday interactions, this conception underestimates the way that power really does accrue in some institutions such as the military or in particular social **classes**, which are able to force their will on others in a manner closer to Weber's concept of coercive power.

Lukes's radical view of power is also open to the charge that sociologists can never really know what other people's interests are. How do we decide? The adequacy of the radical view rests on how this question is answered, but that has proved very difficult. Even if we ask people themselves, the three-dimensional view suggests they may give a 'false' answer because their wants and needs are no longer their own but have been manipulated. A second, related problem is that the three-dimensional perspective asks us to study 'non-decisions' and the unobservable influence of ideologies on people's desires. But how can we study things that never actually happen? Some suggest that the concept is not really a theory of power at all but an acknowledgement that social structures impinge on individual lives.

Continuing Relevance

The concept of power, however defined, is fundamental to political sociology, and students simply have to appreciate the debates on what it is and how it operates in order to reach their own view. Lukes produced a second edition of his book in 2004 with two new essays which brought his ideas up to date, defending the three-dimensional view against Foucault's more general concept of power. Foucault's ideas on the power of discourses in society are best approached through applications to real-world situations, and Amanda Henderson (1994) does this in relation to nursing practice in intensive care situations. She argues that the focus in intensive care monitoring is on the physiological condition of the patient rather than on her or his emotional state and that this knowledge has clear consequences for the quality of nurse–patient interactions. Nurses gain medical power as a result of their ability to interpret this information, but their power is reduced in relation to the traditional 'caring' role of the nurse. This analysis may have implications for our understanding of recent health scandals in hospitals and care homes.

Taking account both of feminist theories of how male domination is established through the closing down of women's expectations and of Amartya Sen's (1999) work on the concept of 'development' as lying in the *capacities* of people to 'live the kind of lives they value – and have reason to value' – Lukes (2004) argued that power is a 'capacity' or set of human 'capabilities', drawing attention to the way in which these can be denied or enhanced. Clearly political sociology cannot do without the concept of power, but, even with these revisions, it is unlikely that any general agreement will be achieved on what power is and how it works. Perhaps in future, rather than engaging in theoretical debates on the nature of power, the concept will be defined 'in use' when dealing with specific cases.

References and Further Reading

Henderson, A. (1994) 'Power and Knowledge in Nursing Practice: The Contribution of Foucault', *Journal of Advanced Nursing*, 20(5): 935–9.
Lukes, S. ([1974] 2004) *Power: A Radical View* (rev. 2nd edn, Basingstoke: Palgrave Macmillan).
Nash, K. (2010) *Contemporary Political Sociology: Globalization, Politics and Power* (Oxford: Wiley-Blackwell), esp. chapter 1.
Sen, A. (1999) *Development as Freedom* (Oxford: Oxford University Press).

Social Movement

Working Definition

A collective attempt, often via loosely organized networks of people, to pursue common interests through campaigns and actions in **civil society** rather than within or through established political systems.

Origins of the Concept

For most of the twentieth century, social movements were considered by sociologists as rather unusual, even irrational phenomena. Seen as a type of collective behaviour, along with riots, crowds and revolutions, they seemed to be marginal to the practice of mainstream sociology. The Chicago School turned the study of such episodes of collective behaviour into a specialist field of inquiry from the 1920s. Herbert Blumer (1969) viewed social movements as agents of social change, not merely *products* of it, and he devised a theory of social unrest to account for social movements outside formal party politics. Neil Smelser (1962) represented functionalist theories in the 1950s: his 'value-added' model identified stages to movement development, with each stage 'adding value'. In the 1960s and 1970s, a new wave of social movements looked very different and were theorized as 'new social movements' which organized and acted in new ways, requiring new types of analysis. The trajectory of social movement studies in sociology has been from marginalized outsider to a firmly established mainstream specialism.

Meaning and Interpretation

Social movements are collective attempts to change **society**. Examples include labour and trade union movements, women's movements, environmental movements, pro-life movements, lesbian and gay movements, and many more. Social movements are arguably the most powerful forms of collective action, and well-organized, persistent campaigns can achieve dramatic results. The 1960s American civil rights movement, for example, succeeded in pushing through important pieces of legislation outlawing racial segregation in schools and public places. The feminist movement scored important gains for women in terms of formal economic and political equality, and, in recent years, environmental movements have campaigned in highly unconventional ways to promote sustainable forms of development and change public attitudes towards the **environment**.

Social movements tend to have 'life cycles' involving several stages (Goodwin and Jasper 2014). First there is 'social ferment', when people are agitated about an issue but activity is unfocused and disorganized. This develops into a stage of 'popular excitement', in which the sources of dissatisfaction are more clearly defined and understood. In the third stage, formal **organizations** are created which coordinate the emerging movement, making more effective campaigning possible. Finally, the movement becomes institutionalized and accepted as part of society's political life. Of course, some movements succeed only partly while others fail completely. Some endure over quite long periods of time, but others just run out of finance or enthusiasm, ending their life cycle.

Sociologists have used a number of theories to understand social movements. Smelser's (1962) functionalist theory saw movements arising as a result of *structural strain*. This theory argued that six elements were necessary to bring about a social movement. The social context must be conducive to movement formation; activists need to feel a structural strain between their expectations and reality, which leads to frustration and a desire for change; beliefs about the causes must become widespread; and there has to be a triggering event, such as a police crackdown on protest, or a key symbolic incident that drives home the movement's message. If these first four elements are present, mobilization is likely. The building of social networks of protesters and activists and then the response of authorities are the final crucial stages and can often be the determining factor in whether movements take off or fade away.

After Smelser, movement scholars increasingly turned to rational choice theories, especially resource mobilization theory (RMT), which emerged in the late 1960s and the 1970s as a reaction against theories that saw movements as 'irrational' phenomena. RMT argued that social movement participants behaved in rational ways and that movements themselves were purposeful, not chaotic. It examines the ability of movements to gain the necessary *resources* to mount effective campaigns. Resources include finance, campaigning expertise, members and supporters or influential social networks. RMT therefore investigates what kinds of resources are useful, how activists go about gaining them, and how they are then deployed in the pursuit of common interests.

Between the late 1960s and the mid-1980s a wave of social movement activity occurred in numerous countries around the world, involving student movements, civil rights movements, disabled people's movements, women's movements, anti-nuclear and ecological movements, and gay rights movements. Collectively, this group has been theorized as 'new social movements' (NSMs), and they brought new issues, such as the environment and disability, into politics. NSMs adopt loose organizational forms, use new action repertoires, including non-violent direct action, and involve the 'new' middle class, who work in welfare state bureaucracies, creative and artistic fields and **education**. This characterization led to new theories of social movements as carriers of symbolic messages about issues that had long been invisible in modern societies (Melucci 1989), helping to revitalize the flagging democratic **culture** of many countries.

Critical Points

There are many criticisms of sociological theories of social movements. RMT has been widely used, but it has little explanation for social movements that achieve success with very limited access to resources. 'Poor people's movements' in the USA and the unemployed in the UK, as well as black civil rights in the United States in the 1950s, have had major successes in changing legislation and attitudes, and yet they had few resources. What they lacked in other resources, they seem to have made up for with sheer enthusiasm and action. Indeed, once they became more organized they lost that initial enthusiasm.

NSM theory has also come in for some sharp criticism. All of the supposedly 'new' features identified above have been found in 'old' social movements. Post-material values were evident in small-scale communes of the nineteenth century, and many older movements began as loose networks before going on to become formal organizations. Some NSM organizations have followed a similar path and become more bureaucratic than the theory suggested. Greenpeace is the most notable example: originally a loose **network** of like-minded individuals involved in numerous direct actions, over time it has become a very large business-like **organization** with a mass membership and huge financial resources.

Continuing Relevance

Social movements have become more important in the political life of societies. **Globalization** processes bring systematic and more immediate connections across national boundaries and, with this, the possibility of genuinely international or global social movements. The conditions are also conducive for social movement activity, as people seem to have a growing sense that they are losing control of their lives in the midst of rapid socio-economic change. Being a supporter or activist in a social movement gives people more of a sense that they are able to influence the direction of societies. Some have even suggested that we may be moving into a 'social movement society' where the national social movements of the past give way to movements without borders (Meyer and Tarrow 1997).

The so-called NSMs adopted non-violent methods as a symbolic representation of the kind of peaceful society they wished to create in the future, and these movements have been widely seen as ushering in 'velvet' revolutions and an era of non-violent movements. However, Sutton and Vertigans's (2006) analysis of terrorism in the name of Islam argues that this may be mistaken. Groups such as al-Qaeda do adopt many of the forms and tactics of NSMs, but their use of extreme violence carries a very different symbolic message – that the Western powers are not unassailable and can be attacked even on home soil. The authors' conclusion is that, if we are moving towards a (new) social movement society, then it may not be quite as peaceful a place as some imagined.

References and Further Reading

Blumer, H. (1969) 'Collective Behavior', in A. McClung-Lee (ed.), *Principles of Sociology* (New York: Barnes & Noble).

Crossley, N. (2002) *Making Sense of Social Movements* (Buckingham: Open University Press).

Goodwin, J., and Jasper, J. (eds) (2014) *The Social Movements Reader: Cases and Concepts* (3rd edn, Oxford: Wiley-Blackwell).

Melucci, A. (1989) *Nomads of the Present: Social Movements and Individual Needs in Contemporary Society* (London: Hutchinson Radius).

Meyer, D. S., and Tarrow, S. (1997) *The Social Movement Society: Contentious Politics for a New Century* (Oxford: Rowman & Littlefield).

Smelser, N. J. (1962) *Theory of Collective Behaviour* (New York: Free Press).

Sutton, P. W., and Vertigans, S. (2006) 'Islamic "New Social Movements"? Radical Islam, al-Qa'ida and Social Movement Theory', *Mobilization: An International Journal*, 11(1): 101–15.

Index

Note: Page numbers in **bold** indicate the main treatment of a concept